Experimental Politics

Technologies of Lived Abstraction
Brian Massumi and Erin Manning, editors

Experimental Politics

Work, Welfare, and Creativity in the Neoliberal Age
Maurizio Lazzarato

Translated by Arianna Bove, Jeremy Gilbert, Andrew Goffey,
Mark Hayward, Jason Read, and Alberto Toscano

Edited by Jeremy Gilbert

The MIT Press
Cambridge, Massachusetts
London, England

© Éditions Amsterdam, 2009. Published by arrangement with Agence Littéraire Pierre Astier & Associés.

This book was set in ITC Stone Sans Std and ITC Stone Serif Std by Toppan Best-set Premedia Limited. Printed and bound in the United States of America.

Library of Congress Cataloging-in-Publication Data is available.

Names: Lazzarato, M. (Maurizio)
Title: Experimental politics : work, welfare, and creativity in the neoliberal age / Maurizio Lazzarato ; translated by Arianna Bove, Jeremy Gilbert, Andrew Goffey, Mark Hayward, Jason Read, and Alberto Toscano ; edited by Jeremy Gilbert.
Other titles: Expérimentations politiques. English
Description: Cambridge, MA : The MIT Press, 2017. | Series: Technologies of lived abstraction | Includes bibliographical references and index.
Identifiers: LCCN 2016004742 | ISBN 9780262034869 (hardcover : alk. paper)
Subjects: LCSH: Entertainers--France--Social conditions. | Social conflict--France. | Liberalism--France.
Classification: LCC HD8039.E652 F8613 2017 | DDC 331.20944--dc23
LC record available at https://lccn.loc.gov/2016004742

10 9 8 7 6 5 4 3 2 1

Contents

Series Foreword

"*What moves as a body, returns as the movement of thought.*"
Of subjectivity (in its nascent state)
Of the social (in its mutant state)
Of the environment (at the point it can be reinvented)
"*A process set up anywhere reverberates everywhere.*"

* * *

The *Technologies of Lived Abstraction* book series is dedicated to work of transdisciplinary reach inquiring critically but especially creatively into processes of subjective, social, and ethical-political emergence abroad in the world today. Thought and body, abstract and concrete, local and global, individual and collective: the works presented are not content to rest with the habitual divisions. They explore how these facets come formatively, reverberatively together, if only to form the movement by which they come again to differ.

Possible paradigms are many: autonomization, relation; emergence, complexity, process; individuation, (auto)poiesis; direct perception, embodied perception, perception-as-action; speculative pragmatism, speculative realism, radical empiricism; mediation, virtualization; ecology of practices, media ecology; technicity; micropolitics, biopolitics, ontopower. Yet there will be a common aim: to catch new thought and action dawning, at a creative crossing. *Technologies of Lived Abstraction* orients to the creativity at this crossing, in virtue of which life everywhere can be considered germinally aesthetic, and the aesthetic anywhere already political.

*   *   *

"Concepts must be experienced. They are lived."

—Erin Manning and Brian Massumi, editors

Experimental Politics: Its Background and Some Implications

Jeremy Gilbert

Intermittents and Immaterial Labor

For many years, Maurizio Lazzarato was a writer known to Anglophone readers only for a handful of short texts, by far the best known of which was his 1997 essay on "immaterial labor," which has perhaps been cited and criticized more often than it has actually been understood.[1] That essay stands as a now-classic theorization of the changing ways in which, in the post-Fordist service economies, even low-paid and largely manual work is expected to be performed by the worker with a high level of emotional and intellectual investment, which can be experienced both as an intensification of exploitation, and source of potential potency and autonomy for the workers themselves. To be clear, that essay does not, as critics frequently suggest, claim that labor itself is ever truly, purely, immaterial or incorporeal in nature, or that both manual labor and the production of solid manufactured goods have ceased to be crucial to capital accumulation on a global scale. Rather, it is concerned with the ways in which the subjectivity and affective potential of the worker increasingly becomes a part of the productive process in many sectors of the commercial and productive economy. In fact, the concept was developed by Lazzarato and his coauthors Antonio

Negri and the sociologist Antonella Corsani in the context of a substantial study, published in 1996, of the development of such forms of labor in the Paris metropolitan region, which stands clearly in the tradition of "workers' inquiry" pioneered by the Italian "autonomist" school of neo-Marxist theory and activism.[2] Workers' inquiry combines direct investigation of lived working conditions with inventive and rigorous theorization, in a manner that resembles nothing in the English-speaking world more closely than the work of the cultural studies tradition at its best.[3]

The emergence of forms of routinized labor demanding major emotional rather than physical investment on the part of workers is a development that has been observed by sociologists at least since the publication of Arlie Russell Hochschild's *The Managed Heart* in 1979, but Lazzarato brings to bear a number of crucial insights in its analysis. One of his most crucial observations is that the increasing importance of this type of labor in large economic sectors makes certain collaborative and communicative forms of creativity central to the process of capitalist value formation. That, in turn, goes a long way to explaining the huge significance attached by neoliberal governments at all scales (from the global to the submunicipal) to the "creative industries," both as supposed engines of growth and zones of social activity that must be disciplined according to commercial imperatives. The present volume is concerned directly with one key episode in the history of this process of valorization and discipline of the creative industries: the 2003 dispute between *intermittents du spectacle* (intermittent workers in the entertainment industry) and a government intent on "reforming" the unique French system for regulating their incomes during periods of unemployment. This is a pivotal episode in the history of both labor struggles in the "new" economy and the attempt by neoliberals to regulate the zones of creativity on which that economy explicitly depends. The scheme in question is one that became, and has continued to be, a matter of great consternation to neoliberals in the French government, partly because the number of French citizens participating in and relying on it for the regulation of their incomes has grown exponentially since its inception in the 1930s, and mainly because of its overtly collectivist and egalitarian nature.

The scheme itself, initially limited to the film industry, was a creation of the Popular Front government that took power in 1936, and was expanded during the period of social democratic expansion and working-class confidence in the decades after the war—the period that the French call *Les Trente Glourieuses* (the thirty glorious years). At the same time, it is of particular significance today as a prefigurative institution that seems to have anticipated the needs of a particular type of workforce, which while small and marginal at the moment of the scheme's inception, has grown to become increasingly typical of the general workforce of "advanced" capitalist economies since that time.

Membership in the scheme constitutes official recognition of a specific employment status, which is why any translation of *intermittent* as "casual" or "precarious" would not really be accurate. This particular status is reserved for those who work in various cultural industries wherein employment is recognized as being available only at irregular intervals, in relation to particular productions, events, and projects, but who are regarded as specialists with skills that must be maintained through practice and study, and therefore cannot be expected to support themselves through casual labor between jobs. It was initially created

exclusively for key workers in the film industry, being expanded
to include all workers in the cinematic sector, technical staff in
the recording and audiovisual industries, and eventually performing artists during the 1960s. The scheme is effectively a system of unemployment insurance that pays out benefits during
periods of unemployment and is supported by payments from
all members during periods of employment, ultimately fulfilling
a redistributive function across the relevant social sectors.

Since at least 2002, when the scheme was reported to be running an enormous deficit, its functioning has posed persistent
problems for the French government, despite which it has more
than doubled in membership since that time, clearly reflecting the general expansion of both the creative industries and
the condition of precarity, which while once exceptional even
within that broad social sector, is now the norm throughout it
and much of the capitalist world.

Although 2014 also saw intense disputes over attempts to
"reform" and reduce the scope of the scheme, it was the heat
wave months of July–August 2003 that saw the most dramatic
struggle engaged in by *intermittents*, severely disrupting the
program of regional and municipal arts festivals that is such a
distinctive feature of the French summer. In particular, it was
this dispute that gave rise to the *coordinations*, the grassroots
organizations of *intermittents* that operated according to highly
"horizontal," participatory, and democratic procedures, and had
considerable success in mobilizing strike action, campaigning
publicly against the reforms, and formulating alternative proposals for the modernization of the scheme. At the time of this
writing, the website of the largest and most prominent—the
Intermittents and Precarious Workers Coordination of the Île
-de-France (i.e., the Parisian metropolitan area)—is fully active

and up to date, and seems to evince a lively and innovative political culture.[4] The analysis and theses developed in *Experimental Politics*, published in France in 2009, emerge directly from Lazzarato's direct involvement with the *coordinations*, as both a sympathetic activist and sociological researcher, which is documented more directly in the *Intermittents et Précaires* study coauthored with Corsani.[5]

Lazzarato's Theoretical Coordinates

Since the publication of those works, Lazzarato has published several others, three of which have been translated by Joshua David Jordan; two of these are books on the politics of debt,[6] while the other—*Signs and Machines*—is a more general exploration of the specific understanding of relationships between power, language, and affect that informs Lazzarato's work. In the course of these and previous, largely untranslated works, Lazzarato has developed an approach that amplifies the resonances between radical strands of the Marxian tradition, neglected resources in social theory (such as the work of Mikhail Bakhtin and of Gabriel Tarde), the political "microphysics" of Michel Foucault, and above all, the "schizoanalysis" of Gilles Deleuze and Félix Guattari. It is this approach that is put to work with such devastating analytic effect in the present volume. It's worth spending some time now considering the provenance and implications of this approach, and its differences from those of some of Lazzarato's key contemporaries.

A few years after the publication of his essay on immaterial labor, Lazzarato came to the wider attention of English-speaking readers as part of the wave of interest in the Italian autonomist[7] tradition that followed the publication of Michael Hardt and

Antonio Negri's *Empire* in 2000 (which itself drew on that essay in part). As one of the founders of the French journal *Multitudes*, he has certainly played an active role in continuing and intensifying the intellectual debates to which that interest gave rise, particularly in France. This follows from years of engagement with the postautonomist tradition through his involvement with projects such as the journal *Futur Antérieur* (Future anterior; the journal was published in an Italian as well as French edition). An excellent essay published by Alberto Toscano in 2007[8] briefly surveyed Lazzarato's intellectual project along with its relationship to the specific intellectual and political milieu from which it emerges—namely, a largely Parisian network of "exiled Italian activists" (of whom by far the best known remains Negri) and members of the French radical Left, pointing out both the continuity of this context with a history of thought and radicalism going back to the late 1960s in Italy and France, and the extent to which its constituent members—including figures such as Paolo Virno, Franco "Bifo" Berardi, and Christian Marazzi—have pursued increasingly divergent projects in recent years. This observation remains entirely salient today. All these thinkers continue to share a general orientation toward a particular set of themes and approaches, but perhaps the most consistent theme in Lazzarato's work and its differences from these others lies in his fealty and commitment to the project of schizoanalysis, especially as expressed in the work of Guattari.

The affinity between these strands of radical theory has been explored by a number of writers in English, most notably Nicholas Thoburn and Jason Read,[9] but it is worth setting out some basic markers here for the benefit of readers who may not be familiar with them. The autonomist tradition is a strand of Marxist theory and practice deriving from the experience of the Italian radical Left in the 1960s and 1970s—experience that produced a number of breaks with the orthodoxies of the Italian Communist Party and postwar Marxism on multiple levels (organizational, political, and conceptual). Most decisively perhaps, all have continued to pursue the consequences of the "reversal of perspective" in Marxist theory undertaken by Mario Tronti in the 1960s.[10] What is reversed by this analytic gesture is a presumed determinism in orthodox twentieth-century Marxism, which sees the "productive forces" of capitalism as developing according to the endogenous logics of capital accumulation and technological advance, to which workers and their organizations must react in a largely secondary fashion. The reversed perspective instead stresses the degree to which transformations in the organization and technologies of capitalism are themselves provoked by workers' resistance to exploitation.

From this point of view, for example, the adoption of post-Fordist techniques of production and distribution by leading-edge capitalists from the 1970s onward—and shifts in capitalist culture such as the widespread embrace of social liberalism during the same period—were not merely innovative means of increasing profits in competition with other capitalists. They were also, and perhaps primarily, responses to pressure from workers from two directions. On the one hand, they responded to the success of those workers who had learned how to organize successfully in the context of postwar, factory-based production and the mixed-economy welfare state (which gave political parties and their electorates unprecedented leverage over large zones of social and economic life), to the point where capitalist profitability overall was arguably threatened. On the other hand, they were reactions to the revolt of youths, women, subordinate workers, people of color, queer people, and so on, against the social and cultural discipline typical of the Fordist epoch, whose demands for greater autonomy had to be partially accommodated.

This is the position explicitly set out several times by Hardt and Negri, and it is consistent with a perspective that always focuses on the agency of the workers, or as in their own work, the productive and communicative "multitude."[11] It is quite different from the view of more orthodox Marxist commentators, such as David Harvey and Frederic Jameson, who have tended to see the emergence of post-Fordism and its attendant cultural shift as the consequence of an almost-unmitigated set of defeats for the working class since the 1960s.[12] Interestingly, as I have suggested elsewhere, it is also a view typical of the British cultural studies tradition, which as early as the 1970s attributed the breakdown of the social democratic consensus primarily to the rise in militancy among workers and other social constituencies in the 1970s.[13] This is not the only way in which Lazzarato's approach and concerns resonate with those of the cultural studies tradition, as will be discussed further below.

It would be a mistake to see clear dividing lines between any of these positions. For example, Harvey's classic account of "the condition of postmodernity" relies heavily on the economic analyses of the "regulation school," with its stress on the idea of Fordism (a term borrowed from Antonio Gramsci) as a distinct "regime of accumulation" that came under intolerable pressure in the 1970s. Although he makes little explicit reference to the regulation school, Lazzarato's analysis seems to be at least partially indebted to their account, particularly in its stress on the significance of the relative dissolution of Fordism in producing the contemporary conjuncture. At the same time, in marked contrast with Hardt and Negri, but like Harvey, Lazzarato clearly understands neoliberalism as one of the key political phenomena of recent decades. In fact, he offers one of few available accounts to fully synthesize a Marxian perspective on its class dynamics with Foucault's influential analysis of its juridical and institutional forms. As will be discussed further momentarily, Lazzarato brings Foucault, the Marxist tradition, and Deleuze and Guattari all to bear on the analysis of contemporary capitalism along with the struggles imbricated with it.

Another study of the shift from Fordism to Post-Fordism after the social revolt of the late 1960s—which is also focused on the emergence of a post-Fordist ideology of creativity among capitalists and their agents—is Luc Boltanski and Eve Chiapello's 1999 book *The New Spirit of Capitalism*. Lazzarato, however, is at pains to differentiate his account from theirs. Notoriously, Boltanski and Chiapello identify two distinct traditions of anticapitalist "critique": the "social critique," which focuses on the inequality, exploitation, and injustice that typify capitalist social relations; and the "artistic critique," which centers on the ugliness, inauthenticity, or tedium of capitalist culture. The former is associated with the traditions of socialism and the labor movement. The latter they posit as typical of bohemian, artistic, and yet also, it seems, aristocratic responses to capitalism.

Precisely what valence Boltanski and Chiapello attribute to these two critiques and the possible relations between them seems to be a question of interpretation. On the one hand, it is possible to read them as positing no particular superiority to one or the other, and offering a useful analytic perspective, from which it becomes possible to observe that those movements, innovations, and interventions that have historically demonstrated the greatest progressive potential have been those combining the two critiques in some way (consider the alliance between artistic avant-gardism and Communism in the early

stages of the Russian Revolution, or the bohemian libertarian-
ism of the Communards and others, or the radical aestheticism
of English socialists such as William Morris or Edward Carpenter).[14] This is not how Lazzarato reads them, though, citing in
particular an interview in *Multitudes* in which Boltanski does
seem to suggest that it is the social critique that carries greater
moral force and is associated with historically successful efforts
to mitigate capitalist exploitation.

From this perspective, Boltanski and Chiapello can be situated
in a tradition of socially conservative socialism that has a considerable pedigree. There is a long tradition of socialist, labor, and
communist movements valuing working-class "respectability,"
self-discipline, and abstinence. Even Gramsci's classic account of
Fordism speculates that the discipline and emotional disengagement of the assembly-line worker might be just what is required
of an effective communist revolutionary. At the same time, it is
easy to see why commentators from Régis Debray to the British
filmmaker Adam Curtis have seen a direct continuity between
the libertinism of the 1960s' counterculture and contemporary
cultures of consumerism.[15] Taken to their logical conclusion,
such analyses arrive at a position that sees the global working
class as having been led into demoralized, disaggregated deca-
dence by both the hedonism of the counterculture (in the 1960s
and 1970s) and post-Fordist consumerism (since the 1980s),
between which they make no fundamental distinction.

But such narratives are surely inadequate to the complex
truth of recent and more distant history, and it would be unfair
to caricature Boltanski and Chiapello as offering too simplistic
an account. In fact, *The New Spirit of Capitalism* ultimately offers
a historical account that supports the views of the autonomists
and the cultural studies tradition, attributing primary agency

to noncapitalist forces in provoking the emergence of post-Fordism. In particular, that work is clear in evidencing the reluctance of capital to adopt the new strategies, and showing that only after exhausting attempts to renew and extend the postwar welfare settlement did it undertake the general move toward post-Fordism (so, for example, the early 1970s saw significant attempts by nominally right-wing administrations to extend the welfare state settlement and social wage, in countries such as the United States and United Kingdom). Lazzarato's objection to Boltanski and Chiapello's approach is ultimately grounded in a more fundamental observation about the nature of contemporary post-Fordist capitalism, however. The simple but devastating point made by Lazzarato is that precisely what defines some of the most acute struggles of our time is the impossibility of defining them in terms of the social or artistic critiques, because they necessarily incorporate both. The struggle of the *intermittents* is quite plainly a struggle for both social rights and creative autonomy, and cannot be conceptualized as either simply one or the other. In this it constitutes a multidimensional object of analysis—which can only be understood by means of a complex theoretical synthesis—and an absolutely typical example of political struggle in the "creative economy."

The politics of creativity, and its relationship to both capitalistic and democratic processes, is a key theme running through much of Lazzarato's work, which arguably offers the most rigorous and sophisticated approach to it to have emerged from the radical tradition. In earlier works such as *Puissances de L'Invention* (Powers of invention) and *Les Revolutions du Capitalisme* (The revolutions of capitalism), he develops a sophisticated post-Marxist ontology that brings together the autonomist emphasis on collective creativity as the source of all social value with a

Foucauldian concern with systems of regulation and administration. Of course, this brings into play a number of themes that run through a great deal of social theory and critical thought. The balance between "structure" and "agency" is one of the definitive topics of twentieth-century Anglophone sociology. Cultural and media studies have for decades been concerned with the relative agency of consumers and users of cultural products in relation to the corporate agencies that sell them. Historians have debated the capacity of workers and other social groups to "make" themselves and their world at least since the mid-twentieth century.[16]

One of the key resources on which Lazzarato draws to resolve these questions is Deleuze and Guattari's understanding of the mechanics of "flight" and "capture." Deleuze and Guattari's general social ontology was partially inspired by—among many other influences—developments in geology and molecular physics that demonstrated the extent to which even the most seemingly solid material structures can be understood to be characterized by relations of movement, when considered at the appropriate scale. From this perspective, "lines of flight"— trajectories of transformation and mobility—rather than fixed structures are understood as defining the fundamental characteristics of social and cultural (and even physical) formations. At the same time, the power of state and corporate institutions is understood in terms their capacity to direct or retard such processes. This framework offers a particularly useful way to understand the complex relationships between processes of capital accumulation and other political and cultural factors with which such processes must necessarily interact. Capital's tendency to "creative destruction" (in Joseph Schumpeter's famous phrase)— to dissolve all existing social ties in the relentless circulation of commodities, labor, and currency—has been observed since before Karl Marx and Friedrich Engels made it the key opening theme of *The Communist Manifesto* in 1848.

At the same time, capitalists cannot produce surplus value without deliberately coordinating the activities of large and ever-growing numbers of bodies, bringing together vast collectivities in the process: be they in factories, cities, universities, or the huge distributed networks of the Internet. The need for capital to regulate the behavior, modes of organization, interactions, and outputs of these collectivities is clearly what motivates much of the political, administrative, and institutional innovation of the modern epoch. A key point to emphasize here, though, is that this administration cannot be too restrictive in its effects if processes of valorization are to proceed, because the mobility and variability of their interactions are basic to the creative energy and capacities of these collectivities along with their constituent elements. This fact becomes especially visible in the context of the so-called creative economy, where intellectual and aesthetic innovation, collaborative interaction, and intensive long-range communication become indispensable to the generation of profits.

In this context, capitalist and corporate agencies encounter the necessity to regulate the behavior of populations without restricting unnecessarily their capacities for creative innovation. To illuminate this situation, Lazzarato draws mainly on Foucault's and Deleuze's analyses of the relative decline of "disciplinary" forms of power—which impose direct and explicit norms of both behavior and belief on members of populations—toward subtler mechanisms for the modulation as well as monitoring of behaviors and expectations. The apogee of the era of "discipline" is probably the early to mid-twentieth century, when the great totalitarian regimes attempted to impose ideological and even ethnic uniformity on entire populations while coordinating almost all physical and social activity of any kind. Even the "liberal" cultures of the United States and United Kingdom were notable for the level of highly policed social and political conformity during this epoch (think of Joseph McCarthy's anti-Communist witch-hunts or the extreme pressure on women to fulfill the narrow role of the "housewife" during the 1950s, etc.). Importantly, this is also the great epoch of highly regulated Fordist capitalism, when disciplinary mechanisms were used to regulate the labor process, and when conversely—with the development of Keynesian regulatory mechanisms and the modern welfare state—even capital itself became subject to new forms of disciplinary governmental supervision.

Deleuze and Foucault both suggest that this epoch may have given way to one in which more complex forms of regulation and anticipation tend to displace classical disciplinary techniques of government. Foucault uses the term *security* to cover this new type of regime while Deleuze refers to *control society*. The "war on terror" might be thought of as a good example here. Although there is clearly a strong ideological dimension to this project, the Western states' hostility to jihadism does not extend to much in the way of explicit ideological prohibition. Rather, the main focus of security efforts to neutralize the "threat" of terrorism has consisted mainly of attempts to create detailed social maps of potential perpetrators' social networks along with efforts to anticipate and neutralize socially threatening *behaviors* (as distinct from ideological beliefs).

Another example might be the way that consumers now rarely find themselves the objects of the simplistic, didactic, and culturally homogenizing advertising campaigns typical of the mid-twentieth century; indeed, conventional mass advertising is coming to seem increasingly quaint to contemporary audiences. The explicit claims made for the immediate use value of specific consumers goods in previous decades (this soap will make you beautiful, this beer will make you manly, this instant soup will facilitate loving family relations, etc.) today seem positively laughable. Instead, in the post-Fordist (or post-post-Fordist) digital marketplace, rather than attempts being made directly to modify and normalize the behavior of consuming populations, the minutiae of consumers' social interactions are monitored and analyzed in order to supply commercial institutions with information that may enable them to predict the probable preferences and behaviors of consumers. This is absolutely typical of the control society as described by Deleuze. As obviously relevant to our understanding of new forms of power as this last illustration might seem, however, Lazzarato may actually be the first commentator explicitly to have linked the emergence of control societies with the onset of post-Fordism—a crucial insight into the genesis of the contemporary.

Lazzarato has offered one highly intriguing way of understanding what is at stake politically in control societies, where the subtle modulation of populations and their behaviors, through the management of network relations, replaces the centralizing and totalizing—yet individualizing—logic of discipline and supervision. In *Les Revolutions du Capitalisme*, he deploys the mathematical ontology of Gottfried Wilhelm Leibniz in order to posit the management of "possible worlds" as a key dimension of cultural/political struggle. One potential use of this approach is that it enables us to consider the political valence of various types of aesthetic practice—such as, for instance, innovative popular musical forms that might be understood as having the potential to posit—if only at an affective and imaginative level—different possible worlds for the communities that participate in them to those in which they currently find themselves. This is more than merely restating the old truism that those in power must try to limit the imaginations and perspectives of those whom they dominate; possible worlds in this sense would not be mere hypothetical scenarios but instead actual shared experiences of real, if as yet unactualized, social potential. An example might be the real sense of increased collective potency and future possibility that a successful, self-organized political action, or just even a successfully executed party, can engender. From the other side of the equation, those with power are seen here as being keen to limit the range of possible worlds that can be sensed or experienced rather than with imposing any one singular model. Achieving this end, self-evidently, requires the simultaneous cultivation and management of particular modes of collective creativity.

Neoliberalism and Its Enemies

The fact that contemporary capitalism deploys highly sophisticated and nuanced techniques to this end is one of the key observations of *Experimental Politics*. In particular, by using the attempted reform of the *intermittents'* scheme as a concrete instance, Lazzarato is able to offer simply one of the most penetrating and cogent analyses of the mechanics of neoliberalism to date. Here it is important to clarify a still widely misunderstood point. Despite its antistate rhetoric, neoliberalism does nothing to reduce the overall power and scope of government. As Lazzarato puts it, "Neoliberalism is not a struggle of corporations and private interests against the public power but a change in the government of conduct that implies a redistribution of functions between public and private. Contrary to the beliefs of liberal ideology, the legal apparatus and state administration are far from playing a minor or subordinate role in bringing this change about."

In this specific case, the proposed reforms to the scheme followed essentially in the tradition of Anglo-American "workfare" programs, aping their obsessions with the personal tracking and monitoring of individual claimants, and making highly directive interventions required to modulate their behaviors in the direction of a more generally entrepreneurial, individualized, competitive persona. This is exemplary of the tendency of neoliberal policies to intervene in social situations in order to produce and enforce competitive market relations wherever possible.

This follows from Foucault's influential observation as to the difference between classical liberalism and neoliberalism. The former believes competitive, acquisitive, individualistic, entrepreneurial behavior to be natural to humans, who can be expected to behave accordingly when overbearing government agencies do not intervene. The latter recognizes the potential for collectivism and egalitarianism in human culture, and regards it as a tendency that must be actively curtailed, suppressed, and neutralized. A considerable literature has developed already in English and French that builds on this basic observation, but relatively little of it seems able to combine Foucault's insights effectively with both a Marxian analysis of the class relations at stake in neoliberalism and a broader sense of their affective and cultural dynamics.[17]

This is a crucial issue for Lazzarato, who observes clearly that "the generalization of the market, competition, and the logic of the corporation to all social relations is a generalization of mistrust and fear of the other." From this perspective, the production of particular negative affects is central to the dynamic of neoliberalism, just as the production of relations of collaboration and collective invention is central to democratic opposition to it. Lazzarato's analysis draws on both Foucault's histories of "pastoral" power (institutional, governmental power whose object is the management of behavior) and the Marxian tradition, with Deleuze and Guattari often providing the pivotal conceptual hinges that link them together. Here is one key passage in which Lazzarato discusses this approach:

From its earliest beginnings, capitalism has developed a different form of power to sovereignty, right, and democratic institutions—a power that is always in process, an actualized power. To the side of and beneath democratic institutions and laws, to the side of and beneath constitutions, there is a constituent power at work that does not sit in deliberative assemblies but that works in a diffuse and everyday fashion, that constructs, undoes, and fissures, passing through global relations and general hierarchies, in order at once to transform and confirm them. The analysis of pastoral power and capitalist society as an archipelago of heterogeneous power relations has significant implications for the definition of "the political" and the modes of struggle and resistance. To the singularity of techniques for the exercise of power corresponds the specificity of refusals, revolts, and resistances, which all express the will not to be governed or to govern oneself. This is not to imply, as Foucault emphasizes, that there was first the pastorate and then the movements of resistance, revolt, and counterconduct. The microphysics of power and micropolitics open new dimensions of action, bringing in a multiplicity of practices that the classical tradition, and almost all critical and revolutionary theories, define as nonpolitical. The whole originality of Foucault, on the one hand, and Deleuze and Guattari, on the other, was precisely that they not only analyzed power as a multiplicity of apparatuses and relations but also affirmed the multiplicity of modalities of resistance and revolt, and the multiplicity of modes of subjectification.

This particular set of concerns—this commitment to understanding, in their full complexity, the relationships between multiple forms of power and the equally diverse and complex modes of resistance to them—may well strike the Anglophone reader as close indeed to the classical concerns of the cultural studies tradition, and its key canonical figures, Raymond Williams and Stuart Hall.[18] It is striking from this perspective that Lazzarato sits uneasily in the contemporary universe of the French academy, not holding any formal post, and describing himself explicitly as "philosopher and sociologist" in a gesture whose defiant interdisciplinarity shows no regard for the mutual suspicion often exhibited by philosophers and social scientists in France. At the same time, in the present volume, Lazzarato is explicitly dismissive of those figures most closely associated with the revival of "philosophy" as a master discourse on the intellectual "Left": Alain Badiou and Slavoj Žižek. A million miles away from their aristocratic brand of disengaged system building, Lazzarato's work, as exemplified here, is much closer to the spirit of the cultural studies tradition in its commitment to both the productive relationship between activism, analysis, and theory, and a certain tradition of radical thought that is valued for its analytic efficacy and conceptual fecundity, rather than for its fashionability or dogmatic orthodoxy.

It is this approach that enables some of Lazzarato's most acute observations on the political dynamic of neoliberalism, and lends these observations such an air of relevance today, even to social contexts apparently distant from those described in the book. For example, a key theme in the present work is neoliberalism's attempt to turn workers into "entrepreneurs of the self," making speculative investments in their own "human capital" as opposed to identifying themselves and others as workers bound together by a common set of class interests. The analytic point that Lazzarato derives from this observation is one with wide applicability. "De-proletarianization by means of individual access to private property: this is one of neoliberalism's most potent instruments of depoliticization." One only has to consider the centrality of homeownership and asset inflation to the political economy and mainstream culture of countries such as the United States and United Kingdom to realize the general value of this observation. In the United Kingdom since the early 1980s, for example, the transfer of housing stock from the public to private sectors, accompanied by the deliberate engineering of successive housing bubbles, has been central to the ongoing hegemony of neoliberalism. Declining real wages throughout the period have been partially offset by consumers' ability to secure cheap credit using the rising value of property assets as collateral. In recent years, the inability of young workers to access the property market before late middle age, if at all, has been widely understood as a more significant social problem than the aforementioned decline in real wages; that decline, in fact, is never acknowledged or discussed in public political discourse, its effects being masked by the rise in personal debt and the falling prices of critical consumer durables manufactured in China. This masking of wage decline, augmentation of debt, and facilitation of consumption are all crucial to discouraging organized or even spontaneous resistance to neoliberalism.

The multidimensional nature of Lazzarato's broader approach and his specific analysis allows him to give attention to the complex modes of resistance to neoliberal regulation and capitalist exploitation that the *coordinations des intermittents* exemplify. In this, again, Lazzarato is close to the classic objectives of cultural studies, aiming to grasp both the multidimensional nature of power relations in any given conjuncture and multiplicity of forms of resistance to which they may give rise.

At the same time, this approach is clearly close to that taken by other post-Marxist thinkers such as Ernesto Laclau and Chantal Mouffe, despite crucial conceptual and political differences between them. The similarities lie in the commitment to supplementing a generally Marxian understanding of the dynamics of capitalism with a general expansion of the terrain and types of power relationship under discussion, in particular through attention to the various forms of pastoral power mentioned above and their institutional manifestations. The differences turn fundamentally on the specific theories of the psychosocial that inform their approaches. Where Lazzarato builds on Guattari's schizoanalysis, and might be said to be one of relatively few writers actually to extend schizoanalysis as a political and intellectual project (instead of merely offering exegeses of Deleuzian philosophy, as most followers of Deleuze and Guattari seem to), Laclau and Mouffe remain committed to a generally Freudian-Lacanian model of group formation and decision making, with its rather more pessimistic implications for the limits and necessary forms of democratic struggle.[19] Nonetheless, a common commitment to theorizing the social conditions and organizational tendencies necessary to any genuinely pluralistic radical politics, which does not demand that any particular struggle take necessary permanent precedence over any other, is a strong point of commonality between these different approaches. Lazzarato sums up his position in relation to the analysis of the *intermittents'* struggle in the following passages:

The counterconducts and processes of subjectification that we have been able to observe in the struggles of the *intermittents* are as multiple and differentiated as the power apparatuses that are supposed to regulate them. They express themselves in different fashions (at the molecular level by flight, diversion, and cunning; at the molar level by the attempt to overturn the situation of domination, by direct and open confrontation with power apparatuses, etc.), which are nonetheless not mutually contradictory. They can express at the same time defensive and offensive attitudes, and can act simultaneously according to a logic of resistance, according to a logic of political experimentation. ...

The individual who is caught up in the cultural labor market is simultaneously *"intermittent,"* "artist," "technician," "wage earner," "professional," and "unemployed" (to stick to the vocabulary of the organization of work and social security). Each one of its definitions opens up a specific semantic field and heterogeneous manners of relating to the world, others, and oneself. The choice of one of these words so as to name a political mode of organization is not at all anodyne, as it in fact organizes a "power takeover " by one relation over others—a part and partial totalization of the situation.

It is worth reflecting that this last point is really identical to Laclau's model of the relationship between the universal and particular, wherein some particular element of an ensemble of relations and political demands may achieve the status of representing many others, but only ever temporarily and relatively arbitrarily. What Lazzarato really adds here, however, is a specifically Foucauldian understanding of "power/knowledge" as a key element of any such struggles, with particular forms of knowledge and expertise, and the deep understanding of their own conditions of work, being put to work by the *intermittents* in their attempts to counter the neoliberalization of their unemployment insurance scheme.

Ecology, health, poverty, new social rights, new rights linked to communication, and new subjects enter the public space of conflict, confrontation, and interlocution. This enlargement of democratic action and the power of problematization goes together with the diffusion of the capacity for expertise and counterexpertise.

The *coordination* of the *intermittents* and precarious workers has a relationship that is at once both continuous and discontinuous with these post-Foucauldian struggles bearing on knowledges. If one confronts its practices with those of the majority of forms of citizen expertise, one notices that they are characterized by remarkable specificities. The formal and informal types of expertise produced by the *coordination* are distinct from the experience of the majority of forms of citizen expertise because even if the latter continue to produce effects of delegitimation on representation-politics, most often they confine themselves to playing a role of control, vigilance, and surveillance of the apparatuses of power. They claim to be forces of denunciation, interpellation, and the solicitation of power, or organize themselves into pressure groups and lobbies, whereas the expertise of the *coordination* is conceived as one of the dimensions of the struggle and an instrument in the process of constitution of a collective "self." From this point of view, it enters into resonance with the tradition of a "knowledge of struggle" that Foucault speaks of: it is a matter of an apparatus at the heart of which knowledge is not limited to the interpellation of power or public opinion but where it serves instead to structure and bear a demand as well as collective action. Expertise thus tends to form part of the process of the construction and transformation of the collective subject in struggle. But it also expresses "knowledge in struggle" *against* the knowledges of the unions, media, scholars, and experts. As such, it arises from the construction of a "memory of conflicts."

Molecular Politics

Lazzarato refers several times to the idea that what Foucault calls disciplinary power is equivalent to *hegemony* (in the Gramscian sense). Although this is consistent with quite a widespread understanding of the latter term, which sees it as designating only centralized, relatively authoritarian forms of social leadership, it is worth reflecting that this is really not how the term is understood within the Anglophone traditions that we have been comparing Lazzarato's ideas with here. The cultural studies tradition along with the post-Marxism of Laclau and Mouffe both treat hegemony as a complex process by which particular social groups, or sets of political demands, achieve a degree of authority and capacity to affect the general direction of social change, always operating across multiple nodes, and never simply unifying or homogenizing social spaces.

This is not the place to carry on a discussion of this issue, or try to correct Lazzarato's perfectly clear and comprehensible usage of the term hegemony (which in no way affects his argument). The point worth making here is simply that from the point of view of these Anglophone intellectual currents, what Lazzarato presents is actually a highly congenial framework within which to understand the complexity of hegemonic and counterhegemonic processes, by making a deft use of the schizoanalytic conceptual toolbox. In particular, he offers a sophisticated understanding of the complex relationships between the *molar* and the *molecular* as understood by Guattari. From this perspective, the molar is understood as the scale at which component elements are aggregated into a coherent whole: people become a population, regions become a nation, and workers become a corporation. The molecular is conversely understood as the level at which things fragment and become mobile, for better or worse, disintegrating coherent entities and opening up the possibility of new configurations: the nuclear family loses its normative status and a range of social possibilities emerges; the factory is closed, and the workers are freed or condemned to do something more or less productive with their lives. The molecular is about transformation; the molar is about stabilization.

The great mistake is always to assume that it is one or the other of these processes that is necessarily to be welcomed or opposed: sometimes they're good, and sometimes they're bad. A nuanced attention to their mechanics is always required. Lazzarato cites Deleuze and Guattari's observation that "molecular escapes and movements would be nothing if they did not return to the molar organizations to reshuffle their segments, their binary distributions of sexes, classes and parties," and Guattari, writing with Suely Rolnick, arguing that "if the processes of molecular revolution are not taken up on the level of the real power relations (social, economic, and material power relations), they may begin to revolve around themselves as imploding processes of subjectification." He goes on to write as follows:

What one sees emerging is an articulation between different functions of the collective assemblage *"coordination"* that overturns the principles around which the workers' movement had organized itself from the end of the 19th century. If, in this tradition, being-together and the subjectivity that emerged from it were functions of being-against, of the manner of fighting, of the way of conceiving the enemy and power, in the experiences of contemporary struggles, this relations effectively seems to reverse itself: the efficacy of being-against, its duration and even its possibility, now depend on the modalities of constitution of being-together. ...

[H]ow is the relation between the molar and the molecular to be articulated at the heart of the macropolitical and the micropolitical, when revolutionary action no longer aims at taking power (peacefully or violently)? Only experimentation with new social practices and new forms of activism can provide the response. Without seeking to compartmentalize or to specialize, they have instead to establish a continuum between political, social, economic questions, between practices and techno-scientific transformations, artistic practices and modalities of production of knowledges. Political action should not aim to reconcile and unify the at once independent and inseparable elements of the micro and macro, of the molar and molecular.

In a fascinating move, Lazzarato deploys Deleuze's concept of *disjunctive synthesis* (which both conjoins and separates terms at the same time, placing them into a situation of mutual relation that is never one of simple totality) in order to theorize the relationship between the new social movements and "lifestyle" politics that emerged in the 1960s—key examples of the "micropolitics" of subjectivity referred to by both Foucault and Guattari—and the tradition of working-class struggle that preceded them.

Disjunctive synthesis refers us to the movements of the 1960s and 1970s, which by integrating the question of the production of subjectivity and transformation of the self into their actions operated a radical displacement in relation to the Marxist method of struggle, for which secondary power relations (men/women, nationals/immigrants, etc.) have to be subordinated to the principal relation (capital/labor). Minoritarian movements reverse this point of view: instead of containing the other relations, the capital/labor relation is, in reality, a specific, partial, singular relation that can only function when assembled, and thanks to the relations of sexual, racial, and cultural domination. The contribution of micropolitics to political action has given rise to numerous misunderstandings, although it restricts itself to affirming that if one wants to attack the principal relation, one must also attack the secondary relations. Disjunctive synthesis is the method for politicizing" the multiplicity of power relations that are entangled with one another. It is necessary to disarticulate the "common world" in which the relations of exploitation along with racial, sexual, cultural, and other forms of domination fit together yet assert the singularity of each one.

Far from being a "spontaneism," a "movementism," a simple affirmation of "forms of life" (a "vitalism" as Jacques Rancière and Alain Badiou say, with a hint of contempt), micropolitics requires a high level of
organization, forceful differentiation of functions and political action,
multiplicity of initiatives, and certain intellectual and organizational
discipline. It demands a rigor and great capacity to read conjunctures
in their specificity as well as intervene in different and always-singular
situations.

Lazzarato makes a convincing case that the struggle of the
intermittents has been exemplary of such disciplined yet creative
organization, and that as such, it has constituted a set of political experiments with far wider relevance.

The Politics of Creativity

Clearly, one of the major stakes of that struggle is both the concept and actuality of creativity, and claims made on it by competing constituencies of specialists, capitalists, and administrators.
Lazzarato draws on one of the important artistic innovators of
the twentieth century, Marcel Duchamp, in order to formulate
a radical politics of creativity that both sheds unique light on
these issues and offers a normative basis for future analysis and
intervention. Duchamp occupies a similar position to Franz
Kafka in the present work, in which the latter is understood as
having precognized the bureaucratic maze of control societies
in his writings rather than having merely allegorized the disciplinary mechanisms that were reaching their apogee during
his lifetime. Both Duchamp and Kafka provide key points of
reference for Lazzarato deriving from the historical moment of
the first emergence of postdisciplinary culture (which Lazzarato
has consistently located in the early decades of the twentieth
century). Discussing the expansion of the concept of art during

and since the nineteenth century, and Duchamp's critical rejection of the notion of art as a professionally specialized activity as opposed to a dimension of all human endeavor, Lazzarato writes as follows:

The social and ontological expansion of the concept of art marks a paradigm shift that concerns society in its entirety. In order to grasp the political consequences of these changes, it is necessary to make explicit the "new division of the sensible" that it implies. By means of this idea, Rancière describes the division between ways of doing and ways of saying that determines who has the power to name the possible, the sayable, and the thinkable in an epoch and a society. This "division of the sensible" thus allows us to grasp in a particularly profound manner the distribution of roles and functions that were proper to industrial capitalism during the nineteenth century, marked as it was by the dualisms active/passive, culture/nature, and sensibility/ understanding. These dualisms are political: they separate and hierarchize society according to relations of domination that organize the powers held by people of "refined culture" (activity) over people with "simple natures" (passivity), the power of people of leisure (freedom) over working people (necessity), and the powers of the class of intellectual labor (autonomy) over the class of manual labor (subordination). This distribution of the sensible corresponds to a dualist divide within the population between the "cultivated classes who have access to the totality of lived experience," on the one hand, and "the savage classes, mired in the fragmentation of work and sensible experience," on the other.

Yet it seems to me that this division of the sensible represents the politico-cultural and semiotic conditions from which Duchamp marks the exit with his conception of art as coefficient to different degrees in each human activity. While the disciplinary model poses a difference of kind between art and nonart, nature and culture, material and intellectual labor, the new division of the sensible that Duchamp intuited is no longer marked by dualisms, but by a chain, series, or continuum that expresses differences in the power to act.

Lazzarato sees this newly differentiated continuum as typical of the entire world of work in the contemporary affective, creative economy that typifies the advanced capitalist societies:

The disciplinary division of functions, roles, and identities intersects perfectly with the divisions between dominant (capitalists) and the dominated (proletariat): refined culture, art, mastery of speech, developed sensibilities, and intellectual labor fall to the dominant class while nature, a poor facility with language, rough sensibilities, and manual labor fall to the dominated. Rancière's "division of the sensible" also presents us with another opposition: the "two humanities." Yet in our society today, there is but one population that engages in activities all of which contain "coefficients" of creativity, speech, developed sensibilities, intellect, and refined culture—in other words, all that once constituted the exclusive "heritage" of the bourgeoisie (or the aristocracy). Salaried workers, the unemployed, and welfare recipients represent a continuum that encompasses and mixes manual and intellectual labor, which were once separated between different classes, in the same way that cultivated and rough sensibilities are no longer distributed between "bourgeoisie" and "proletariat," but are distributed in a differential fashion within a single population. Moreover, we are living through a veritable reversal in relation to the old division of the sensible as there is today an injunction to "equip" oneself (in the way one once spoke of equipping a machine) for that which the dominated were once excluded from: speech, autonomy, intellectual work, refined culture, art, and educated sensibilities. In the new division of the sensible, the problem is less the divide between activity and passivity than the requirement to become "autonomous," and assume the responsibility and the risks that these behaviors carry. The issue resides less in the division between mastery of "speech" by the bourgeoisie and the inarticulate "cry" (of pain) from workers and the proletariat than in the inciting of everyone to expression; it is less in the separation between the cultured people and the uncivilized than in the continuous training and acculturation that we are obliged to undergo throughout our lives.

Lazzarato makes a crucial observation with reference to the specific politics of the *intermittents'* scheme and neoliberal reforms of it: it works in some senses to reestablish a clear distinction between "proper" "professional" artists and everyone else, even while it functions within a context wherein the very logic of contemporary capitalism makes visible the persistent instability and purely institutional nature of that distinction. One of the key objectives of the reformers has always been to establish much clearer, objective, and certifiable criteria according to which artistic professionals can be identified, and by means of which their numbers can be strictly controlled.

Contemporary societies provide us with a good example of how techniques of government intervene into the double expansion of art and culture outlined by Duchamp. Art and culture, as Duchamp sensed at the beginning of the last century, can be used as two techniques, heterogeneous yet complementary, which enable the impoverishment of subjectivity and limit governed subjects' capacity to act.

As we already noted in the French context, the *economic* impoverishment of artists and technicians is produced through the organization of a cultural labor market that accentuates competition along with the difference in revenues between employees in order to construct human capital as precarious, flexible, and subject to the production of content in the cultural industries. Nevertheless, the *subjective* impoverishment of artists and technicians (but also of publics), develops according to two logics that appear contradictory at times: first, industry incorporates and "depotentializes" the critique of the division between art and nonart initially raised by avant-garde movements, while second, reestablishing this distinction.

What is crucial to understand is that, once again, Lazzarato is not merely positing a simple mechanism of "recuperation" of the avant-garde here (to use the Situationists' term). Rather, what is at stake is, again, a logic of potentiation, disruption, and capture, whereby the creative possibilities engendered by the breakdown of established social forms and distinctions must be channeled in specific ways if they are not to pose a threat to the conditions necessary for capitalist exploitation and profit. Nowhere is this more apparent than in the ways in which Duchamp's idea of subjectivity as creative medium and his "anartistic" problematization of the very notion of "art" are taken up and given new, relatively impotent form in the contemporary creative economy.

Duchamp asks us to think the act of creation as a process of subjectivation and the artist as a medium. "A work in itself does not exist. It is the viewers who make the picture": this is the well-known aspect of Duchamp's position. The work is a coproduction, "a product of two poles; there is the pole of the one who makes the work and the pole of the one who looks at it. I give the ones who look at it as much importance as the one who makes it."

We find an initial problematization of these questions through an interrogation of the practices of resistance as well as creation found in the movement of the *intermittants*, anartistic work of Duchamp, and more conceptual practices of Guattari. Artists and technicians in struggle have pointed to three fundamental questions beyond those we have already considered: the new figure of the artist/intellectual, the relationship between time and money, and property rights in neoliberal societies. The *intermittants'* movement is one expression of a double expansion of art ("sociological" and "ontological"), which transforms the figure and functions of the artist and the intellectual. The transcendent intellectual, organic intellectual of Gramsci, and even specific intellectual of Foucault, along with the image of the artist found in the romantic tradition, is here substituted with what Guattari called "a collective intellectuality." This collective intellectuality was labeled "mass intellectuality" in Italy as early as the 1970s:

Since the 1980s, corporate management and the government of the social has turned to techniques of expression in order to encourage the implication of subjectivity and an incitement to activity and "performance." The neoliberal motto "express yourself, be creative" has taken its place alongside the liberal motto "Make yourself rich!" Expression is not only solicited, but has become the condition of employability. But the incitement to creativity has no corresponding social right. On the contrary! Neoliberal governmentality reinvents new "copyrights" and new rights for intellectual property and imposes a massive reduction in "social property" and collective rights. However, this strategy isn't new to the history of capitalism; Walter Benjamin, who described this process in the period between the two World Wars, describes this as one of the origins of fascism.

In contemporary capitalism, the permanent employee is caught between the hypermodern and neoarchaic actions of the business. According to a modulation that follows different hierarchical levels, the permanent employee must implicate oneself subjectively, invest their sensibility, and become "human capital" that is autonomous and performs while always staying within the structures of hierarchical subordination. The injunction to be creative and perform at a high level is a paradox. First, this is because the autonomy that the salaried employee must acquire does not change the conditions of their heteronomy within the organization of labor. Furthermore, because creativity and performativity must be transformed, directly or indirectly, into an increase in productivity and efficiency (the transformation of a nonfinalized action into an instrumental action.) And finally, because the injunction to be creative corresponds to neither new revenues nor new rights, but instead a taking in hand of risks and responsibilities by salaried workers themselves when they should fall on the lone entrepreneur.

Here we come to one of the ultimate and politically crucial conclusions of Lazzarato's analysis. There is no question that what he is advocating is any form of simplistic bohemianism, and it is here that his differences with Boltanski and Chiapello perhaps come most clearly into focus. For it is not in the name of any kind of individualized or aristocratic aestheticism that any of his arguments are made, even while he defends the value of a certain tradition of avant-gardism that values the "artistic" dimension of all endeavor. Rather, the key point is that all creativity is social creativity, and all political efficacy depends to some extent on this fact. With reference to the kinds of subjective experiments to have emerged from radical strands of cultural experimentation since the 1960s, Lazzarato comments that "if it's true that we are unable to imagine radical political changes that are brought about little by little by means of molecular behaviors, it is also true that the possibility of such radical change is unimaginable without these same behaviors." Referring to the core issue raised by these political-philosophical issues, he remarks that the "assertion that subjectivity is first of all a collective assemblage, even when it is expressed through an individual, is essential to the dismantling of the neoliberal ideology of the 'creative class' or the theory of the "cognitive worker," which maintains belief in the creativity of individuals or social groups defined by certain socioanthropological characteristics."

Here we come finally to the overall historical importance of the *intermittents'* struggle and political significance of Lazzarato's theorization of it. Both the political movement itself and remarkably coherent conceptual framework developed by Lazzarato demonstrate the efficacy of a politics as well as analysis that is at once libertarian, antiessentialist, and rigorously anti-individualist, recognizing the creative nature of collectivity and collaborative dynamic inherent in all real creativity. It is these facts that neoliberalism is predicated on attempting to refute at all costs. It is their irrefutability that remains neoliberalism's— and perhaps capitalism's—greatest point of vulnerability.

Introduction to the French Edition

The three chapters that constitute this book[1] are the product of an experience and an experiment: an inquiry undertaken by a collective of researchers and "nonresearchers" (casual and precarious workers) into the conditions of work, employment, and unemployment among casual workers in the entertainment industry, between September 2004 and November 2005, during the unfolding of a dispute over the reorganization of their unemployment insurance scheme. The methods and objectives of the inquiry were above all socioeconomic, and if the results that we obtained (and gathered in a book)[2] are important, they are equally limited. The present book therefore results from the necessity of bringing to the inquiry a perspective slightly detached from the hypotheses from which it proceeded—the socioeconomic grid of the analysis of practices of employment, work, and unemployment of casual workers allowing too many things to slip through it. The "power effects" of economic and social *dispositifs* (of the salariat and welfare state mechanisms); the power effects of discursive practices (of the scientists, the experts, and the media, whose pronouncements accompanied and punctuated the progress of the dispute); the complexity of the modalities of subjection of neoliberal politics, and the refusals to submit to government and the processes of political subjectification: all could become apparent only in an oblique form from a purely socioeconomic analysis.

In order to try to grasp what slips through this socioeconomic grid, we wished to integrate the analysis of the dispute with other approaches—approaches developed in the 1960s and 1970s by Michel Foucault, Gilles Deleuze, and Félix Guattari. In our view, social critique has thus far not taken sufficient stock of, or sufficiently exploited, the political pertinence and heuristic fecundity of these approaches.

These two books (this one and that based directly on the inquiry), these two different approaches to the same events, bear witness to a theoretical difficulty that is also, in fact, a political impasse. In the context of the "great transformation" through which we are currently living, they problematize the difficulty of combining analysis and modes of intervention and organization founded on the great dualisms of capital and labor, economics and politics, with analysis and modes of intervention and organization that have been experimented with since the era of 1968, constructed according to a logic of multiplicity, which acts beneath, transversally and to the side of the aforementioned grand dualisms. These two books, at the same time that they bear witness to this difficulty, would hope to contribute to the sketching out and following up of some leads in the search for means to remedy the impotence of which this difficulty is the cause.

1 The Government of Inequalities: Critique of Neoliberal Insecurity

The dispute in which *intermittents* (short-term contract workers) in the French entertainment industry were engaged in 2003, over the issue of their unemployment insurance, put into play a set of political, economic, and social issues that concern the whole society.

The contemporary economy is characterized by a disjunction between work and employment, to which casual workers of this type are particularly sensitive. The time during which they are actually employed does not last long enough to be described as a full period of real work; periods of employment only compensate partially for their practices of "work" (training, apprenticeship, forms of cooperation and voluntary labor, the circulation of knowledge and competences, "downtime," breaks, moments of hesitation understood as necessary conditions for activity and work on oneself, etc.). Correlatively, a phase of unemployment cannot be reduced to a time without work, because a part of what we have called here "work" goes on during such periods of "unemployment." For the clear opposition between work and unemployment is substituted an imbrication of periods of employment with periods of absence-of-employment, such that unemployment changes in nature, and its "production" requires new institutions and new norms. Under these conditions, unemployment allowances, far from being limited to covering the risks of loss of employment, are used by some "*intermittents*" as "financing" for their activities, as a "social investment" that permits a relatively flexible arrangement of different temporalities: times of employment, times of work, times of unemployment, and times for living.

The "reform" wished to call into question what exactly characterized "intermittence": unlike in every other sector of precarious and temporary employment—in which no continuity of revenue and social rights is available to support the discontinuities and the imbrications between unemployment, employment, and work—in the case of the *intermittents*, the cost of flexibility and precarity did not fall exclusively on the employee. Furthermore, according to the initiators of the reform (MEDEF [Mouvement des Enterprises de France, or Movement of French Businesses], the organization of French employers; the CFDT, one of the five major confederations of unions in France), in the flexible and precarious labor market in which individuals pass from one job to another, changing employer each time, the payment of unemployment benefits should become the principal instrument for the control of their mobility and behavior.

From this perspective, the flexible and precarious workforce resembled—to use a distinction of Michel Foucault's—a "floating population," a "multiplicity in movement," rather than a fixed and stabilized population like that of the workers of the postwar "golden age" that could be mapped on a grid by disciplinary techniques, by the "mute" organization of movements and actions of individual and collective bodies in the closed space of the factory. This "floating population" is not—far from it—specific to the cultural labor market but prefigures the becoming of the whole of the workforce in contemporary societies, which Foucault called "security societies." It was therefore surely in order to establish a new discipline of mobility, and precarity beyond the walls of the enterprise, by means of a social policy that the first testing ground of the political program of the French bosses (their program of "social reconstruction") was a reform of unemployment insurance.

For these reasons, we can take this conflict as a point of reference from which to analyze the conditions of production and reproduction of the market in precarious employment (and "unemployment," which corresponds to it), and disclose the new forms of subjectification and subjection that this production entails. This "little" conflict actually has general implications: at stake are, on the one hand, the categories of work, employment, and unemployment and the functions of the welfare state, and on the other hand, the conditions for a politics conducted at the highest level of contemporary capitalist organization.

Foucault, at the Heart of the *Intermittents'* Conflict and of the Neoliberal Transformation of Society

In order to describe the modalities of the formation and functioning of the cultural labor market, we will follow the clues offered by Foucault in one of his published lecture courses, *The Birth of Biopolitics*, as the concepts and the arguments that are developed there are to be found, by a strange convergence of circumstances, at the heart of the *intermittents'* conflict. The restructuring of their unemployment insurance regime was the final element in constructing the first testing ground for the whole program of social reconstruction advocated by the bosses. François Ewald, student and editor of Foucault's posthumous writings, is, with Denis Kessler, the former number two at MEDEF, at once the promoter and the intellectual cover for the bosses' project, which seems on the evidence to have been inspired, directly and indirectly, by Foucault's lectures on neoliberalism.

To begin to interrogate the work of Foucault from this perspective, we can ask ourselves some questions that touch on all of the key stakes in the conflict and the major axis that traverses the employers' reform project. Why does the constitution of the labor market in the culture industry occur by way of the management of "social policy"? Why does this project encounter, falter, and stumble over a problem of unemployment insurance? And why do French employers use the adjective "social" to qualify their politico-economic project? The response that Foucault's course offers to us is as follows: liberal government is, from its earliest origins, a "government of society." Liberal government is not an economic governance that limits itself to recognizing and observing economic laws; it is a governance that takes the totality of society as its objective and target. Liberal politics is "a politics of society" for which the market is at once its instrument of intelligibility, its system of measurement, and the source of its functional rules.

What Is the "Social"?

The "social" was introduced as a mode of governance from the moment when the relation between the capitalist economy and politics became problematic. Foucault explains it as follows: the power of the sovereign must be exercised in a territory and on subjects of right, but this space is inhabited from the eighteenth century on by economic subjects who instead of bearing rights, have (economic) interests. *Homo economicus* is a figure hetero-geneous to, and not superimposable on, *Homo juridicus*. Eco-nomic man and the subject of rights give rise to two equally heterogeneous processes of constitution: each subject of rights integrates itself into the political community by way of a dia-lectic of renunciation. The political constitution assumes that the juridical subject transfers its rights to another. Economic man integrates himself into the economic totality through a spontaneous multiplication of his own interests. One does not renounce one's interests. On the contrary, it is only by persever-ing in one's selfish interests that there is a multiplication and satisfaction of needs among the whole of society. According to Foucault, neither juridical theory nor economic theory, neither the law nor the market, are capable of reconciling this heteroge-neity. This requires a new domain, a new field, or a new plane of reference that will be neither the totality of subjects of rights nor the totality of economic subjects. Each will only be govern-able within a scale of measurement according to which it will be possible to define a totality that encompasses them both while bringing to light not only their relationship or combination but equally a series of elements that amount to interests but that are not reducible to economic interests. This totality is named "civil society," "society," or the "social."

In order for governmentality to be able to conserve its global character, in order that it not be separated into two branches (an art of governing economically and an art of governing juridi-cally), liberalism invents and experiments with a collection of techniques (of government) that is exercised over a new plane of reference: civil society, society, or the social. Here, society is not the space where a certain distance or certain autonomy is con-stituted in relation to the state but the correlate of techniques of government. Society is not a primary and immediate reality but something that forms a part of the modern technology of government, of which it is the product. It's at this crossroads, it's in the management of this interface, that liberalism constitutes itself as an art of government.

In the twentieth century, the social government of conduct had a specific political function. If it is true that social policies are consubstantial with the birth and the development of capitalism, it is also the case that they are installed at the heart of capitalist strategy as a response to "the politics of revolution" and notably its actualization in Russia. The problematic relationship between economics and politics had been pushed over into an irreducibly antagonistic dualism by the Soviet revolution. The government of conduct was henceforth precisely for the purpose of producing polarizations of power and revenue in the process of neutralizing and depoliticizing the dualisms that these polarizations always risk crystallizing, by way of processes of differentiation and individualization that were increasingly driven by social policy. Such social policies are therefore very much at the heart of liberal strategies, even if they play this role differently in the case of Keynesian liberalism and the "ordoliberalism" that is the cornerstone of German postwar liberalism and contemporary neoliberalism. It is a question therefore of understanding what the neoliberals mean by the terms "market" and "society," and knowing how they understand their relationship.

The Market according to the Neoliberals

For the neoliberals, the market is not spontaneous at all; it is not the expression of a supposed natural tendency of humans to trade, as Adam Smith believed. By contrast with classical liberalism, what the neoliberals most powerfully emphasize is not trade but competition as the organizing principle of the market, and most notably competition between firms and workers. If trade implies equality, then competition implies inequality. The new mode of government of the market substitutes the pairing inequality and enterprise for the pairing trade and equality. For the neoliberals, introducing the market as a principle of regulation means making competition rather than trade the regulatory principle of society. At the same time, in the neoliberal conception, competition is not the result of a "natural play" of appetites, instincts, and behaviors. It is rather a "formal game" between inequalities—a game that must be instituted, and continually maintained and sustained. For the neoliberals, appetites and instincts are not given; only inequality has the capacity to produce a dynamic that pushes them to compete one with the other, which thereby sharpens the appetites, the instincts, and the brains of individuals, and therefore maximizes their capacity to act. The neoliberal conception of the market, contrary to the more widely held view, is therefore antinaturalist. The market and competition are not natural and automatic mechanisms but the result of an active construction that requires a multiplicity of interventions, notably by the state, in order to exist and function. To be able to be "laissez-faire," it is necessary to intervene a great deal, and intervene simultaneously in the economic conditions and the not directly economic conditions of the functioning of the market and competition. It is not necessary to intervene in the market, but for the market; to intervene so that the "fragile mechanisms" of competition can function means to manage the conditions, notably the social condition, of its functioning. Neoliberal government must act on society itself in its weft and warp, taking account, and even taking charge, of social processes in order to make a market mechanism internal to them. The "social reconstruction" desired by the French bosses inherits this tradition directly when Kessler makes competition, at the moment of its launch, the regulatory principle of the social: "The principle of competitiveness reintroduces economic exigency into a social domain, which has, at times, too great a tendency to play up its autonomy from it, or even to want to dominate it."

Inequality and Competition in the Cultural Labor Market

In the specific case—which we maintain on several grounds to be exemplary—that we analyze here (the cultural labor market, and the conflict to which its "reform" gave rise), we are going to try from hereon in to understand the role played by the institutions for the regulation of unemployment, and notably of UNEDIC. UNEDIC (Union nationale pour l'emploi dans l'industrie et le commerce, or National Professional Union for Employment in Industry and Trade), administered jointly by the employers' organizations and the trade unions,[1] is a body charged at the same time with the administration of unemployment insurance, putting in place the regulations decided by the social partners, and furnishing the necessary means of putting it into operation and of coordinating the work of the ASSEDIC (Association pour l'emploi dans l'industrie et le commerce, or Association for Employment in Industry and Trade) network. Within the cultural labor market, competition was already widespread, even though according to the logic of the "reformers" (MEDEF and the CFDT, administrators of UNEDIC), it was subjected to strong distortions by virtue of the (relative) redistribution of revenues introduced by the system of unemployment insurance for casual workers in the entertainment industry: the unemployment benefits effectively redistributed a part of the revenues of those who earned a lot, and had been heavily employed, to those who had been less employed and whose earnings were weaker.

If we refer to the results of the research that we carried out[2] into the conditions of work, employment, and unemployment of *intermittents*, one sees very well the problem that this mode of indemnification poses for the "reformers." In terms of causal workers, 13.5 percent earn a salary that does not reach 30 percent of the annual SMIC (*Salaire minimum interprofessionnel de croissance*, or the national minimum wage, usually given as an acceptable annual salary for full-time work).

The greatest number, 56.4 percent, earn a salary equivalent to between half of SMIC and slightly more than SMIC, while 9.1 percent of *intermittents* earn a salary equivalent to more than double SMIC. The differential between salaries is very significant and has several causes. But for our purposes here, it seems that unemployment benefits not only constitute, on average, nearly half the income of an *intermittent* (the average income of whom in 2003 was €23,374, of which €10,671 were unemployment benefits) but furthermore compensate in part for the gap between the salaries of the richest and the poorest.

For the *intermittents* earning less than 30 percent of SMIC, the average proportion of their income consisting of benefits is 70 percent; for those earning 40–50 percent of SMIC, the proportion is 59 percent; for those earning 50–60 percent of SMIC, it's 57 percent; and so forth. For those earning 150–200 percent of SMIC, the proportion consisting of benefits is 33 percent; for those who earn between three and four times SMIC, the proportion is 17 percent. The coefficient of variation of salaries is 7.21, although the coefficient of variation of benefits is 3.44. The difference between salaries is therefore significantly reduced by the allocation of benefits.[3]

The Meaning of a Neoliberal "Reform"

The system that UNEDIC wanted to "reform" is a combination of a "mutualist" system of indemnification—in which indemnities compensate in part for low salaries—and a system of indemnification on an insurance model, within which the indemnities paid out are proportional to salaries. The reform was supposed to reduce and eliminate what remained of the mutualist logic, and generalize the insurance logic that was already partially at work. That a growing number of individuals are able to "profit" from this mode of indemnification—which offers relatively better protection from the precarity and instability of the labor market than other comparable systems—is exactly what neoliberalism calls an "anticompetitive system."

A system that flattens out inequalities, even at the margins, corrects "irrationalities," and interferes with the effects and regulates the "excesses" of the market is, according to neoliberal logic, an anticompetitive system. A system that "mutualizes risks" distorts competition, as it introduces "social justice"— that is to say, a noneconomic logic that impedes the proper functioning of the market, even though the market is conceived as only capable of a "rational" and "efficient" allocation of resources.

From the perspective of the reformers, the mechanisms of unemployment insurance must not compensate for the inequalities produced by the system: it is not part of their function to reduce inequalities but on the contrary to maintain each individual in a position of differential inequality in relation to all others. The government of the market founded on the principles of competition and enterprise must see to it that everybody finds themselves in a state of "equal inequality." It is therefore necessary to intervene in the domain of social policy in order to individualize it. During the postwar period, the German liberal school of Freibourg (ordoliberalism) significantly called this kind of politics "individual social policy" in order to oppose it to "socialist social policy," meaning the policy of collectivizing and socializing social expenditure. Foucault observes that what is aimed at here is an "individualization" of social policy that takes as its goal not to assure individuals of a social protection against risks but to constitute an economic space inside of which they can assume and confront risks *individually*.

Mixed Techniques of Discipline and Security

To inscribe this logic of "individual social policy" in the mechanisms of social protection, the reform of the regime of unemployment benefits had at the same time to put to work earlier disciplinary techniques and the most recent techniques of security. The former—supervision, sanction, examination, and exclusion—are reorganized and adapted to new functions that require the latter—incitement and mobilization for employability—by way of the modulation and the individualization/differentiation of social policy. Simultaneously, the activation of these technologies of discipline and security results in an inflation of juridical and legal acts, at the same time as a reduction in the number of norms and regulations imposed by the state and the institutions charged with regulating the labor market.

The reform aims therefore to reduce the "excess" of *inter-mittents* who enjoy rights to unemployment insurance. "There are too many *intermittents*, too many companies, too many shows, too many artists," asserted the minister of culture, Jean-Jacques Aillagon, who was forced to resign one year after taking office by the radicalism of the conflict. In order to reduce the number of *intermittents*, the reforms first make use of a toughening up of the conditions necessary for access to rights to unemployment insurance. They would like, subsequently, with the encouragement of the Ministry of Culture, to bring into play other techniques of disciplinary selection: the division between "the incapable and the incompetent" and "the able and the competent"—an old disciplinary division used to categorize "the poor" is put to work by creating a distinction between "good" (employable) artists and technicians, and "bad" (meaning "unemployable" by the culture industry). A new system of national diplomas must filter, classify, select, and format in order to ensure that only the "employable" enter into the indemnification regime of the *intermittents* and careers in the culture industry, with the "unemployable" being returned to the care of the state. Kessler, explaining MEDEF's point of view, expressed regret that our epoch has forgotten the fundamental distinction of social politics, between the "able-bodied" and the "infirm";[4] "the latter have the right to assistance, but the former must find their means of subsistence in work." The "branding" of individuals takes on the character of ancient divisions: the unemployed are marked out as if they were plague victims, with the double objective of blaming them (they are not good artists) and defining them as deliberate refuseniks (they will not accept the reality of the labor market in the culture industry, and its outputs and modalities of production).

More a Political Issue Than an Economic Problem

Denis Gautier-Savanc, MEDEF representative at UNEDIC—and indicted for "lubrication of social relations" (distributing funds to unions, politicians, etc.) in 2008—declared in 2005, after having based the entire campaign to publicize the "reform" on the supposed deficit engendered by a lax system of indemnification, that the problem of unemployment insurance for the *intermittents* was not exactly a deficit problem but a problem of numbers (of individuals indemnified). He thus indicated that the problem was less an economic one than a political one: a problem of control. The method of indemnifying *intermittents* did not permit mastery over their entrance to and exit from the regime, or control of their behavior according the principle of "free competition" and capitalization; it allowed too much space and too much freedom to strategies of circumvention and redeployment of the insurance system, making it possible for participants to extract themselves, as we will see, from the logic of the corporation and "human capital." The problem of the *intermittents* is therefore a problem of the government of conduct under the new conditions of flexible production.

The reform was thus an operation of power before being an economic operation. Reducing the deficit, subjecting the accounts of the social welfare system to the logic of the enterprise, was a means of reasserting control over "the social," reasserting control over the behavior of the governed, who were attempting, according to Kessler, to emancipate themselves from the market by means of "the progressive dissociation of social protection from work."[5] This reduction in the number of *intermittents* is comparable to an "exclusion," but here the excluded are included in a "population" (the totality of the labor market)

on which governmental power is exercised in the form of a differential management of inequalities. The disciplinary technology of exclusion is incorporated into the functioning of a
security technology of managed disparities.

The action of the security government bears on a continuum that runs from the welfare recipient to the permanent
employee who benefits from the employee savings plan and
share-ownership schemes, by way of the unemployed, the poor
worker, the precarious, the *intermittent*, the temp, the part-time
employee, and so on. This continuum is regulated by a jungle
of laws, norms, and rules that create proliferating divisions
between types of work contract, modes of insertion, requalifica-
tion, training, indemnification, and access to (social) rights and
minimum social standards. This continuum, it is necessary to
observe, is not only "salarial" but also "social," as implied by
the project for "social" reconstruction, since it includes welfare
recipients, the poor, workers outside the formal economy, and
so forth.

This continuum is traversed by discontinuities, thresholds,
which the technologies of security make it possible to govern
as a whole, as a single "floating population." The proper function of government will always be, on the one hand, to set out
differences between the legal status of different group, their revenues, the training appropriate to them, the social guarantees
that they enjoy, and so on, and to make these inequalities efficacious in relation to each other. On the other hand, it will act to
amplify the politics of individualization within each segment
and each situation in order to incite further the spirit of competition: individualization of salaries and careers, individualization
of support for the unemployed, individualization of the government of the poor, and so forth. Within this continuum, no

position of relative inequality must feel stable and sure of itself. The construction of the precarious, the unemployed, the poor, and the poor worker; the multiplication of "cases" and "situations" (youths, disadvantaged youths, ghetto youths, qualified youths, etc.); and the deepening and intensification of individualization: all aim at weakening not only the individual who finds themselves in this situation but in an obviously differential manner, every position in the labor market.

Individualization as Depoliticization

In order to understand the working of the neoliberal strategy of government, it might be interesting to compare it with that of a great part of the political and trade union Left. The latter "thinks" and "acts" very often with reference to a single norm: the permanent work contract, which it wishes to generalize to the entire population. The bosses and the state, but also each successive government of the past thirty years, act and think following another logic: marking out, constructing, and consolidating a *multiplicity* of "normalities" (unemployment, precarity, part-time work, full-time work, full-time work with benefits, etc.). The government of these "differential normalities" is not aimed at their reorganization in terms of the norm of the full-time permanent contract but instead, as we have seen, at maintaining them in a state of "equal inequality," competition, and differences between situations in order to perpetuate a "mobilizing" insecurity and uncertainty. Inclusion and exclusion, normal and abnormal, do not therefore define, as they do in disciplinary societies, a "great divide." Inclusion and exclusion are "variables" of governmental action, which furthermore have a tendency to multiply cases, situations, and statuses between these two limits. Government thus acts ultimately less by way of *partition* than through the *modulation* of divisions and differences. The society of security is not a "society in which a mechanism of general normalization and the exclusion of those who cannot be normalized is needed."[6]

Unlike disciplinary societies, wherein the "inside" and the "outside" was given a priori, in the society of security they are reversible, mobile, and unstable. The apparatuses of security work continually at the limit, at the frontier between the interior and the exterior, the inside and the outside. The limit between the inside and the outside is not defined by a prior norm, since it is necessary to bring it into existence. Theories of exclusion, or even disaffiliation,[7] seem to us to hark back to disciplinary societies and not to grasp the specificity of the apparatuses of power that have been at work since 1968. Of course this is not to say that there is no exclusion, disaffiliation, and marginality but rather that their functions and objectives change within the contemporary practices of neoliberal government.

Current labor and "workfare" policies (which aim to force and encourage welfare recipients into work) introduce, to varying degrees, insecurity, instability, uncertainty, and economic and existential precarity into the life of individuals. They render insecure not only the lives of individuals but also their relationships with all the institutions that used to protect them. The insecurity of the unemployed and the precarious is certainly not the same as that of the employee of a large multinational, with employee savings and profit-sharing schemes, but there is a differential of fears that runs the entire length of the continuum. How else can we explain the generalized insecurity (which is not only economic) that reigns in a society that has nonetheless never been so "protected"? Differential management of such social differences emerges and proceeds from these differential fears, which constitute the "affective" foundation of the government of conduct through inequalities. Such inequalities play their role so much better than those that establish greater and clearer divisions. Nevertheless, thresholds and gaps are relative to what a determinate society can "tolerate" or "stand."

Gilles Deleuze and Félix Guattari found doubtless the most adequate name for what Foucault chose to call the "apparatus of security." For their part, they speak of a "micropolitics of insecurity": "the administration of a great organized molar security [that] has as its correlate a whole micropolitics of petty fears, a permanent molecular insecurity, to the point that the motto of domestic policymakers might be: a macropolitics of society by and for a micropolitics of insecurity."[8] The differential management of the labor market has a fundamental function that responds to a very precise political question: How to produce polarizations of revenue and power inside the capital-labor relation without them crystallizing into irreducible political dualisms? The government of conduct is an ensemble of techniques whose objective is the neutralization and depoliticization of that "revolutionary politics" that emerged between the end of the nineteenth and the beginning of the twentieth centuries—a politics that was capable of overturning these inequalities in a fight "to the death" between "workers" and "capitalists."

The Manufacture of "Human Capital" Entrepreneurs

How does neoliberal government intervene in the social? By making the social a function of the enterprise. It intervenes in favor of multiplicity, differentiation, and competition, and to incite, encourage, and constrain each individual to become an entrepreneur of the self, to become "human capital." Neoliberal policies involve as much state intervention as Keynesian policies did, but with the difference that unlike the latter, they cannot support "demand" but must support "supply."

Neoliberalism is, according to Foucault, a mode of government that consumes freedom, and that in order to do this, must first produce and organize it. For the neoliberals, freedom is not a natural value that preexists governmental action, the exercise of which it would act to guarantee (as in classical liberalism); rather, it is that which the market requires in order to function. The freedom that neoliberalism incites, encourages, and produces is then simply the correlate of the apparatuses of security. The great difference between neoliberal liberalism and Keynesian liberalism is that the freedom that it acts to manufacture and organize is from the start that of the entrepreneur, to which the freedom of the worker and the consumer—which was one of the Keynesian instruments of intervention—must be radically subordinated. The neoliberals do indeed therefore have a "social politics," since society is—as in the case of Keynesianism—the target of a permanent governmental intervention. What changes in comparison with the latter are the objects and aims of the intervention: it acts to turn society into an "enterprise society" and to turn the worker into "a sort of enterprise."

How can this form of government be translated into a project for the construction of the cultural labor market? For the differential government of competition in the market to become possible, it is necessary that the system of unemployment insurance functions at the same time as a system of capitalization and individual insurance. The contributions paid by entrepreneurs and workers must not amount to a form of mutualization of risks but to an individual investment against risks. It therefore represents an invested capital that must be remunerated as such. Thus, in the terms used by the reform, the period of compensation for *intermittents* is now to be referred to as the scheme-member's "capital" of indemnified days—days that the individual must manage as capital.

What does this little word "capital" do in the case of the wage earners? How does it work? It expresses the fact that unemployment benefits form part of the multiplicity of investments (in training, mobility, affectivity, etc.) that the individual (the "human capital") must make in order to maximize their performance. Consequently, benefit levels must not have the effect of redistributing revenues from one part of the population of *intermittents* to another; they must be proportional to the investment made; those who earn the most and contribute the most—because they have been employed the most—are those who must be best compensated. The model of individual insurance must everywhere replace the model of the mutualization of risk: it is not a matter of organizing the transfer of revenues from one part of society to another in order to compensate for the imbalances created by the market but on the contrary, making the mechanisms of capitalization and individual insurance function in all areas of life (health, retirement, training, etc.).

It's for this reason that the proposals for a new model of compensation put forward by the *coordinations des intermittents* (the coordinating groups of the *intermittents* struggle against the "reforms") were unacceptable to the managers of UNEDIC, even if we know today that the reform adopted is more expensive that the previous system of compensation, introduces more glaring inequalities, and encourages abuse by employers. Despite the cost of the reform that was implemented—despite, therefore, its economic "irrationality"—the *coordinations'* alternative proposal was inadmissible from the point of view of the "political rationality" of neoliberalism: it proposed a system of renumeration still more redistributive than that which existed hitherto, since in setting minimum and maximum benefit levels, it actually increased the capacity of the scheme to transfer revenues from one part of the insured population to another. For neoliberal theory, it is precisely the distribution and transfer of revenues from one part of the insured population to another, in order to correct the inequalities and excesses of the market, that transform individuals into "dependents" (*assistés*) and "passive consumers" of benefits.

The "nanny state" is defined by Kessler as the direct consequence of the "dissociation of contributions from benefits,"[9] which is in turn the consequence of the disjunction between "work and benefits." Conversely, differences in revenue, status in power, and training would have the power to transform the passive conduct of the benefits-consumer into an active conduct of entrepreneurship, a commitment of the individual to the production of their own capital. It would make of this same individual a producer, an entrepreneur who accepts the rule of the competitive game, and who undertakes to optimize their investments (in this case, their investment in insurance against the loss of employment). It's exactly this function of incitement to be an entrepreneur and an entrepreneur of the self, to play the competitive game, that the social politics of mutualization neutralizes.

Capitalization is therefore one of the techniques that must contribute to the transformation of the worker into "human capital" that must ensure for itself the formation, the growth, the accumulation, the improvement, and the valorization of the "self" to the extent that it is also "capital," through the management of all its relations, choices, and conduct according to the logic of costs and benefits, and the law of supply and demand. Capitalization must contribute to the making of the worker into "a sort of permanent and multiple enterprise." What is therefore demanded of individuals is not to ensure the productivity of labor but the rentability of a capital (of their own capital, of a capital inseparable from their own person). The individual must think of themselves as a fragment of capital, a molecular fraction of capital. The worker is no longer a simple factor of production; the individual is not, properly speaking, a unit of labor power but of skill capital, a "skills-machine," which goes along with a "life style, a way of life,"[10] a moral choice, a "form of relation between the individual and itself and, at times, its peers, the future, the group and the family."[11]

Social policy must not only be reformed in order to encourage the flourishing of the enterprise and the individual entrepreneur: it must also transform its only services into enterprises, on the terrain of accumulation and rentability. Kessler translates these precepts as follows: on the one hand, "in future, all social policy will have to be subjected to the scrutiny of economic rationality: what costs, what benefits? It will have to justify its differences and its singularities, its exceptions and its specificities according to their comparative advantages";[12] on the other hand, businesses must "reinternalize" the social welfare functions that they had externalized during the era of Fordism by delegating them to the state.

Social reconstruction is therefore the harbinger of a "new capitalism" within which the savings of employees and the general population, pension funds, and health insurance, "because managed within a competitive universe, will become once more a function of business."[13] Kessler estimates that in 1999, the value of public spending to businesses in the service sector amounted to a booty of some 2,600 billon francs, or 150 percent of total government spending. The privatization of the mechanisms of social insurance, the individualization of social policy, and the will to make social welfare into a function of business are at the heart of a project of "social reconstruction," and thus the project of restructuring unemployment insurance.

This amounts to a reversal of the logic of the welfare state. In 1939, the liberal economist John Maynard Keynes was able to describe the ends of the "welfare" that he wanted to create in Great Britain as still dominated by logics that were not exclusively economic: "a system where we can act as an organized community for common purposes and to promote social and economic justice, while respecting and protecting the individual—his freedom of choice, his faith, his mind and its expression, his enterprise and his property."[14] The generalization of business and competition used to encounter limits, even in the thinking of the ordoliberals who put in place and ran the economic policy of postwar Germany. Competition was considered by them to be a "principle of order" in the economy, but not as a "principle on which a whole society can be built."[15] By contrast, the generalization of competition by contemporary neoliberals is on a certain level absolute and without limits. It is for them a matter of generalizing the economic form of the market "throughout the social body and including the whole of the social system not usually conducted through or sanctioned by monetary exchanges."[16]

Some Remarks on the Limitations of the Foucauldian Analysis of Neoliberalism (1): Risk, Protection, and Financialization

Before pursuing our study of the struggle of the *intermittents* through the prism of Foucault's analyses of neoliberalism, it is doubtless useful to reflect on their principal limitations. Even if *The Birth of Biopolitics* constitutes one of the most complete and elaborated works on neoliberalism that we have at our disposal, there are nonetheless, in the reconstruction of apparatuses for the government of conduct that this book proposes, certain gaps and absences, which nevertheless concern an essential aspect of, if not the master key to, neoliberal practice today. For Foucault completely neglects the role of money in the changing "regime of accumulation" (the passage from "managerial" and "industrial" to "shareholder" and "postindustrial" capitalism, to use the terms currently employed by economists).

This is astonishing on several grounds. First of all, because the neoliberal conquest of the economy and society has been led and directed by finance. The transformation of part of the direct and indirect salary into financial assets, for a significant number of employees (those who are solvent), is ordered and governed by finance. Second, because financialization is the starting point for a new conception of risk and security, which has direct and immediate repercussions for the labor market and the welfare state. Since the end of the 1970s, we have without any doubt witnessed a new distribution of risks as well as the forms of protection that respond to it. Within the terms of the Fordist pact between bosses, unions, and the state—as moreover, in the French system of work and social welfare, which still thrives—the right to social protection was legitimated by the asymmetrical power relations between employer and employed that every contract of work implies. Social protection was (and still is) conceived—including legally—as compensation for the subordination of the employee. However, this conception has been completely overturned by the financialization of the economy, which introduces an entirely different conception of risk and protection that is wholly contemptuous of such codes and laws, and breaks radically with the pact or the compromises issuing from the Second World War. It therefore seems difficult to ignore the monetary question.

Deleuze and Guattari, unlike Foucault, have given us—by way of an elaboration of Marxian theory—a remarkable interpretation of money and its double nature: exchange money and credit money. In the Deleuzian schema, there are three types of money that draw three lines or designate three types of power (or impotence). First, there is money as *financial* structure (enabling the creation or the destruction of money), which draws a primary "abstract or mutant line," " a nonrealizable quantity," producing its own singularities. It is important to underline the fact that here the concept of abstraction does not refer to Karl Marx's theory of abstraction but to the idea of the virtual. Money is an abstract/virtual flux: nonfigurative, indifferent to all production, and can give rise to any figure and any production. There follows a second line, "entirely different, concrete, consisting of perceptible curves: money as method of payment, segmentable." Money, as a method of payment, allocated as wages, profits, interest, and so on. Money conceived as a method of payment implies a third line: the "totality of produced goods" of a given epoch.

The power of institutions that regulate "the production and destruction of money" (the banking system under managerial capitalism, and the financial sector under shareholder capitalism) manifests itself in the control of the operations that convert the first line into the two others by means of the manifestation of credit. Finance, in regulating the frequency and level of investment, can give rise to any figure/production. The power imbalance of capitalist societies is inscribed in the power imbalance between credit money and exchange money. The money that circulates on the stock exchange, in pension funds, in the banks, that appears in business accounts, is not at all the same as the money that we have in our pockets, or that comes to us in the form of salaries or various allowances.[17] These two moneys— exchange money and credit money—belong to two different regimes of power. What is called "purchasing power" is in reality a "powerlessness," as Deleuze very usefully calls it. It is a matter of monetary signs, which are impotent because limited to the possibility of extracting from a flux of consumption that has already been determined by the flux of credit, by the abstract line of money as capital. "A cosmic swindle," the philosopher calls it. Credit money (nonfigurative abstract line), by contrast, has the power to rearticulate "economic chains directed toward the adaptation of flows of production to the disjunctions of capital,"[18] to play on the constitution of possibilities.

Deleuze therefore introduces a notable innovation into the theory of money, conceiving it as a capitalist appropriation of virtuality insofar as it amounts to power over possibilities. The contemporary economy, as is becoming clearer and clearer, is an economy of possibilities, an economy in which finance assumes the power to name, delimit, and circumscribe the possibilities for a society and an epoch. The contemporary economy presents itself as a proliferation of choices, options, and possibilities offered to consumers. At the same time, it represents itself as a power of assemblage (it's up to the consumer, it says, to assemble its range of products: "assemble your universe!"), even though in reality the consumer has no choice outside the alternatives fixed and determined by the actualization of the "abstract line" drawn by credit money.

Under Fordism, the conversion of the abstract line, the actualization of money, was conditioned by political disagreements whose integration into the regime of accumulation was accomplished by means of political compromises (on employment, effective demand, and sharing the gains of productivity—what one can call "socialism of capital," the fruit of capital's effort to integrate the class struggle into its regime of accumulation). The hatred that the liberals vowed for the New Deal was a class hatred, directed against a counterpower that encroached, even if only partially, on the sovereignty of capitalist money. Neoliberalism is fundamentally a politics of the reprivatization of money—that is to say, a reprivatization of the power to determine and circumscribe possibilities.[19] It is therefore necessary to integrate an analysis of money from an economic as well as a political perspective into the analysis of the competitive market: "this is money and the market, capitalism's true police."[20]

What changes to notions (and practices) of risk—and protection against it—are introduced by the financialization of the economy and the privatization of money? We have discerned them in the stakes of the *intermittents'* struggle.

For a long time, to be waged meant precisely to benefit from the security of the waged condition, risk being left to entrepreneurs who received in exchange the opportunity to enrich themselves. Contemporary capitalism has inverted this equation. Henceforth, it is the wage earner who is exposed to the risks of industry and it is the entrepreneur, the shareholder, who is protected from them. This is one element of the breach of that implicit contract which previously used to link wage earners to businesses. ... The breach amounts to this: today, management—

modeling itself on the financial sector—knows how to protect itself, individually or collectively, from risk through the use of stock options and golden parachutes, but it no longer protects the wage-earners. ... The real breach, before being quantitative, is qualitative: which is much more serious.[21]

The reality of shareholder capitalism therefore leads us to refine the observations that Foucault draws from the liberal texts on competition, since the latter concern from the start and above all the workers and the "nonpropertied" population. There is a fundamental asymmetry between, on the one hand, the shareholders, the beneficiaries of the employee savings plans, and so forth, who can count on a continuous increase in income (in particular from personal assets), and who can transfer their risks onto the stock market or insurance policies, and on the other hand, the poorer section of workers and the wider population (or rather, the majority of the population) that are seeing their incomes (dependent on salaries) frozen for several years, and cannot count on a system of protections gnawed away at by the continuous and systematic reduction of social spending.

Some Remarks on the Limits of the Foucauldian Analysis of Neoliberalism (2): Private Property

But more profoundly, what does this passage from managerial to shareholder capitalism signify? It signifies that the bosses and the state, beginning in the 1970s in the United States and the 1980s in France (at the moment of the first socialist presidency), have progressively disengaged themselves from their pact with the unions (the US New Deal, exported, as it were, to Europe after World War II). According to Foucault, this pact antici-pates an accumulation founded on full employment (of men, as women were dependent on the security of male employment), support for consumption (the politics of demand), the growth of GNP, the redistribution of profits and wealth, and the provision of social goods or the allocation of collective goods. The slowing down and the impotence of social and wage/incomes policies driven by the unions became apparent when, as Foucault already signaled in the 1970s, neoliberals aimed at the final liquidation of the Fordist pact's objectives and politico-economic priorities. At the European level, the objective of neoliberal policies is "full activity," and no longer full employment, if one understands by "employment" work that is relatively assured in its duration (preeminence of the permanent contract, firmly fenced in by the right to work and covered by the system of social protections). Everyone will have to work under whatever conditions. What is aimed at, as in England and the United States, is the *precarious full activity* of a growing section of the population and all age categories.

This calling into question of the Fordist pact, implying a new distribution of risk and protections, allows us to introduce another concept that is equally strangely absent from these Foucauldian lessons on neoliberalism: the concept of "private property." Neoliberal policies are, in the final analysis, a revenge on the New Deal and the compromises that the "propertied" were forced to make with the nonproprietorial classes, under threat of "civil war" and an irreversible crisis of capitalism after the crash of 1929. The New Deal crystallizes all the class hatred of liberals such as Friedrich Hayek, because it strikes at the very source of the liberal conception of freedom and right: private property.

Robert Castel uses the concept of "social property," in opposition to the private property from which the workers were excluded, to define the conquests of the labor movement (protection against the risks of illness, unemployment, old age, etc.). Social property is the means for the propertyless to get access to property by collective rights—that is to say, by means of the institution of the waged workers as a "class," as a political subject. Situated in the history of property, neoliberalism is a politics whose meaning and principal goal are the reversal of these political conquests in order to reduce, wherever possible, these forms of socialization and mutualization of wealth and property, and prefer to them a "de-proletarianization" that takes place by means of individual access to property. De-proletarianization by means of individual access to private property: this is one of neoliberalism's most potent instruments of depoliticization.

Theories of risk, which have flourished with the rise of neoliberalism, smother the concept and the reality of "private property," which constitutes the essential motor of shareholder capitalism, under a vocabulary that obscures the real political battle and the stakes that are in play around the question of "risk."[22] The affirmation of theorists of the "risk society," according to which we are leaving behind a "world of enemies" and entering into a "world of risks and dangers," is emblematic of this way of thinking. The observed reality is entirely different: if there is a conflict around unemployment insurance, it is because there is hostility, because there is a political disagreement that bears directly on the question of knowing who has the right to name risks, and who has the right to decide the modes according to which they will be protected against and how they will be financed (who pays?).

In France, MEDEF, through the theory of the risk society, exhibits all its class interests, since the substitution of individual insurance for social welfare is one of the means of reestablishing the power of private property over social property, and determining a redistribution of power and income in favor of the former. In 2005, in the United States—the country where the neoliberal program has gone furthest—the income differential between social classes had returned to the level of 1928. The neoliberals have succeeded, at least at the level of incomes, in effacing the New Deal.[23] The "socialism of capital," this specter that the welfare state more or less used to represent, must be systematically dismantled, wherever the relations of force permit.

Some Remarks on the Limits of the Foucauldian Analysis of Neoliberalism (3): The "Silent Revolution" in Pension Funds

There remains to take into account a third great change introduced by contemporary capitalism that Foucault did not include in his lectures on liberalism in the 1970s. The financialization of the economy surely constitutes a part of the apparatuses for the government of conduct because it outlines a new alliance or a new form of integration between capital and work, no longer founded on employment, the redistribution of the proceeds of productivity, and so on, but on shareholdings and savings.

Neoliberalism was born at the moment of the monetarist turn on the part of the US administration and the Federal Reserve, which in multiplying the range of instruments for profiting from savings, drove them toward the financing of business and the economy via the stock market. The "silent revolution" in workers' and employees' pension funds, in effect the investment of earned savings in the market economy, constitutes the essential element—from the point of view of the government of conduct—of the monetarist turn. The mobilization of pension funds for investment in the stock market, for example, has one very precise goal: it is a matter of "eliminating the separation between capital and labor implicit in the Fordist salary relationship by strictly tying workers' savings to processes of capitalist transformation/restructuring."[24] The new US alliance between certain fractions of capital and sections of the salariat no longer proceeds from the sharing of industrial profits, or on the basis of secure employment or consumption, as was the case during the Fordist era, but instead proceeds from the profits and rents generated on the stock market (that is, on the basis of savings and investments).[25]

What interests us more particularly in this neoliberal turn is the fact that the "revolution" in pension funds was started by the fiscal crisis of New York State in 1974–1975—that is to say, with a crisis of the social regulation (and not only the industrial regulation) of capitalism. The pension funds of public employees were used to fund the *welfare* deficit of the state, with the unions thereby replacing the traditional investors in public expenditure. The crisis, before being industrial, was social, and it was in response to this crisis that new techniques and apparatuses capable of managing it were developed. The investment of employee savings for the reduction of the deficit of the New York welfare state achieved a double objective: implicating state employees in the regulation of social spending (blackmailing them with the threat of deficit) while cutting the ground out from under the feet of any possible alliance between the "dependents" (the poor, the unemployed, single mothers, young people, etc.) and the providers of social services.

The de-proletarianization that the German ordoliberals wished for (the construction of small units of production, aids to homeownership, "popular" shareholding, etc.) is here achieved on the basis of a new way of managing the savings of permanent workers. From this perspective, the aim of neoliberalism has always been the same since then: "a wage earner who is equally a capitalist is no longer a proletarian," despite the fact of the "growing proletarianization of the economy."[26]

These policies exert a certain power over the conduct of wage earners because they "divide" them internally, making them "schizophrenic": the wage earner and the investor, while they may be merged in the same person, nonetheless clearly do not possess the same rationality. Shareholder capitalism creates new divisions and new inequalities, which in breaking apart the solidarities of class, plunge trade union politics into impotence and constrain them in an exclusively defensive attitude. Corporate restructurings, redundancies, relocations, and productivity drives—in businesses whose risks are the responsibilities of their employees—are all demanded by the corporate investors representing the pension funds of other wage earners.

This analysis of pension funds brings to light a new terrain of struggle, which must not limit itself to the defense of the social gains of Fordism. For the neoliberal program introduces a remarkable innovation that we must find the capacity to turn against neoliberalism itself: shareholder capitalism everywhere promotes and generalizes the disconnection between income and employment, between income and work. The objective of restoring the value of work—as sought by French president Nicolas Sarkozy—is absolutely ridiculous and fallacious in the context of a capitalism that systematically favors income from investments, property, oil resources, and intellectual property rights (the logical outcome of the reestablishment of rent is the reestablishment of inheritance—the exact opposite of the meritocratic principle advocated by the neoliberals—as exemplified by Sarkozy's initial economic program in 2007, with its massive reduction of inheritance tax). This is the point of disconnection that we must shift in order to open up the possibility of new forms of socialization and mutualization. What must be generalized is not employment but the disjunction that shareholder capitalism would like to reserve exclusively for the owners of capital.

Subjectification, Responsibility, and Workfare

The conception of the individual as "entrepreneur of the self" is the final outcome of capital as a machine of subjection. For Deleuze and Guattari, capital acts as a formidable "point of subjectification that constitutes all human beings as subjects; but some, the 'capitalists,' are subjects of enunciation that form the private subjectivity of capital, while the others, the 'proletarians,' are subjects of the statement, subjected to the technical machines."[27]

With the idea of "human capital," we can speak of the accomplishment of the double process of subjection and exploitation. On the one hand, "human capital" takes individualization to its ultimate extreme, as the subject draws on all its "immaterial," affective, and cognitive resources of the self in all its activities. On the other hand, the techniques of "human capital" lead to the identification of individualization and exploitation, as the "entrepreneur of the self" is at the same time their own boss and own slave, capitalist and proletarian.[28] As Foucault notes, with neoliberalism the practices of government become focused on the individual and their subjectivity, behavior, and style. Where classical economic analysis confines itself to the study of mechanisms of production, exchange, and consumption, it allows the choices and decisions of the worker themselves to escape scrutiny; by contrast, the neoliberals want to study work as economic conduct, but as economic conduct in practice, put to work, rationalized, and calculated by the one who works.

The techniques of security are therefore procedures that ceaselessly integrate new elements (behaviors, reactions, and opinions) and new expert knowledges (from doctors, psychologists, economists, sociologists, and social workers), which bear on the diagnosis and eventually the reform of individuals. The tracking of the unemployed, introduced by MEDEF's "social reconstruction" project (and the reform extended to *intermittents*), can be understood as a security technique that works for the transformation of the "excluded" worker, the unemployed, the minimum-wage earner, and the nonaffiliated precarious worker into "human capital"; that is, as a technique that mobilizes the individual and their talents and competences in order to adapt them to the supply of available work. Here we are far from the appealing image that labor policies normally create for themselves, as it is the disciplinary technique of punishment, obedience, obligation, subordination, and culpability that is most often mobilized, reactualized, and redeployed by "workfare" (obligatory work) programs. For all that unemployment has become embedded in socioeconomic reality as an "endemic illness," the government of conduct largely focuses on this disciplinary dimension, on the construction of a disciplinary logic adapted to the needs of security. Unemployment therefore appears as the fault of the unemployed, as a "moral" sickness of the individual. Subjection works through the attribution of responsibility, or still more through the attribution of culpability.

According to Kessler, the "progressive dissociation of work" leads to a distribution of rights "without those rights depending on any prior or subsequent participation in productive activity. … Rights without responsibilities, rights which are not the counterpart to a contributive effort, this is what we call that dependence … which, as used to be said unquestionably in an earlier epoch, demoralizes."[29] This new theory of risk implies the moralization of "workfare." On the one hand, "for the traditional social risks—accident, illness, old age—are progressively substituted the risks of not being "employable," of not being able to fit in."[30] On the other hand, risks today are "more endogenous than exogenous; they depend in part on behavior. The vector of risk is not independent of the vector of behavior."[31] The notion of employability, as deployed by Kessler, expresses precisely this change of paradigm, which addresses directly the subjectivity of the individual, as the risk of unemployment "can no longer be considered as unconnected to the behavior of individuals" and their "lifestyles." To be employable means to match one's behavior and lifestyle to the demands of the market. Risk is thereby characterized as a complex mixture of "random events and more or less predictable events in which the intrinsic characteristics of individuals and their behavior play an important role."[32]

According to the terms of the bosses' project for "social reconstruction," we are therefore going to enter into the era of *monitoring*, the "individual tracking" of behavior and lifestyles, the injunction to demand of benefit recipients that they "take responsibility for changing their behavior" and their ways of living. Ernest-Antoine Seillière, interviewed by Ewald, summarized the new functions of social policy as follows: "Social welfare thereby changes from the constitution of a universal right into the management of a lifestyle."[33]

Workfare is precisely the retooling, the adaptation, of an old disciplinary technique (the control of the worker), which acts on the movements of the body in a closed space, to the new techniques of security and control (*monitoring* and individual tracking). The politics of *workfare* is a good example of the way in which disciplinary techniques can be integrated and rendered functional within the apparatus of security, integrating heterogeneous apparatuses of power into a new modality of government.

The Effects of the Power of Money: Debt as a Technique of Training for the "Responsibilization" (Culpabilization) of "Human Capital"

Among the effects of the power of money over subjectivity, the most important are those exercised by "debt." The origin and foundation of money is not the exchange of commodities (Marx) but the contraction of a debt (Friedrich Nietzsche). The system of debt (financial and moral; according to Nietzsche, their origin is identical) causes responsibility and culpability to circulate simultaneously among the governed.

Contemporary capitalism, on the one hand, encourages governed individuals to incur debts. In the United States, where total savings are in deficit, one makes use of all kinds of credit (to consume, buy a home, pursue one's studies, etc.) while absolving molecular indebtedness of all blame; on the other hand, it makes the same individuals culpable by rendering them responsible for the molar deficits (of social welfare, health insurance, unemployment insurance, etc.), which they must dedicate themselves to repaying. This incitement to take on debt and this obligation to make sacrifices to reduce the "excesses" of social

spending are not contradictory, as they act to install the governed in a system of "infinite debt": we are never finished with
debt within financial capitalism, simply because it is just not
repayable. This "infinite debt" is not primarily an economic
apparatus but a security technique for reducing uncertainty
about the time and the behavior of the governed. By training the
governed to promise (and honor their debts), capitalism disposes
of the future in advance, since debt makes it possible to predict,
measure, calculate, and establish equivalences between current
and future behavior. These are the effects of the power of debt on
subjectivity (culpability and responsibility) that allow capitalism
to construct a bridge between the present and the future.

In Nietzsche's *Genealogy of Morals*, the possibility of extracting a "civilized man" from the "wild man"—that is, a man who
is "predictable, regular, calculable"—depends on the capacity
to promise—that is, on the fabrication of a memory of debt.
The memory of contemporary civilized" man is the memory of
employability, availability, and docility before the laws of the
labor market and consumption, since this leaves him liable for
a debt.

According to neoliberal logic, unemployment benefits are
not a right acquired by virtue of paying one's dues but a debt
that must be repaid with interest: it must be paid in the form
of the constant efforts of the debtor to maximize their employability. The "services" of the welfare state are therefore not social
rights won through struggle but a "credit" that the system has
kindly extended to you. If the mnemotechnics that neoliberal
government puts in place are not, most of the time, as atrocious
and bloody as those described by Nietzsche (execution, tor-
ture, mutilation, etc.), their meaning is identical: constructing
a memory, inscribing obligation in the body and the mind. In

order for these effects of the power of money over subjectivity to function, it is therefore necessary to exit the logic of individual and collective rights, and enter into the logic of credit ("investments" of human capital).

The capitalists who "burn up" hundreds of billions of dollars with every financial crisis without encumbering themselves with any memory or any obligation are the same who, faced with a €900 million deficit in the unemployment insurance regime of the *intermittents*, evoked economic and social catastrophes on an apocalyptic scale.[34] Despite the claims of the band of "social reconstructors" (Ewald, Kessler, and Seillière), financial capitalism is anything but a "riskophile" capitalism, since as we have seen with the "subprime" crisis, it is not the "entrepreneurs" but others (the taxpayers) who are obliged to settle the debts that they did not themselves contract. The miracles of capitalism ...

Money not only shapes the general laws that the economists assure us to be natural but also produces these effects over power on subjectivity by means of specific techniques of individualization. Your banker knows your account's flows of debit and credit with a precision that makes it possible to draw up a precise and specific cartography of your "lifestyle," govern your "conduct," and modulate your access to credit. The utilization of techniques tied to "infinite debt" for the individualizing training in culpability and responsibility begins very early for "human capital," even before entry into the labor market. In the United States, 80 percent of students who complete a masters of law accumulate a debt of $77,000 if they attended a private institution and $50,000 if they attended a public university. The average debt of a medical graduate is, according to a study by the Association of American Medical Colleges, $140,000.[35]

The Tolerable Equilibrium of Precarity in Neoliberal Capitalism

One of the first consequences of the intervention of neoliberal politics in the social, as we can state easily with reference to the construction of the cultural labor market, is the increase of poverty. The creation of human capital that is employable by the culture industry and creditworthy to the insurers is accomplished at the expense of a growing number of "new poor." Poverty within neoliberalism is not linked to a lack of development. It is not the symptom of a backwardness that economic growth will reduce. Poverty is entirely created within the interior of an "objectively" rich society by the apparatuses of segmentation, division, and differentiation. Neoliberal poverty is completely different from the poverty with the countries of the North such as Italy knew until the 1960s. The new poverty is the product of a political will in a capitalist society that has "vanquished" "material poverty."

Neoliberal politics utilizes the formidable accumulation of wealth, knowledge, and possibilities, placing humanity on the threshold of "the end of material poverty" in order to produce and reproduce a new poverty, a new precarity, and a new insecurity. Its problem is not the elimination or the diminution of precarity, or the absorption or reduction of inequalities. Neoliberal society is at ease with a certain level of precarity, insecurity, and inequality, just as disciplinary societies were at ease with a certain level of illegality that they themselves had created. Neoliberal logic wants neither reduction nor the elimination of inequalities for the good reason that it plays on these differences, and governs on the basis of them. It seeks merely to establish a tolerable equilibrium—an equilibrium between different normalities that society can stand: between the normality of poverty and precarity, and the normality of wealth. It no longer concerns itself with "relative poverty," the income gap, or their causes. It is interested only in that "absolute poverty" that prevents the individual from playing the game of competition. It must therefore define a threshold, a vital minimum above which the individual can become once more an "enterprise," and above which the gaps between incomes can and must be considerable, and below which the individual falls outside the social game, the game of competition, at which point they must be helped, but in a fashion that is specific and limited, and not systematic.

To establish this tolerable equilibrium, to produce a new form of poverty, the neoliberals use the institutions of the welfare state (to which they are always violently opposed because they create social property), but reversing the functions and the goals for which they were created. In the same way that they have tamed the democratic institutions against which they had always fought (universal suffrage,[36] for example, mastered by virtue of the fact that "representation" is always dominated by the "oligarchy of wealth"), the neoliberals are now able to master the institutions of the welfare state, as so many apparatuses for the government of conduct, the production of inequalities, and the manufacture of poverty. According to neoliberal logic, all protections against risk, all institutions of social property, are institutions that must function minimally (minimum wage, minimum age of retirement, minimum income, etc.), and the minimum has a political meaning, since it defines a threshold below which there is a risk of "civil war," a breach of the social peace. Via these techniques of the minimum, we can see well how neoliberal policies effect a reversal of the institutions of protection, transforming them into apparatuses for the production of insecurity, the limits of which are set by the level of the risk that those who are being rendered insecure will be mobilized and politicized. The theory of the risk society would therefore have everything to gain by integrating into its development the risk thresholds to which the neoliberals are sensitive: the risk of revolt, politicization, and the abrogation or even the simple reduction of their "privileges," including the right to private property, which they regard as the most "human" of rights.

The State as Precursor

The interventionism of the state (focused on the market and the company), as highlighted by Foucault in his analysis of ordoliberalism in postwar Germany, has been intensified still further by neoliberal policies. In all the countries of the capitalist West, it is the state that puts in place the laws and norms that open the way to the neoliberal reconstruction of the market as a supposedly self-regulating system.

State interventions to favor the construction of a competitive market have been very numerous in France: liberalization of financial markets, corporate tax breaks, the public valorization of the entrepreneurial model, the establishment of precarious work contracts, the implementation of the RMI,[37] labor policies (up to the introduction of the thirty-five-hour week, which made possible a flexibilization of work within the company by allowing the calculation of overall workloads and renumeration on an annual basis), "workfare," the implementation of neoliberal fiscal policies, reduction of "fiscal pressure" on the most affluent (negative taxation, etc.). Sarkozy's "fiscal package" was, at the time of its introduction, only the latest (and most grotesque) charitable measure in favor of the rich.

On the more specific terrain of unemployment insurance, the apparatuses—implemented in the context of the boss class's "social reconstruction"—of behavior monitoring, the management of lifestyles by way of "individual tracking" of the unemployed with a view to adapting them to the demand for labor and adding value to them as human capital, are largely inspired by the RMI, introduced and managed by the state. The state practiced the individualization of social policy long before the "social reconstruction" of the bosses, to which it opened the way. According to the terms of the "inclusion contract" managed by the state, just as much as those of "individual tracking" managed by the "social partners,"[38] benefits are no longer thought of as a universally shared social right, but as a right that is dependent on the implication of the subjectivity and the behavior of the recipient—a right guaranteed by the signing of an individual "employment plan." The individualization of social policies, the new management of poverty (the RMI), the introduction of fiscal incentives to work, and the management of the labor market by way of precarity have all been tested extensively by government administrations, long before the moment of "social reconstruction."

In the *intermittents'* dispute, the state, even if it is not the immediate origin of the reform, has played a decisive role. We can distinguish two broad types of state intervention in the conflict. On the one hand, the state took charge of the management of the crisis created by the cancellation of the main festivals of summer 2003, and its cost. On the other hand, the minister for culture opened a "new front," shifting the struggle over social rights onto the terrain of cultural policy. What we can see in effect already from September 2003 is a strategy that catches opponents of reform in a pincer movement, trapping them like a vice: on the one side, UNEDIC's initiative to reduce the deficit and the overall number of *intermittents*; on the other side, a series of state interventions involving regulation, limitation, and employment in the culture sector that would have the same effects.

The Management of the Dispute

Faced with the radicalism and the determination of the movement—and notably the *coordinations*, which were designed for the conduct of a medium-term campaign—the state brought all its financial might and power apparatus to bear on the implementation of the reform, in an attempt to weaken and divide it. The continuity of the dispute, the doggedness and the variety of initiatives and types of struggle with which the *intermittents* prolonged their mobilization (the performers' strike of spring 2005, two and a half years after the triggering of the dispute, was the biggest in the French arts sector since 1968), forced the state to put in place a policy of 'recovery" of those *intermittents* who had been expelled from the system by the reforms (the "transitional allowance fund"),[39] preventing, until April 1, 2007, the full implementation of the protocol signed in June 2003.

According to Michel Largave, the administrator for the fund, 41,337 *intermittents* had drawn on it by February 2, 2007. By the end of 2006, the fund had cost €220 million since its creation.[40] The transitional fund is a double-edged policy, clearly representing a political victory for the movement, which guaranteed a continuous income to thousands of *intermittents* for two years, but also forming a part of the state's strategy for normalizing the sector, the aim of which was to give the reform time to do its work of selection and exclusion—even if this cost money in the short term.

The ministerial interventions aimed at managing the dispute (contrived consultation exercises, ceremonious public announcements, proposals for the construction of a "just and equitable" regime, threats of recourse to law if the social partners did not arrive at a satisfactory agreement, expert studies, etc.) all amount to delaying tactics. But these maneuvers also have another, equally important, function: blocking the contagion and circulation of demands to other sectors and into the very interior of institutions. The government entrusted the management of the crisis to the minister for culture and not to the minister for employment and social cohesion—the point being to define the problem of unemployment insurance for *intermittents* as a cultural problem and not as a problem of relative social rights. The minister for culture exerted all his might to try to prevent a parliamentary vote on the alternative proposals for reform of the insurance system put forward by the committee established by some members of the *coordination* and a Green member of Parliament—proposals that had gathered the support of representatives across the political spectrum (with the exception of the National Front).

Cultural Politics

The implementation of the reforms required an engagement on the part of the state that unfolded in three stages, each having as its objective the reduction of the number of *intermittents*. The first stage is constituted by the cultural labor policy, which, on the one hand, aims to replace wherever possible *intermittents'* contracts with permanent contracts, and on the other hand, indexes the financing of cultural projects to the creation of jobs and particularly the creation of permanent jobs. An economic principle—permanent employment—becomes at the same time the standard against which to measure artistic or cultural work, and the instrument of social differentiation. The state enunciates and applies a logic of "regulation": fewer *intermittents*, but "better" paid, "better" insured, more employable by the culture industry, and more permanent posts, while the "surplus" are taken charge of by state welfare services. This enables the state to find a vast network of alliances, for the only actors in the conflict who oppose this discriminatory logic of permanent employment, even among the *intermittents'* organizations, are the *coordinations*.

The second stage, which like the first, generates consensus among UNEDIC, the unions, the political parties, and the state, still with the exception of the *coordinations*, concerns the "professionalization" of the sector. This comes down to the erection of barriers to entry into the entertainment professions through the creation of state diplomas[41] and the restriction of the field (excluding all "nonartistic" trades, reducing the number of trades and professions that can enjoy *intermittent* status). The "professionalization" of the *intermittents* amounts to a restoration of state control over access to *intermittent* status and the career trajectories of *intermittents*, returning power to the state to determine who is and is not an artist.

The final proposal, which once more isolated the *coordinations* and ensured the consensus between the social partners, was for "regulation." The administrative regulation of small companies (above all in the performing arts) organized by ASSEDIC and the regulation by the state in order to discourage "cheats"—that is to say, those who use the unemployment insurance not within the "normal" limits of a system of insurance against the loss of work, but effectively expand its scope to include the financing of plans for work, training, and life in general for *intermittents*— shares the same will to division and differentiation, with a view to reducing the number of beneficiaries. It is therefore a matter of mobilizing state structures and the civil service in order to drastically reduce the incidence of "intermittent" work and replace it with permanent employment.

The state, therefore, not only accepted the logic of the reform but also, in imposing the permanent contract as the norm against which to measure cultural and artistic work, aggravated and deepened the effects of division and exclusion in the labor market that it brought about. This is typical of the ways in which, above and beyond this particular dispute, the state works for the generalization of the norms and techniques of corporate governance across the totality of social relations, while itself adopting, soliciting, and organizing the generalization of the idea of "human capital" and its associated behaviors within every domain of society. The state, as so often in the history of liberalism, far from being a force that is external and hostile to *Homo economicus* and his laws, is the very institution that initiates, experiments with, installs, and diffuses the new modalities of the government of conduct. Neoliberalism is not a struggle of corporations and private interests against the public power but a change in the government of conduct that implies a redistribution of functions between public and private. Contrary to the beliefs of liberal ideology, the legal apparatus and state administration are far from playing a minor or subordinate role in bringing this change about.[42]

In the case of the *intermittents*, without these interventions, it would never have been possible to implement the reforms, and the supposedly automatic mechanisms of the market would never have been able to function and produce their effects. The state disengagement called for by neoliberal policies concerns only the financing of social welfare, and the means of protecting workers and the wider population—never the financing of corporations. On the contrary, during just the period of the neoliberal "rolling back" of state power over the economy, public spending in the form of "corporate welfare" has exploded.[43]

According to a study carried out in 2006 by the inspectorates of two ministries—finance and social affairs—at the request of the prime minister, following questioning by the Employment Advisory Council (Conseil d'orientation pour L'Emploi, or COE), the "welfare benefits" that France contributes to businesses far exceed the ten billion registered by the European Commission. These "welfare benefits" amounted in fact to some sixty-five billion in 2005, or 4 percent of GDP. "This," explain the inspectors, "is a little more than the national education budget, almost double the defense budget, [and] equivalent to the total spending on hospitals." In its public report of 2004, the Court of Audit evaluated at 2.4 percent of GDP the total sum spent on public support for employment (in other words, on "welfare benefits" for businesses). And shortly after this, President Sarkozy announced, with regard to the purchasing power of the citizenry, that the "coffers are empty."[44]

We can draw a partial conclusion from the preceding observations. The hypothesis that we believe ourselves to have verified throughout the course of the *intermittents'* dispute is as follows: the subjection of the "wage earner," the subjection of "human capital," and the neoliberal logic of the corporation, on the one hand, and the logic of the defense of the rights of the standard salariat, on the other, establish together a new government of conduct that is precisely what the behavior and struggles of the *intermittents* refuses, flees, deflects, and combats. As we have been able to discern over the course of the *intermittents'* dispute, neoliberal logic is not the only one that incites competition. The trade union logic of permanent employment encourages a competition that is no less fierce between workers (permanent and precarious wage earners, the employed and the unemployed, workers and poor workers, etc.). The logic of division and separation is not produced solely by the neoliberal policy of "reform" of the unemployment insurance but also by the policies favoring "cultural employment" based on permanent contracts, promoted by the Left as much as by the Right. These employment policies (or policies of full activity), in multiplying both economic and social differences and inequalities, favor the differential management of liberal government and are completely subordinate to the neoliberal politics of the optimization of differences.[45]

The Critique of the "Artistic Critique" and Its Discontents

Liberal policies not only create and intensify inequalities between different social layers; they have just the same effect *within* each social stratum. The case of the *intermittents du spectacle* is a very illuminating example of the segmentation, the fragmentation, and the displacement to which neoliberal policies have subjected the "unlocatable middle classes." Contemporary capitalism polarizes and fractures the middle classes, entailing new modes of behavior and subjection in the fields of employment, unemployment, and work.

The New Spirit of Capitalism[46] by Luc Boltanski and Eve Chiapello is quick to subsume these mutations into the category of
the "artistic critique." More generally, in the work of sociologists and economists concerned with the changing nature of
capitalism, and more specifically the artistic and cultural labor
market, there is a marked tendency to see artistic work and its
modes of operation as the model from which neoliberal economics draws its inspiration. This discourse is ambiguous and
warrants interrogation. At the same time, the definition of the
"artistic critique" and the role attributed to it in contemporary
capitalism by these authors raises a number of problems. For the
movement of artists and technicians in the performing arts that
would have been expected to incarnate this "artistic critique" is
the one that in reality, has made the fiercest and most articulate
critique of it.

The thesis that runs through *The New Spirit of Capitalism* is as
follows: the "artistic critique" (founded on the freedom, autonomy, and authenticity that it demands and asserts the value of)
and the "social critique" (founded on the solidarity, security, and
equality that it demands and asserts the value of) "are often carried out by distinct groups" and are "incompatible." The torch
of the "artistic critique" was passed from the artists and students
of May 1968 to the "creatives" at the "top of the sociocultural
hierarchy" who work in the media, finance, advertising, show
business, fashion, new media, and so on. The "social critique,"
by contrast, was passed from the workers of 1968 to the "little
people," the subordinated and excluded of neoliberalism. The
artistic and social critiques are "largely incompatible."

The "artistic critique" provokes in Boltanski and Chiapello
a degree of unease, even mistrust, which they conceal poorly.
From their perspective, this is easy to understand, since the

"artistic critique, once again, is not spontaneously egalitarian: it always runs the risk of being reinterpreted in an aristocratic sense," and "unchecked by considerations of equality and solidarity, it can very quickly play into the hands of a particularly destructive liberalism, recent years have shown."[47]

Besides, the artistic critique is "not, in itself, necessary for the efficacious indictment of capitalism, as is shown by the prior successes of the labor movement that were obtained without the help of the artistic critique. May 1968 was, from this point of view, exceptional." Not only is the artistic critique unnecessary, except in order to "moderate the excessive egalitarianism of the social critique" that risks "dismissing the importance of liberty" [sic], but it is furthermore the Trojan horse of neoliberalism, to which it is allied by virtue of their shared aristocratic taste for freedom, autonomy, and authenticity, which the artists first passed on to the "students," having found its realization in the lifestyles of the "bobos."[48]

Reading this book, one feels that it is shot through with the resentment toward May 1968 that for some years has run through the French intellectual elites, from certain sections of the extreme Left to the conservative and reactionary Right, by way of the nebulous "republican" center, for which Foucault, Deleuze, and Guattari paid the price, to the extent that they, supposed masters of the improbable "thought of 1968," are thought to have planted the seed of liberalism in people's heads without realizing it. Boltanski and Chiapello here revive for us the opposition between liberty and equality, autonomy and security—an opposition that belongs to another epoch, and on which historical socialism and communism both broke their teeth.

The Political Limits of the Concept of the "Artistic Critique"

There are many problems with Boltanski and Chiapello's critique of the "artistic critique," but the biggest is precisely the existence of the resistance movement among "artists" and "technicians" in the arts, and the emergence of the *coordination* of *intermittents* and precarious workers of which it constitutes the most fully realized expression. The five words of one of the slogans of the *intermittents'* movement—"no culture without social rights"— suffice to shake Boltanksi and Chiapello's entire theoretical edifice, and make clear the limits of their analysis of contemporary capitalism. Translated into their language, the slogan "no culture without social rights" becomes, in effect, "no liberty, autonomy, or authenticity without solidarity, equality, and security." That which Boltanski and Chiapello consider to be potentially "aristo-liberal," as incompatible with social justice, becomes a terrain of struggle—the only one, perhaps, starting from which we can confront and wreck the logic of neoliberalism.

The movement of 2003 demolished the supposed separation between, on the one hand, the "creatives" of the new liberal professions, and on the other hand, "the poor," "the little people," and "the precarious" of the new labor market. The *coordination* of *intermittents* and precarious workers of the Île-de-France proposes, simply in its name, a refutation of the supposed incompatibility between "artistic critique" and "social critique." The *coordinations* bring together the artist and the temporary worker, the artist and the precarious worker, the artist and the unemployed worker, and the artist and the welfare recipient. And this is certainly not a matter of some vague political solidarity.

The artists and technicians have given an account of themselves such as the sociologists have visibly been unable to give:

the precarious, the new poor, the unemployed, and the welfare
recipient are not opposed to the artists and technicians, because
the majority of artists and technicians live or will live in a state
of precarity, often experiencing unemployment and dependence
on welfare. Boltanski and Chiapello bemoan the fate of the "little people" [sic], the "poor," and the "unemployed," but what
this leads them to underestimate, if not to negate, is their capacity for action and struggle:

> The mobility of the little people, being usually a forced mobility, does
> not really permit them to play an active role in the creation of networks.
> They are tossed about at the whims of their employers, according to the
> terms of their contracts, moving from one to another in order to avoid
> disappearing completely from the scene. They circulate like commodi-
> ties in a network which they never weave themselves, and on the other
> hand are exchanged by others in order to maintain their own connec-
> tions. As we explain when we describe the nature of exploitation in a
> network, the mobility of the great—a source of flourishing and profit—
> is exactly the opposite of the mobility of the small, which for them
> amounts to nothing more than impoverishment and precarity. Or, to
> repeat one of our formulas, the mobility of the exploiter has for its exact
> counterpart the mobility of the exploited.

And yet ... and yet the little people, the poor, and the precarious don't just complain. They invent the new weapons that
are necessary in order to fight flexible finance capitalism on its
own terrain—the terrain of mobility and discontinuity—in an
effort to reverse the disconnection from revenues and work that
the new bosses would like to guarantee exclusively to the owners of capital. Even within the very real asymmetries of power
that characterize social relations under capitalism, "mobility"
is far from being merely "forced," and the capacity to construct networks is far from being an exclusive prerogative of
the "great." The struggle of the *intermittents* has been possible

because it has relied on a tremendous density and differentiation of the networks that have constituted the real logistical basis for the struggle. The same thing could be said of the unemployed workers' movement that Pierre Bourdieu described as a "miracle."

The strongest, most determined, and most lucid resistance to the liberal project of the French boss class ("social reconstruction") has come from the "poorest" and most "precarious" of the artists and technicians in the performing arts—those who find themselves at the bottom of the income scale. It is the *coordinations* of *intermittents* and precarious workers who have proposed a new model of compensation that for all that it proceeds from the specificities and modalities of employment, unemployment, and work in the cultural sector, is extendable and adaptable to all "temporary workers," and not only to artists and technicians in the performing arts. This model, elaborated from the side of the "artistic critique," is founded on solidarity, security, and justice, which Boltanski and Chiapello call "the social critique." It's the *coordinations des intermittents* that have demonstrated that the terrain of struggle (for a system of unemployment insurance) is adequate to the nature of finance capitalism—which is to say, is capable of securing at the same time equality and autonomy, and even mobility. The "poorest" and the "smallest," the least well off of the *intermittents*, called for a system of insurance against flexibility, because they knew how to construct networks of solidarity and cooperation in order to resist the injunctions of the cultural labor market. It is these networks and this flexibility (which one more time, even among the poorest, is far from being always forced) that during the struggle, have been invested as highly effective instruments of mobilization. Can we now seriously maintain the opposition between "artistic critique" and "social critique"?

The Sociological Perspective

From a sociological perspective, the concept of the "artistic critique" surely brings with it a host of misunderstandings. The social divisions created by neoliberal policies bear no resemblance to the caricature of the social composition and the cartography of inequalities depicted in Boltanski and Chiapello's book.

Let us return to the description of those social groups that, according to Boltanski and Chiapello, are the bearers of the "artistic critique" and try to see why it is a caricature, and a demagogic one at that:

> Moreover, it is crucial to see that the artistic critique is today carried out above all by well-placed persons, college graduates, often working in the "creative sector" (marketing, advertising, the media, fashion, new media, etc.), or even on the financial markets and for consultancies, and that their awareness of the lives of those at the other end of the social scale—casualized workers, who in themselves have no interest in mobility—is close to zero.

The fissures produced by neoliberal policies do not run between the new liberal professions and the new proles, the connected and the unemployed, a "new creative class's" working in the "creative industries," and an old working class that works in the "traditional industries." Rather, these inequalities are internal to the aforementioned "creative professions," which according to the authors of *The New Spirit of Capitalism*, are the bearers of the "artistic critique." None of the professions that they present as typical of the heralds of the artistic critique is a homogeneous entity; each corresponds to an ensemble of situations that are highly differentiated in terms of status, salaries, social protection, workloads, length of employment, and so forth. It is possible to work in the performing arts, the press, architecture, and so on, and be rich, with a secure position, or poor and in a situation of extreme precarity. Between these two extremes, there exists an infinite variation and a very wide modulation of situations and relative statuses. The fissures of neoliberal societies do not run between those individuals who work in the media, advertising, the theater, and photography, on the one hand, and the workers, employees, precarious, and unemployed, on the other. These fissures run through the new liberal professions, the "creative" professions, because, very simply, a proportion of the individuals who work in those professions are themselves poor, precarious, and lacking in security.

We could say exactly the same thing about almost all the professions mentioned by the authors, notably university researchers whom they should—it is not unreasonable to imagine—know a bit better. The "precarious researchers" movement contributed to the clarification—some months after the *intermittents'* movement—of the true position of a section of the "creative" or "intellectual" professions in the universities and research institutions. The movement against the CPE[49] and its order words, against "precarity," would not have been possible without these two movements of "creatives" at the "top of the social hierarchy" that preceded it.

Furthermore, if we want to complete the picture of cultural labor that we have begun to draw in broad strokes, by incorporating the modifications implied by considering the issue of *intermittence*, we have to take into account the number of "artists" who are not covered by the regime of unemployment insurance. We can therefore add to the inequalities produced inside the system the social divisions that emerge outside it. An indeterminate number of artists subscribe to the scheme without ever accumulating enough hours to acquire rights to benefits. An inquiry into those musicians (the most numerous group among the *intermittents*) who claim RMI by the statistical department of the Ministry of Culture[50] produced the following results: on December 31, 2001, 12.3 percent of musicians and 9.5 percent of other performing artists received RMI; on December 31, 2002, the figures were 11.4 and 8.8 percent, respectively; on December 31, 2003, 11.6 and 9.4 percent; on December 31, 2004, 12.3 and 10.1 percent; on December 31, 2005, 13 and 10.3 percent; and on December 31, 2006, 12.2 and 9.4 percent.

If we add to these "excluded" the visual artists and all those whose "artistic" professions are not included within the scope of the unemployment insurance scheme, a more complete picture of the situation emerges. Among visual artists, the only ones who really get by (excepting the very small numbers of artists who make a living from the highly speculative contemporary art market) are those with a teaching post. The others are, once again, unemployed, receiving RMI and living on the social minimum. Recall once more that in Paris, 20 percent of RMI recipients describe themselves as engaged in an "artistic" occupation.

We find data comparable to those that we have established from our inquiry into the *intermittents* in studies bearing on the "the middle classes adrift." The new capitalism "only really delivers for a tenth of newcomers, whose living standards remain very uncertain because of the generalization an 'up or out'—ascension or exclusion—mechanism." Only a "very upper middle class" reaches the heights of the private salariat (corporate lawyers, expert accountants, finance and management executives, etc.), but "at the other extreme, precarity goes hand in hand with a very modest standard of living."[51]

As in the case of the *intermittents*, there would seem to have been a "structural excess." The young, children of the "former middle classes," are considered "superabundant" and "overqualified":

For the generations aged thirty to forty today, while the level of qualifications is increasing, the social starting points themselves improve, and so the number of potential candidates for entry into the middle classes is rising, half of mid-level public posts have simply disappeared and their private sector equivalents have grown too slowly to absorb the growing number of candidates. This discrepancy is nowhere so pronounced as for intermediate level positions.[53]

In the United States, these same phenomena of downward mobility and precarization are in the process of killing the supposed "American dream," and the central role, as much political as economic, that the "middle class" used to play in it. "Welcome to Middle Class Poverty" is one of the most effective slogans of the New York–based Freelancers Union. Thus, even in the United States, the "new professions" ("Film/Television, Advertising, Graphic Design, Health Care, Journalism, Fashion, Financial Services," etc.)[52] are very far from identifying with the false image conveyed by *The New Spirit of Capitalism*, as they are at the starting point of a new wave of "unionization," mutualization, and solidarity. In brief, the "creative class" does not exist, even in the United States,[53] because the "new professions," the "creative sectors" (media, fashion, culture, etc.), are not homogeneous blocs. The new professions are therefore not analyzable with the "molar" categories used by the authors of *The New Spirit of Capitalism*.

Equality and Freedom: "Social Critique" and "Artistic Critique" in the Welfare State

The logic of autonomy and freedom, and the logic of solidarity and equality, are in reality far from being incompatible. In accordance with the strategy of the *intermittents*, they must, on the contrary, unfold together, in harmony, if we wish to think of a new politics of social rights. In confining ourselves to the classic terrain of the "social critique,"we concede to the neoliberals the possibility of criticizing the welfare state in the name of "freedom" and "autonomy."

The neoliberals, in order to legitimate their policies of transformation and reducing public spending, make use of the critiques that the movements of the 1960s and 1970s made of the increasingly invasive controls being exercised by the state over the lives of individuals. The struggles that got under way around 1968 had known very well that the "securitization" of existence, the welfare state's program after the Second World War, was also a technique of the government of conduct, as it "facilitates the direction of individuals, albeit according to a totally different method from disciplinary mechanisms."[54]

For Foucault, to whom we owe this analysis, the major drawback to the system of social welfare constructed over the course of the twentieth century is the "dependence" of individuals on the state. But this dependence is not only understood as dependence by virtue of "exclusion" or "marginalization."[55] (the poor, the weak, and the "abnormal," dependent on the state for their survival); it is dependence by virtue of "integration" in the case of the wage earners themselves. "Social welfare," in fact, does not fully benefit the individual except when the latter is integrated, be it in their familial, occupational, or geographic milieu.[56]

Thus will be protected that which is "already protected," says Foucault.

Social welfare is not a simple insurance against social risks (unemployment, accident, or old age) but a technique of government based on a particular way of life to which it subjects individuals, and any person or group that does not want to accede to this way of life finds themselves marginalized. Integration into the welfare state on the part of the "salariat" implies subjection to a "lifestyle" that imposes a series of linear passages and programs leading from one enclosure to another (school, army, factory, or retirement). The securitization of existence during the so-called *Trente Glorieuses*[57] had as its direct counterpart the acceptance of this "destiny."

The welfare state and "social rights" of Fordism are ambivalent; they amount to indisputable social victories, and yet on the other hand, they exercise equally manifest power effects over individuals. It's this ambivalence that, if we wish to resist neoliberalism effectively, we must recognize, think through, and deal with. The social struggles of the 1960s and 1970s show precisely that it is possible to carry on a struggle for "new social rights" that allies autonomy with equality, and operationalizes the critique of the welfare state's "power effects," and its effects of subjection and individualization. For Foucault, "the objective of optimal social protection combined with a maximum of independence is quite clear." In the face of the new dependencies and new power effects, according to Foucault, there "is most certainly one positive demand: for a security that opens the way to relationships that are richer, more numerous, more diverse, and more supple with oneself and one's milieu, which at the same time ensures for all a real autonomy."[58]

The *intermittents'* struggles take place precisely at the point of articulation of these two realities: "protection" and "dependence," "subjection" and "autonomous subjectification." It is not because these struggles take on "government by individualization" and highlight, by contrast, "everything that can make individuals truly individual" that they open the way to liberalism.[59] It is rather because the "social critique" of the traditional Left refuses to confront the "power effects" of the welfare state and does nothing but defend the "social gains" that it remains impotent in the face of neoliberalism. If the "social critique" does not move onto the terrain indicated by the *intermittents*, where freedom and equality are not opposed, it will have no chance of winning out against the neoliberal initiative. It will remain, as it is now, subordinated to the apparatuses of the government of conduct.

New Forms of Governmentality

In the glorification of "work," in the unwearied talk of the "blessing of work," I see the same covert idea as in the praise of useful impersonal actions: that fear of everything individual. Fundamentally, one now feels at the sight of work—one always means by work that hard industriousness from early till late—that such work is the best policeman, that it keeps everyone in bounds and can mightily hinder the development of reason, covetousness, desire for independence. For it uses up an extraordinary amount of nervous energy, which is thus denied to reflection, brooding, dreaming, worrying, loving, hating; it sets a small goal always in sight and guarantees easy and regular satisfactions. Thus a society in which there is continual hard work will have more security: and security is now worshipped as the supreme divinity.
—Friedrich Nietzsche, *Daybreak*

The evolution of the liberal mode of government poses a series of questions that Foucault was little able to anticipate. The picture of new forms of the government of conduct that he draws is still that of the first phase of the deployment of neoliberalism, which came to a close with the first Gulf War. At this moment, the horizon of government became that of the internal and external war of security. The resplendent neoliberals of the *new economy*, the epic of the entrepreneur of the self, the freedom to create and innovate, are succeeded by the somber neoconservatives of the "clash of civilizations," the war of good against evil, and the reestablishment of "eternal" Western values (nation, family, and work). The logic of competition has transformed into the logic of "security" war, and into racism both internal and external to a nation-state, whose authority it would like to reassert. The new *Homo economicus* who takes on the task of economic and social innovation transforms very quickly into a bringer of destruction and restoration. The "freedom" of enterprise that liberalism asserts against the "equality" of "state socialism"—incarnated in the welfare state and its politics of "care"—transforms into the suspension of habeas corpus even in the homeland of neoliberalism.[60]

From this perspective, the work of Deleuze and Guattari suffers from none of the "ambiguities" that litter Foucault's lectures on neoliberalism, to the point where one sometimes has the impression that he himself fell under the spell of neoliberal "governmentality." According to them, contemporary capitalism's government of conduct is characterized at the same time by the institution of "hypermodern" mechanisms (finance, communication, marketing, management of "human capital," etc.) and the deployment of mechanisms of subjection that they call "neoarchaic," in that they produce and reproduce anew that which the former seem of necessity to bypass (racism, war, the nation, class divisions, the values of family, work, authority, merit, etc.). Hypermodernity and neoarchaisms are not contradictory processes but the two complementary faces of the same mode of governing our societies.

The capitalist process of deterritorialization with the "continuous upheaval of production, uninterrupted disruption of all social categories, insecurity, and unending movement ... while referring always to universalizing perspectives, has never been able to achieve anything, historically, except to fall back into reterritorializations of a nationalist, classist, corporatist, racist, paternalist order."[61]

The German ordoliberals had, in their own fashion, perfectly grasped this problem. The generalization of the logic of the market and the corporation implies an increased need for political and social integration, as competition is a "principle that dissolves more than it unifies." The market and the corporation systematically unmake that which society holds together. The ordoliberals therefore oppose the "warm values" of state, nation, the social, civil society, and so on, to the "cold values" of competition, the market, and the corporation.[62] The economic relation is incapable, on its own, of informing something like a community, and so is obliged to seek it elsewhere, in dimensions of social life that are not strictly economic, outside the logic of capital.

Neither economic nor juridical subjects are able to guarantee social integration. "Human capital" and "the subject of Right" mobilize and represent only partly "partial aspects," "abstract" "ideas" of subjectivity that are incapable of guaranteeing, as such, the conditions of a common life, a community. For that to be possible, they must be integrated into a far vaster and more complex ensemble: society, the social. On the one hand, the market is a universal principle that establishes a link between economic subjects that "is, if you like, non-local. ... There is no localization, no territoriality, no particular grouping in the total space of the market."[63] On the other hand, contrary to the claims of the famous liberal motto, private vices do not lead to public virtues. Economic interest is a selfish interest that in undermining the social and political conditions for the community, needs "disinterested interest"[64] (sympathy or malevolence, love or hate)—that is, noneconomic interests—in order to integrate itself and function within society. Economic subjects, without the production and reproduction of bonds of "sympathy and benevolence" toward certain individuals, and without the production of bonds of "repugnance" and malevolence toward other individuals, would never be able to play their economic role. Only "disinterested interests" are capable of defining the territories, the singular regroupings that territorialize the selfish and ideal interests mobilized by *Homo economicus* and *Homo juridicus*. In other words, the economic bond and the juridical bond "strengthen the community, but in another way undo it."[65]

The social that territorializes, that makes it possible for economic interests to exist, can only be a social characterized by "malevolence" and repugnance, insecurity and fear, since the market, competition, and the corporation constitute the dynamic and the tempo of all action. If the dynamic of the economic phenomenon is not constituted by exchange as in classical liberalism, but by competition and the corporation, then mistrusts, fear, and insecurity are not phenomena external to the market but directly and forcefully exuded by it. The trust necessary to the working of the market presupposes a prior mistrust because the other is a competitor, a rival, an enemy who must be vanquished. The generalization of the market, competition, and the logic of the corporation to all social relations is a generalization of mistrust and fear of the other. US neoliberalism, having destroyed what remained of the "benevolent" and "socialist" territorializations of "welfare," naturally adopted the "malevolent" values of Christian fundamentalism and internal and external war in order to underwrite its integration into society. For the same reasons, war was an intrinsic necessity for the "Third Way" of Blair's new social democracy, which made the market and competition into society's governing principles.

Racism (internal, toward immigrants, and external, toward other civilizations) is one of the most potent phenomena of "repugnance" and "malevolence" that contributes to the constitution and the fixing of the territories, the "identities," and the "values" that "capital" lacks. In practice, the government of conduct today in all the capitalist West is structured by this phenomenon, which emerging at the end of the nineteenth century, has undergone an explosion and a neoarchaic reconfiguration with the growing power neoliberal economic policies. In Italy, Sylvio Berlusconi, in order to assure the hypermodernity of his politics, needed the racism of Lega Nord (Northern League) and the authoritarian neofascism of Alleanza Nazionale (the National Alliance). In France, Sarkozy's discourse of "rupture,"[66] "reform," and "modernization" had to be connected to a Ministry of Immigration and National Identity, and the affirmation of the values of "work, family, and nation." We return, therefore, to one of our starting points. "The social" not only constitutes the plane from which the heterogeneity of the economic and juridical dimensions is to be managed but will also have the function of ensuring the integration of the different power apparatuses through the exclusion and hatred for the other of which the immigrant is the symbol.

As regards the "hypermodern" dimension, Foucault describes neoliberal governmentality as a politics that brings us out of the "disciplinary society." It takes us beyond disciplinary mechanisms, as it puts in place policies for the government of conduct that operate through the "optimization of the system of differences"—in other words, through the differential management of disparities in situation, income, status, training, and so on, as we have seen in the case of the *intermittents*. From the point of view of its "modernity," the problem of "securitized" government is not that of the normalization of heterogeneity but that of the management of differences.[67] The optimization of these disparities is obtained by a modulation of rights, norms, and rules, which espouse and form a "supple" segmentation of the population. The divisions, fissures, and differentiations are "fractal" rather than dualistic. They even occur *within* the old class divisions, as we can see in the case of pension funds (some have access to this form of savings, and others pay the price), or across the whole terrain of the fragmented and displaced "middle classes."

More generally, we can assert that alongside a *dialectical* and *hegemonic* implementation, a *differential* management of power takes up position. In the disciplinary society, the deployment of power is hegemonic in the sense that is founded on the division between the normal and abnormal, inclusion and exclusion, and the hegemony of the first over the second. In contemporary neoliberal society, the deployment of power is not hegemonic but differential, because for it, the abnormal, the excluded, and the marginal are not other or exterior but are differences that must be managed in conjunction with others.[68]

The securitized society, which Foucault saw emerging at the
end of the 1970s, would need neither to comply with "an exhaus-
tive disciplinary system" nor incite an "indefinite need for conformity." On the contrary, the security societies that Foucault
saw emerging "would tolerate a whole series of different and
varied behaviors, bordering on the deviant, and even mutually
antagonistic."[69] In security societies, power would be "subtler,
more skillful," with room for maneuver for a "tolerated pluralism." Its modalities of government would be exercised through
an optimization of difference, leaving the field free for "oscilla-
tory processes, and a tolerance for individuals and for minor-
ity practices." The apparatuses of power would act in order to
limit deviant, seemingly antagonistic differences, minorities,
and behaviors "within acceptable boundaries, rather than imposing on them a law that says 'no.'"[70] On the "hard segmentarity"
of industrial capitalism, structured according to the "either-or"
dichotomy (the exclusive disjunctions between work and unemployment, masculinity and femininity, the intellectual and the
manual, the heterosexual and the homosexual, etc.), which stri-
ates perception, affectivity, and thought in advance, enclosing
experience in predetermined forms, is superimposed a more
"supple" segmentarity that seems to multiply possibilities, differences, and social groups. The production of dualisms and the
management of differences are superimposed and effectuated
according to the relations of force—the strategies and the objectives of political situations that are specific in each case.

Alain Badiou and Slavoj Žižek are saying nothing new when
they assert that the logic of "minorities" (women, homosexual,
intermittents, Arabs, etc.) fits perfectly with the logic of capital
since these "differences" and "communities" can easily constitute new markets for corporate investment.[71] Not only, as

Foucault suggests, does the capitalist organization of society "tolerate" subjective territories that escape its grasp, but "it has itself set about creating its own margins," and "has furnished individuals, families, social groups, and minorities with new subjective territories." If capitalist logic multiplies the forms of intervention by causing "ministries of culture, ministries for women, for black people, for the insane, etc." to spring up everywhere, "it is so as to encourage particularized forms of culture, so that people should feel themselves to inhabit some kind of territory, rather than feeling lost in an abstract world."[72]

But it is important here not to mix everything up—in particular, to confuse that which distinguishes minorities as "states," as "communities," of which the identitarian contours effectively configure new market niches, and minoritarian politics, the "minor becomings" that are something else altogether. The workers as revolutionary subject, bearer of the universal, through which Badiou and Žižek think they can bypass the question of minorities, once blocked in their "becoming revolutionary" (i.e., becoming-minor), were moreover, long before the "minorities," the first great mass consumer market.

"Ethnic diversity" can be considered in several ways one of the matrices of new forms of the government of conduct and new forms of accumulation. The "orthodoxy of power is multicultural," asserted the historian Michel de Certeau, thereby anticipating the success of multiculturalism in the 1980s and 1990s on both sides of the Atlantic: "The dominant society deals with diversity itself through means that render all differences accessible to everyone, that detach them from the specific meaning according to which a particular community assigns them, and that thereby levels ethnic heteronomies in submitting them to the general code of individualized diffusion." The government of society through the optimization of inequalities and differential management is, for de Certeau, a "hybrid monism" (a term that echoes Foucault's "tolerated pluralism"), which "transforms, rewrites, homogenizes, and totalizes the supple contents into a rigid grid."[73] The grid is not that of the disciplinary enclosure but of the circulation of differences, the singularity of which has been neutralized in the open space of security societies.

From the Government of Souls to the Political Government of Men

The disciplinary apparatuses and security apparatuses, whose actions in the "reform" of the *intermittents'* labor market we have just described, make up part of a new and original form of power. Different apparatuses of power operate, and heterogeneous relations of power are exercised within the labor market. On the side of general and universal laws, decreed by Parliament, defining, for example, the length of the working day, on the side of rules and norms negotiated by the social partners—bosses' unions and wage earners' unions—which can just as well concern business agreements as the mechanisms of financing and compensating unemployment through ASSEDIC, there exists an "archipelago" of power relations that are neither global nor general, but local, molecular, and singular. The individual tracking of the unemployed, the techniques for the integration of RMI recipients, business management, the coaching of wage earners as of the unemployed, generalized continuous training, the apparatuses of credit and repayment, and so forth—all institute processes of subjection that differ from submission to a law, a contract, or a democratic institution.

The techniques of differentiation, individualization, and molecular subjection, outlined or prefigured by what Foucault calls "pastoral power," have been inflected, modified, enriched, and augmented first by "policy,"[75] and then by the welfare state (whose French name—*l'État-providence*, or "providential state"—recalls its religious origins) in the early nineteenth and late twentieth centuries, thus transforming the techniques for the "government of souls" into techniques for "the political government of men." This genealogy allows us to specify the molecular nature of the power effects of neoliberal governmentality. Christianity, the only religion to have organized itself into a church, "gave rise to an art of conducting, directing, leading, guiding, taking in hand, and manipulating men, an art of monitoring them and urging them on step by step, an art with the function of taking charge of men collectively and individually throughout their life and at every moment of their existence."[74]

This art of government is, so to speak, completely unknown to political philosophy and theories of right. "The strangest form of power, the form of power that is most typical of the West, and that will also have the greatest and most durable fortune. ... This form of power so typical of the West and unique, I think, in the entire history of civilisations," in contrast with the majority of modern and contemporary political models, maintains no relationship with the Greek and Roman political tradition.[75] Pastoral power and its modern avatars must not be confused with the processes used to subject men to a law, a sovereign, or democratic institutions. Governing, says Foucault, is not the same as "reigning," it is not the same thing as "commanding," and it is not the same as "making the law." Such are all theories and practices of sovereignty (the king, the prince, or the people), theories and practices of the *arkhè*—that is, a form of political organization founded on the question of knowing who is entitled to command and who is entitled to obey (at the root of the political analyses of Jacques Rancière and Hannah Arendt), all juridico-democratic theories and practices, not forgetting most currents of Marxism, which neglect the processes of the government of conduct, despite their centrality to power relations under capitalism, especially contemporary capitalism.

Foucault enumerates the characteristics of this "micropower," highlighting what distinguishes each of them from ancient and modern theories of "macropower." Pastoral power establishes between men a series of complex, continuous, and paradoxical relationships that are not political in the sense understood by democratic institutions, political philosophy, or almost all revolutionary and critical theories. Pastoral power is "a strange technology of power, treating the massive majority of humans as a flock with a handful of shepherds."[76] By contrast with sovereignty, it is not exercised over a territory (city, kingdom, principality, or republic) but a "multiplicity in movement" (a flock for the practices of the church and a "population" for governmentality). Instead of addressing individuals as subjects of right, "capable of voluntary action," capable of transferring rights and delegating their power to their representatives, capable of assuming the magistracies of the polis, pastoral power targets "living subjects," and their everyday behavior, subjectivity, and conscience.

The pastor, remarks Foucault, is not fundamentally a judge or a citizen but a *doctor*. Pastoral power is a "beneficent" power: it cares at the same time for the flock and the sheep in the flock, taking charge of them one by one. By contrast with sovereignty (or the law), which is exercised in a collective fashion, pastoral power is exercised in a "distributive" manner (it is deployed "from individual to individual," step by step, communicating by singularities). It is preoccupied with each soul, with each situation and its particularity, rather than with the higher unity constituted by the whole. Its action is local and infinitesimal, rather than global and general.[77] Pastoral power—like its legatees, which are "policy"[78] informed by "raison d'état" and the welfare state—concerns itself with details and intervenes in the infinitesimal, on the molecular level of a situation and a subjectivity. It is a continuous and permanent power. It is not exercised intermittently, like power founded on rights, sovereignty, or citizenship (transfer of rights by contract, delegation of power by vote, the execution of public offices, etc.), but all day long and lifelong. Pastoral power is individualizing. The pastoral technologies of individualization operate not through categories of birth or wealth but a "subtle economy" that combines merits and demerits, their trajectories and circuits.[79] This economy of souls institutes an absolute dependence, a relation of submission and absolute and unconditional obedience not to the law or "reasonable" principles but to the will of another individual. "Obey because it is absurd" is the motto of Christian submission, of which the monastic rules constitute the ultimate fulfillment, while the Greek citizen only allows himself to be governed by the law and the rhetoric of men, such that according to Foucault, "the general category of obedience" does not exist for the Greeks.

The pastor is also a doctor for the soul, teaching modes of existence. The pastor must not limit himself to teaching the truth but also and above all must direct consciences, by means of an action that is "not global or general" but specific and singular. Saint Gregory therefore enumerates up to thirty-six different ways of teaching, depending on who is being addressed (rich or poor, married, sick, happy or sad, etc.). The teaching takes place not through the enunciation of general principles but "an observation, a supervision, and a direction that is exercised over conduct at every moment, and in the least discontinuous manner possible." Pastoral knowledge thus produces a "perpetual knowledge that will be the knowledge of people's behavior and their conduct.[80] The technologies of the confession, the examination of conscience, and so on, constitute equally instruments for examination of the relation to self and relations with others that make it possible to act on the affects and sensibility of each subjectivity. The pastor must "account for every action of each of his sheep, everything that happened to every one of them, everything they have done, for good or ill.[81]

Pastoral power's direction of conscience does not have for its end the mastery of the self, autonomy, and liberty (from dependence on the passions), as in ancient society, but to the contrary, the complete renunciation of the will, humility, and the neutralization of all individual, personal, and self-centered activity. Pastoral power is not a power that institutes a community of equals, of peers, ruled by the principles of equality and liberty. It favors and exalts not the active citizens of the republican and democratic tradition, but rather, a generalized system of reciprocal dependencies. The techniques of pastoral power aim at the production of a subject who is "subjected" to networks that imply the general servitude of everyone to everyone. The assimilation and transformation of these techniques of individualization by "policy" in the service of raison d'état, in the sixteenth and seventeenth centuries did not fundamentally change its nature. Policy secures "an ensemble of controls, decisions, and constraints that bear on men themselves, not to the extent that they have a status, not to the extent they occupy a place within the social order, structure, and hierarchy, but to the extent that they do something, to the extent that they are capable of doing it, and to the extent that they carry on doing it throughout their lives."[82] The economy of *merits* and *demerits*, the direction of conduct in everyday life, today constitutes the motor of those practices and discourses that are supposed to individualize, control, regulate, and order the behavior of the governed at work, in training, unemployment, health, consumption, communication, and so forth.

These management techniques—which from the corporation, have extended themselves to individualizing regulation (the unemployed, the RMI recipients, and the poor) and society in general (the school, the hospital, communication, and consumption)—still draw inspiration from these molecular practices, which distribute merits and demerits, which produce dependence and subjection, even when dependence and subjection are produced, as in the case of the "entrepreneur of the self," by the activation and mobilization of the initiative and freedom—or capacity to act—of the individual. Pastoral power is not exercised in the light, in the transparency and visibility of public space, but in the opacity of the "microrelation" (individual to individual, institution to individual), in the dark everydayness of the factory, the school, the hospital, and social services. It is the molecular model for power relations—manufacturing fractal and multiple hierarchies and divisions, subtler and more mobile than those deployed by the traditional oligarchies of wealth and birth—that will see a continuous extension and exponential growth under capitalism.

The Archipelago of Power Relations and the Definition of the Political

The transformation of pastoral power into the political government of men does not replace sovereignty or disciplinary mechanisms. On the contrary, it renders the problem of sovereignty more acute since the government of men introduces other subjects than the subjects of rights. Government no longer substitutes itself for disciplinary mechanisms; instead, it uses them to individualize the population and intervene, deeply and delicately, in the mass, on the details and the infinitesimal of each situation and subjectivity. This form of power is not exercised in opposition to the law, democratic institutions, or sovereignty. It slides under global power relations, constituting a series of micropolitical techniques that pass through the nets of the codes (of work and social welfare, etc.) and laws, causing them to evolve. A problematic relationship (but an often very effective one, as we have seen in the case of the reform) has thereby been established, since the earliest days of capitalism, between macropolitics and micropolitics, between governmental techniques and the collective, general, global logic of sovereignty, rights, and democratic institutions. Thus power works according to increasingly heterogeneous logics: totalization and individuation, collective action and distributive action, power dualities and power differentials, centralization and decentralization.

From its earliest beginnings, capitalism has developed a different form of power to sovereignty, right, and democratic institutions—a power that is always in process, an actualized power. To the side of and beneath democratic institutions and laws, to the side of and beneath constitutions, there is a constituent power at work that does not sit in deliberative assemblies but that works in a diffuse and everyday fashion, that constructs, undoes, and fissures, passing through global relations and general hierarchies, in order at once to transform and confirm them. The analysis of pastoral power and capitalist society as an archipelago of heterogeneous power relations has significant implications for the definition of "the political," and the modes of struggle and resistance. To the singularity of techniques for the exercise of power corresponds the specificity of refusals, revolts, and resistances, which all express the will not to be governed or to govern oneself. This is not to imply, as Foucault emphasizes, that there was first the pastorate and then the movements of resistance, revolt, and counterconduct. The microphysics of power and micropolitics open new dimensions of action, bringing in a multiplicity of practices that the classical tradition, and almost all critical and revolutionary theories, define as nonpolitical. The whole originality of Foucault, on the one hand, and Deleuze and Guattari, on the other, was precisely that they not only analyzed power as a multiplicity of apparatuses and relations but also affirmed the multiplicity of modalities of resistance and revolt, and the multiplicity of modes of subjectification. Different forms of resistance intervene and act in the same struggle: resistance to power as sovereignty, resistance to power as economic exploitation, and resistance to power as the government of bodies and souls (as the direction of conducts and consciences). If these heterogeneous modalities of resistance always manifest themselves together during a revolt or a revolutionary sequence, they nonetheless retain their singularity and specificity. During each such revolt or sequence, there is always one of these forms of resistance and subjectification that takes precedence over the others.

In the nineteenth century, what generally took precedence was the claim for political rights and universal suffrage. With the Communist movement at the beginning of the twentieth century, it was the question of sovereignty (the taking of power) that took precedence over the others. With the "strange revolution" of 1968, it was resistance to modern pastoral power—the refusal of the government of bodies and souls—that seemed to prevail. It was neither the claim for political rights nor the fight for sovereignty (to take power), nor the revolt against economic exploitation, that was preeminent within the movements of 1968, although all these elements of revolt and refusal were present. It was the struggle against the form of management in the school and the factory, in relations with the self and others (the power of women over men, teachers over pupils, parents over children, doctors over patients, administration over all ways of life, etc.), that was at the heart of 1968. Struggles against being governed and to govern oneself seem thus to be characteristic of contemporary forms of refusal. The Marxist tradition maintains a paradoxical relationship with the modern form of pastoral power. On the one hand, in opposing the separation of the political from the social, it grasps—on the side of juridical relations, beneath the functioning of democratic institutions (and their principles of liberty and equality), other power relations that express themselves in the factory and in the direction of the economy.[83] But on the other hand, its discovery of relations of power heterogeneous to the classical definition of the political is limited to industrial labor and blocked by its exclusive focus on this. This tradition thinks it can contain the microphysics of power, and the counterconducts that it both incites and regulates, reducing them to economic and productive relations. Its definition of the political and the political subject flows from this, according to which there is only one significant strategic power relation (the relations of production) and only one revolutionary subject (the working class).

Between 1750 and 1810–1820, suggests Foucault, the concept of political economy was understood in at least two ways. Sometimes this expression aims at "a particular strict and limited analysis of the production and circulation of wealth," and sometimes at "a sort of general reflection on the organization, distribution, and limitation of powers in a society.[84] Marxism did not follow this path (powers—in the plural—and society), and locks itself, like the whole discipline of economics, into the first.

The heterogeneity of the power relations of political economy to those of sovereignty and democratic institutions is interpreted within a frame that defines the former as the material base of the latter. The economy is seen as the foundation of right and political representation, even though, if we follow Foucault, it is really a question of heterogeneous apparatuses of power that act on the same plane but according to heterogeneous logics. The relation of *modern* pastoral power to Marxism would appear therefore to be somewhat paradoxical: it is at once recognized, disfigured, and neutralized by political economy.

It is important here to clarify one point. Foucault's microphysics and Deleuze and Guattari's micropolitics have nothing to do with the order-word "small is beautiful," or the valorization or exaltation of marginality. On the one hand, they bear on specifically capitalist power relations, and their relation to sovereignty, democratic institutions, and the state. On the other hand, they force us to problematize the models of political struggle that we have inherited from the workers' movement. The political question that the struggle of the *intermittents* can help us to raise is,

How do people coordinate[85] the struggles for rights, the struggles on the terrain of political representation and sovereignty, and economic struggles, with the struggles against being governed and to govern oneself?

The Production and Regulation of a New Type of "Unemployed"

We have mobilized the micropolitical approach of Foucault and Deleuze and Guattari to analyze "economic" categories such as "work," "employment," and "subjectivity," and their power effects on subjectivity. Our understanding of economy and these categories finds itself thereby reconfigured within a new theoretical and political frame. Unemployment, employment, and work are not "natural" realities with an objective existence, an economic existence in itself, which would be anterior to the pastoral institutions and techniques that are supposed to govern them. Unemployment, employment, and work are the results of a construction that operates at the intersection of apparatuses that enunciate the law, the norm, opinions, categories, knowledges, and other apparatuses and techniques of individualization that manage and regulate the conduct and behavior of the governed.

The Deleuzian and Foucauldian distinction between "discursive" and "nondiscursive" formations[86] can help us to map the power apparatuses of production and government that the conflict has brought to the fore. We can thereby distinguish the different apparatuses to which the struggles of the *intermittents* have been opposed according to their relative objects. Nondiscursive apparatuses or practices intervene in what we can *do* (our possible or probable actions), while discursive apparatuses or practices intervene in what we can *say* (our possible or probable utterances). By "nondiscursive practices," we understand the apparatuses (the ANPE[87]—managed by the state and its agencies—and UNEDIC and ASSEDIC—managed by the unions, businesses, and workers) that inscribe, fix, monitor, summon, distribute benefits, decide on expulsions and sanctions, and organize tracking of the unemployed (interviews, files, and training). Through interventions in the level of benefits, the length of period of entitlement, the conditions of access to benefits, the checks, the expulsions, the tracking, and so on, these apparatuses shape the limits of the possible or probable actions of the insured (by equating time without work with time spent looking for work, encouraging workers to train according to the dictates of the market in "human capital," etc.). These practices aim to govern "the unemployed" according to two different logics: as "subject of right" and "living individuals" as "citizens," and as "the governed." Unemployment insurance is one of those welfare state apparatuses within which relationships are negotiated between political power—exercised over civil subjects (who have rights)—and "pastoral" power, which is exercised over living individuals, over concrete and singular subjectivities (who have an age, skills, a sex, and particular ways of doing, thinking, behaving, etc.).[88]

By "discursive formations" or "discursive practices," we understand an ensemble of heterogeneous apparatuses of enunciation. The assemblages of enunciation and their functions have very different characters. Parliament enunciates laws (in this case, the laws concerning the right to work and the right to social welfare), UNEDIC enunciates norms, ASSEDIC and ANPE the regulations, the universities produce scholarly statements and classifications, the media produce opinions, and the experts produce expert judgments. "Unemployment," "work," and "employment" as categories, opinions, and judgments, materialize at the intersection of these different regimes of enunciation. These statements and enunciations act on a multiplicity of publics (citizens, media, university teachers, national and local representatives, socioprofessional categories, etc.) by using different techniques for the production of meaning and communication, according to a logic of differential management of publics and the constitution of opinion. At the intersection of discursive and nondiscursive practices, we can describe unemployment, employment, and work as "global effects" or "mass effects" of this mutually supporting multitude of discursive and nondiscursive processes and apparatuses (economic, political, and social; producing statements and knowledges).

"The economy" is an ensemble of activities regulated at once by the different corporeal techniques and procedures that are exercised on the possible or probable action of the governed, and by the semiotic apparatuses that are brought to bear on the speech and the possible statements of the governed. As such, there is no properly and simply economic reality of capitalism, or capital, that "pastoral" law, norms, and techniques and apparatuses of enunciation should then regulate and represent. Capital does not have a logic all its own, autonomous and independent laws, that it would then be a matter of limiting, of regulating through rights, opinions, knowledges, and techniques of subjectification; it needs endlessly to be instituted. Capitalism has no historical existence except when an institutional framework, positive rules (legal and extralegal, like pastoral techniques of individualization), and "disinterested interests" ("the social") constitute its conditions of possibility. The economic process and the institutional framework, writes Foucault, "call on each

other, support each other, modify and shape each other in cease-
less reciprocity."[89]

Governmentality carries out the composition and integration
of this multiplicity of processes by using first one apparatus and
then another, now this procedure and now another, by foster-
ing technologies that are sometimes corporeal and sometimes
discursive. But government is also, and primarily, a strategic
relation between *governors* and *governed*, wherein the first try to
determine the conduct of the second, while the latter develop
practices "to not be governed," to be governed as little as possible, to be governed in another fashion, according to other
principles, by other technologies and knowledges, or even to
govern themselves. Foucault names these strategies of resistance
and creation "counterconducts"; they open up onto "autonomous and independent" processes of subjectification—that is,
processes of self-constitution.

The counterconducts and processes of subjectification that
we have been able to observe in the struggles of the *intermittents* are as multiple and differentiated as the power apparatuses
that are supposed to regulate them. They express themselves in
different fashions (at the molecular level by flight, diversion,
and cunning; at the molar level by the attempt to overturn the
situation of domination, by direct and open confrontation with
power apparatuses, etc.), which are nonetheless not mutually
contradictory. They can express at the same time defensive and
offensive attitudes, and can act simultaneously according to a
logic of resistance, according to a logic of political experimentation. Unemployment, employment, and work not only appear,
therefore, at the intersection of apparatuses of regulation and
incitement and assemblages of enunciation; they appear also
at the intersection of different strategies, which draw on the

government of conduct as well as the refusal to be directed or the desire to govern oneself, as much at the molecular as at the molar level. This preliminary sketch of the cartography of contemporary power apparatuses gives us just an overall view of the domains wherein they are exercised, using different technologies, forms, and strategies of government. At the same time, it gives us a map of possible terrains of confrontation.

2 The Dynamics of the Political Event: Micropolitics and the Process of Subjectification

Uprisings belong to history, but in a certain sense, they escape it.
—Michel Foucault, "Useless to Revolt?"

The Demise of Classical Forms of "Revolutionary Politics"

In this chapter we ask what "revolutionary politics" and the "revolutionary subject" have become, in light of the micropolitics of Deleuze and Guattari as well as Foucault's microphysics of power, and draw some lessons from the struggle of the *intermittents*, both very distant from and very close to these theoretical questions.

Is Deleuze and Guattari's micropolitics, as Badiou suggests, a theory "sucked up, so to speak, by the *doxa* of the body, desire, affect, networks, the multitude, nomadism and enjoyment into which a whole contemporary 'politics' sinks, as if into a poor man's Spinozism? On the other hand, is Foucault's microphysics of power 'always a blend of a genealogy of symbolic forms and a virtual (or desiring) theory of bodies ... which may be called a linguistic anthropology?'"[1] Contrary to what these arrogant and disingenuous statements suggest, micropolitics and microphysics can be said to be the first great theories that have really problematized the neutralization of "revolutionary politics" and the "revolutionary subject" that capitalism has been carrying out since the Soviet revolution. According to Foucault, power and politics as they developed in Christian Europe were radically disrupted by the birth of political economy.[2] At the end of the nineteenth century, the workers movement, especially its Marxist wing, and the revolutions that broke out at the end of World War I, managed to exploit the problematic relationship between the economy and the political, and turn it against capitalism. Carl Schmitt, whose concept of power was certainly neither juridical nor economic, believed that under capitalism it was impossible to speak of the "political" and the "political subject" without going through the economy.[3] By the time Foucault engaged with the liberal theory that emerged after the Soviet revolution, and read its transformation of power and politics, the problem had completely shifted. After the 1970s, the working class that had been previously integrated in industrial society in the interwar US New Deal and the Fordist pact after World War II was defeated and "de-proletarianized" (as the ordoliberals would say), while industrial society was being dismantled as the center of the world economy. The introduction of a "new domain, a new field," which Foucault calls the "social," now "neutralized" (or depoliticized) the problematic relation between politics and the economy, which the "revolution" had exploited and overturned. As we have seen in the previous chapter, this growing panoply of techniques (semiotic, scientific, cultural, communicative, and of insurance) significantly blurred the borders between the economy and politics, and deeply transformed the role of the state,[4] thus rendering inoperable the tactics and strategies devised by revolutionary politics.

According to Foucault, by means of overlapping apparatuses of sovereignty, discipline, and biopolitics that simultaneously give rise to and produce large binary divisions (classes, sexes, etc.), and through the "optimization of systems of difference"—similar to the macro- and microphysics of power that constitute the two inseparable sides of governmentality—power is configured as the government of "subjects of rights" and "living subjects." Similarly, according to Deleuze and Guattari, in contemporary capitalism power is exercised through molar and molecular apparatuses, constituting distinct but inseparable moments.[5] The social subjection that assigns roles, functions, and identities to individuals is coupled with the machinic subjugation that traverses both the preindividual dimension of affects, perceptions, and desires, and the realm of their transindividuality. The techniques and apparatuses that "neutralized," continuously defused, and newly instituted the dualisms of class that revolutionary politics was able to turn into a "class war" are both macro- and micropolitical, and tie the economic, social, political, cultural, and technological together, displacing the field of struggle and requiring new weapons.

The "Marxian" gesture reclaimed by Deleuze and Guattari and practiced by Foucault (it is impossible to speak of politics and political subjects without going through the apparatuses of capitalism as they are) seems to make no sense to Badiou and Rancière, for whom politics takes care of itself, and the subject is exclusively defined by the act of its own declaration. In order to save a politics destroyed and completely reconfigured by the capitalist response to the October Revolution, they take refuge in universalism and formalism, where the whole singularity of power relations, conflicts, and processes of subjectification in contemporary capitalism is lost, even though the only question is ever that of the event, excess, and rupture. This singularity is the real question that Foucault's microphysics of power and Deleuze and Guattari's micropolitics address. How should a "war machine" function when the objective is not war (or the seizure of power in its institutional or armed forms)? When the power it confronts manages dualisms through the optimization of differentiations and individualizations? How does subjectivity act at the molar and molecular level to subtract itself from the designations of the government of conducts and subjugations? How does it affirm itself both as a political and an existential subject? What is the relationship between ethics (the transformation of the self) and politics given the conditions of contemporary capitalism?

Micropolitics and microphysics have another important function. They substantiate what had been rediscovered in 1968—that "the revolution in modern Europe was not only a political project but also a form of life"[6]—and what 1968 had affirmed politically—that changes in individual conducts and changes in the configuration of the world go together. In the twentieth century, Communism had dulled the relationship between politics and ethics, politics and "lifestyle," and Stalinism had wiped it out. The "care of the self and others" that Foucault refers to, and the production of the world and subjectivity that Deleuze and Guattari wrote of, activated a "new activism" that is deeply rooted in the history of the West.[7] The movement of the *intermittents* was invested by all these questions, and rooted in a specific situation, its responses were partial but meaningful.

The Event and History: Against Idealism

The first great innovation introduced by the micropolitics and microphysics of power is the theory of the event, which

questions the relation between time and history in order to distance action from the idealism of the philosophy of history. To
start with, the dynamics of the birth and constitution of the
political movement of the *intermittents* can be described through
this theory of the event. The event is what crops up from history and sinks back into history without being itself history. The
event is immanent to economic, social, and political history,
but not reducible to it. What is called "history" here must be
understood as the product of the multiplicity of discursive and
nondiscursive devices of subjectification and subjugation that
we have already described. As far as the conflict of the *intermittents* is concerned, these are: the condition of their employment,
work, and life; the processes of subjectification in which they
are caught (waged, entrepreneur, poor, or unemployed); and the
public space as it is constituted and codified by the logics of
representation and mediation. Following Foucault, the place of
the intellectual in relation to the event lies in the reconstruction
of a part of the history of the movement of the *intermittents* by
a political collective (les Précaires associés de Paris, or Associated
Precarious Workers of Paris) that from the end of 2002, keeps
"looking out for, almost from underneath history, what disrupts
it and agitates it," watching over what will come "slightly at the
rearguard of politics" as it is exercised. The Précaires associés de
Paris watches over and prepares an event that it can only anticipate in a very indeterminate way. Working for the event means
working for the unpredictable.[8]

The movement of the *intermittents* of course has its own
historical, social, economic, and political conditions, but in
its emergence as an event, it departs from those conditions
to create something new: new possibilities of action and new
modes of subjectification. There is something in the event that
cannot be reduced to the social determinisms of causal series,

in the sense that its conditions do not contain all its effects. The *coordination* of *intermittents* and precarious workers, and its practices, its way of doing and speaking, are neither directly deducible from their conditions of work, employment, and unemployment, nor can they be reduced to the codifications of existing social and political spaces, or their devices of subjectification and subjugation. For them, the question is to understand the continuities and discontinuities (of action, problems, and practices) that the socioeconomic and political situation entertains with the event. Therefore, the event cannot be *completely* deduced from history, from whence it comes and in which it inscribes itself anew.

In the case we are most interested in, the event has a date and a place: the night between June 26 and 27, 2003, at the theater la Colline, where thousands of people, motivated by their rejection of the "reform," crossed a political and existential threshold. The crossing of this threshold was instantaneous and collective, and produced a rupture, a discontinuity in "history" and subjectivity. The event does not affect the state of things it emerges from, without first *affecting the subjectivities* that take part and position themselves in it saying "no." Something changed in life and society that asks of subjectivity, What just happened, what's happening, and what's going to happen? This instantaneous subjective change is an act of both resistance and creation: resistance to power, and creation of possibilities whose limits are not clearly established. These possibilities are not just possibilities "pure and simple," or in an abstract sense; they are "living possibilities" because they are already engaged in a given situation, in the specific conditions of *intermittence*, the cultural labor market, the refoundation of the social, the treatment of unemployment by the activation of passive spending, etc. For this reason, they are not already there, prior to the event, but created by the event and emerging with it. The event is a bifurcation, a disengagement from the law, norms, and existing values. Unstable and unbalanced, its emergence opens up a process of subjectification, and its modalities of existence and action are still undetermined. The event and its date are points of reversal and diversion that knock off balance thousands of people, plunging them into a different situation about which they have no preconception. The event is an opening, a possibility for self-transformation, and consequently, for changing the sociopolitical situation. A new universe is opened up, and those who cross this threshold can engage in new relations, new modes of thinking and doing, and new knowledge and affects.

These possibilities are first and foremost *felt* rather than *conceived*, because the subjective mutation is primarily nondiscursive. There is a multiplicity of reasons and causes (economic, political, social, etc.) for refusal and revolt, but the meaning of the act that embodies them presents itself straightforwardly to its agents, in a nondiscursive modality, and with a clarity that is not of the same order as that to which these reasons and causes can be ascribed. It comes as an existential rupture that does not merely transform consciousness and discourse. This must be addressed if we wish to "enrich language, generate and pollinate a new discursive field,"[9] and new modes of action and organization. This nondiscursive rupture sparks off a process of production of subjectivity that, on the one hand, fosters its own rules and norms, and on the other, allows speech to proliferate. This happened, in an exemplary way, during the occupation of the Olympe de Gouge theater, where a few days before the establishment of the *coordination* of *intermittents* and precarious workers of the Île-de-France, the movement moved to another theater in the east of Paris (la Colline).

The event is a source of desires and unknown beliefs to the extent that adding itself to the world, it must measure itself against what is already there, already instituted. The event and its effects add something to the world, and this can change what is already constituted. *Political action entails building the conditions for a transformation of what is, starting from the new possibilities contained in the event.* These conditions for the realization of the possible are not identical to the conditions of its emergence, because the two are open to a process of subjectification that reorients action and changes power relations. Among the actual conditions of the world, some create obstacles; others are favorable to the realization of these possibilities. Among the favorable conditions, some are already there; others must be invented and built; others must be seized in the becoming of the social and political conjuncture. After the first moments of the event (its emergence), a second and problematic moment occurs: the possibilities that have emerged with the event must now actualize themselves in the existing state of things and subjectivity.[10]

Political Experimentation Today

The collapse of the event back into history (the counteractualization of the event) occurs at the crossroads of at least three different processes of singularization: (1) the political struggle with different apparatuses of power (political, economic, media, welfare state, etc.), which in their turn manage to counteract the event; (2) the political struggle between constituted political forces (unions, Trotskyists, Communists, Maoists, etc.) and the forces that are in the process of being constituted (the *coordination*) inside the movement itself, which are about meeting objectives, modes of organization and struggle, building alliances, and implementing strategies; and (3) the relation between this level of molar subjectification and the processes of molecular subjectification that emerges from working practices, unemployment, wage labor, and the life of the *intermittents*. Each process of singularization goes through irreversible points of bifurcation (American pragmatist philosopher William James's notion) that determine their very dynamics.

In the weeks that followed June 26, 2003, nearly every general assembly constituted a point of bifurcation where collective decisions determined irreversible choices that opened up certain heterogeneous possibilities of struggle and organization while closing others. If in these meetings, the "Communist hypothesis" as it was still put forward by Communists, Trotskyists, and Maoists—a hypothesis that the 1970s' movements had already strongly criticized and often liquidated—had not been disowned, had the "Communist hypothesis" been able to impose itself, we would have had to deal with a very different movement, a completely different dynamic and process of subjectification. In fact, we would have simply been confronted with the impossibility of a movement, because the political innovations that had made the movement powerful and ensured its durability would have been prevented. This Communist hypothesis does not present many affinities with contemporary subjectivities and no longer represents a "living hypothesis." Rather, it is a "dead hypothesis" where the movement has recuperated anything that might be necessary to the struggle.[11] The movement of the *intermittents* deploys its political experimentation outside the classical Communist hypothesis because it is forced to conceive of the

relation between the molecular action of employment practices, unemployment, work, and life and the molar action in the
institutional public realm, as one between two levels of political
subjectification that are both distinct and inseparable, heterogeneous and yet communicative, rather than as a relation between
the economy and politics.

The second movement of the event (its subsiding back into
history) is very important as it opens to a process other than
one of simple verification: political experimentation does not
bring about a fidelity to the event but rather something new—a
social and political creation. The new nascent subjectivity must,
on the one hand, change the conditions of employment, work,
unemployment, and the apparatuses of subjugation (to the
wage, "profession," or "artist") that it is enveloped in. On the
other hand, it must introduce institutional changes (the "rewrit-
ing" of unemployment welfare, democracy and its institutions, a
new production of knowledge, etc.). This is necessary not only to
change its economic and political situation but also, and above
all, to open up spaces or build collective agencies capable of operating a "subjective reconversion."[12] In order to measure up to
what is already there, for instance—labor rights, social security,
the cultural labor market, assigned roles and functions, and the
democracy of institutions—it is necessary immediately to invent
and build modes of saying and doing, modes of "being together"
(the desire to self-govern) and modes of "being against" (the will
not to be governed) that are adequate to the discontinuity introduced by the event.

The subsiding of the event into history and its inscription
in the existing state of things determines a new political situation: the mode of this subsiding; this inscription in a scene where
it barges into social, economic, and political institutions, and

subsequently becomes integrated without friction; the mode in which it questions or legitimates the dominant "discourse" on employment, unemployment, and work; or the way in which it eventually defines "these problems" otherwise are all relevant to a "political" struggle. These are questions of political strategy and tactics, of confrontation between heterogeneous points of view.

The subsiding of the event and the management of its effects, the struggle over the meaning that is given to them, are just as important as its emergence, and also seem to point to a more fundamental political question, because this subsiding occurs in a time span that is normally unfavorable to movements: the long term of unions and political institutions, the term of the "professionals" of politics, the time span of those who have time for politics. Starting from this question of the development of the event and history, where history is no longer configured as a leading idea, a guide to action, it might be possible to understand the deep crisis affecting political action today, in both its "revolutionary" and "democratic" forms.

We can draw some lessons by analyzing the practices of the *coordination* of the *intermittents* precisely because their political action is exercised through the development of the constitutive moments of the event: the condition or state of things from which it emerges, the new subjective and objective conditions it determines, and finally, the conditions to seize or construct in order to change the state of things and subjectivities. The three moments or temporalities of the event define three heterogeneous political situations that demand different treatments and modes of expression and action. The event is the condition or the occasion for a political "constructivism" that the *coordination* seems to have adopted.

The Event, the World, and Subjectivity

The political event returns the world and subjectivity to us. It returns the world to its true nature: the world shows those who have been opened and ripped apart by the event that it is not merely *what it is* but something *in the course of making itself* and *something to be made*. The event gives us an open, unfinished, and incomplete world, and in so doing calls on subjectivity, because we can inscribe our actions and exercise our responsibility in this incompleteness, this nonfinitude.

The world in the process of making always requires an ethical perfection, is always searching for an existential closure. In this sense, the opening of the event gives us access to the process of production and transformation of subjectivity. Like the world, individual and collective subjectivity are not given; they are in the process of making and are open to being made. The event returns the world to us as a "matter of choice," and subjectivity as a "crossroad of *praxis*." What is happening to me there? What can or should I do, and how to start from that place there? Am I responsible for what is going on? Am I responsible for what is going to happen?[13] The event brings subjectivity face-to-face with alternatives, decisions, and risks. With the event, one instantaneously goes from one world to the next, from one mode of struggle to another, where boundaries and meanings are not fully perceived but rather felt as being full of promises and challenges.

Choosing to invest and engage in the realization of these promises and challenges entails reshuffling the old world (its old beliefs, desires, and routines) and creating with the new. In this sense, the event is a process of "reconversion" or production of new subjectivity—that is, a reassessment of our own ways of thinking and acting, an interrogation of our very existence. The world and subjectivity are not already given; everything is far from being decided, contrary to the discourse on "the end of history" that has been repeated to us since the 1990s. The US Department of State decreed that history ended when the Berlin Wall fell, Communism expired, and the "working class" became fragmented in a new sociology of social classes.[14] This talk of an "end of history" proclaims that the possible does not overflow the real but is equal to it; more precisely, the possible amounts to what is on offer on the market. The arrogance of the "victors" expresses that any possible that is not already involved in the market does not exist. Therefore, our time is certainly not the end of history but a time when we should pay attention to the way history acts in relation to what is not historical—the event—in a manner that does not sketch out in advance the future of the world.

Counterconduct

The transformations of capitalism are unexpectedly faced with the slow emergence of a new Self as a pocket of resistance.
—Gilles Deleuze, *Foucault*

In order to determine the relations of continuity and discontinuity between "history" and the "event," we must first return to the description of the socioeconomic and subjective conditions of emergence of the event. We have analyzed the transformations and mutations of the government of conducts, and the discursive and nondiscursive apparatuses through which it is exercised, but so far we have neglected what Foucault calls "counterconducts"—that is to say, modes of life and behavior animated by the will to not be led by others, not be governed, govern differently, or even self-govern. In this analysis we must carefully distinguish between two types of counterconduct: the counterconduct of the *intermittents*, exercised and expressed in their condition of work, employment, unemployment, and life, which we call "molecular"; and the counterconducts expressed and exercised in the public space of political, union, and social institutions organized and practiced by the *coordination*, which we call "molar." Finally, we ought to consider the way these molecular and molar counterconducts open up to processes of subjectification.

On the one hand, molecular resistances and inventions express themselves as the outsmarting—an escape and a deviation from—the codes and norms that sustain the market for cultural labor. On the other hand, molar counterconducts, exercised by the *coordination*, try to reverse the situation, and build conditions of open conflict and polemical interlocution with economic, social, political, and media institutions. They demand "new social rights" and work toward the development and institution of a different system of indemnity for unemployment for all precarious workers as well as the "democratic" transformation of the institutions that regulate them. Having said that, molecular counterconducts cannot be reduced, following the dominant logic of the workers' movement, to simple economic behaviors that require the intervention of a trade union organization and a party in order to qualify as being political, because they directly undermine the distribution of places, roles, functions, and apparatuses of subjection at work in the market (the injunction to be waged and self-enterprising). By tackling the effects of the power of laws, norms, and rules, they de-structure the functions of command and obedience, the subordination and autonomy of organization of the labor market. Molecular resistance also manifests itself as a practice of invention and experimentation. Molecular counterconducts add to the refusal of modes of subjugation and the shifting of codes and rules, the invention of modes of life setting out new temporalities assigned to them (times of work, times of employment, times of unemployment, and times of life).

The "Ambiguities" and "Potentialities" of Molecular Counterconducts

According to Deleuze, under capitalism, all social transformations entail a "reconversion of subjectivity" and the emergence of a "new self" as a pocket of resistance. This hypothesis can be verified firsthand at the level of the molecular counterconducts of the *intermittents*. Among the numerous behaviors that we can qualify as molecular counterconducts, we will briefly describe these transformations through the results of our inquiry into what we have named the figure of the "waged employer." What is an *intermittent* "waged employer"? It is an *intermittent* who sets up and manages their own production (company, small structure of production, etc.) while being waged by this structure? This *intermittent* is in fact an employer, who initiates the projects, recruits, seeks funding, and manages relations with the "real" employers of the sector (theaters, local government, audiovisual productions, etc.). Therefore, the employer has the responsibility and capability for initiative that the market logic ascribes to the entrepreneur. But in relation to the institutions that manage the labor market, the employer is a waged laborer like any other, because they are hired and declared as such.[15]

The waged employers elude the traditional codifications of the labor market (employees and entrepreneurs) and social welfare. They are neither employees nor entrepreneurs, nor free-lance workers. They combine these different qualities without being reducible to these codifications. The waged employer is a hybrid figure adopted by the *intermittents* in order to adapt to the new needs of cultural production and bring *their own projects* to fruition. This evolution runs parallel to a hybridization of the functions, roles, and respective responsibilities of employers and employees. Though the waged employer carries out entre-preneurial functions, they are not the one who gives the orders. The theater, local government, television, or cinema production remain in charge, and use these small cultural structures in the same way that large companies in the industry use smaller enter-prises as subcontractors.[16]

The hybridization of these statuses raises a large number of problems for the governing of the labor market, because in the culture industry (and notably in the performing arts), the level of belief of the "employers" is more important than that of the "employees." The Latarjet report, one of the countless reports on performing arts issued by institutions, sees the main cause of the malfunctioning of the labor market in the sector as this: "The considerable development of a number of companies and small employers has meant that the ratio employer–employee increas-ingly tends to approach.[17]

The "excessively large number" of waged employers leads to a degradation of the cultural labor market, because the logic that divides people into (autonomous) entrepreneurs and (sub-ordinated) workers becomes blurred, and the functions of com-mand and obedience, respectively exercised by entrepreneurs and waged laborers, are dangerously put into question. At stake here are the "effects of power" of the labor market, because there seems to be a mass refusal to be governed both by the codes, norms, and regulations of wage labor and the injunction to be "self-entrepreneurial."

The Latarjet report recommends a return to a strict definition of wage subordination and an equally strict definition of entrepreneurial responsibilities, so that each is assigned a role and place defined by the codes of work and social welfare. The good *economic* functioning of the labor market requires as a prerequisite a *political* functioning that clearly distinguishes between those who command and those who obey. The aim of the "reform" was to (re)build a labor market for culture: to reconstruct the effects of power—that is to say, basically, to clearly differentiate command, on one side, from obedience, on the other. In their bureaucratic and academic language, the authors of the report express the need to "regulate" and reestablish the tasks of every person within the division of labor: "To redefine the responsibilities of each one as a prerequisite for an effective political economy of cultural production."

Therefore, molecular counterconducts are not only practices of resistance, but also inventions of new modes of working and living, and a self-transformation that takes place in a space that is only partly institutionalized, somewhere where power relations are in the process of being made and unmade. According to Deleuze, the "movements of subjective reconversion" that occur in the course of all social transformations are "pockets of instability," because they are bearers of "ambiguities" and "potentialities." With Foucault, we can define the nature of this ambiguity, or rather this ambivalence, with much precision: the relations that characterize what he defined as microphysics of power are "unstable, reversible and mobile."[18] They are not completely fixed by norms, laws, and regulations because they partly express "new" relations, and partly elude current modes of subjugation and codifications. These new relations are in the process of being made, and their identity is not fixed; they can still be "here or there." Their reversibility, mobility, and instability give them that character of "ambivalence" that Deleuze speaks of. The nature of social transformation, the "ambivalence" of proliferating counterconducts, has been perfectly seized on by the *intermittents* that we investigated in our inquiry, insofar as they produce and are subjected to them.

An actor we interviewed during our research sums it up well: "Intermittence presents two faces, one libertarian; the other ultraliberal." The regime of intermittence sweeps across all spaces: "I work when I want, where I want, as I want," and "I work when I can, when they want, as they want." On the same topic, an editor remarks: "The positive aspects should not be forgotten: totally free time, absence of routine, multiple encounters"; and these also have a negative side: "Total irregularity and displacement (therefore, the impossibility of investing oneself in outside activities: sports, music, or social life)," and above all, the constant stress due to precariousness, especially when one realizes that they are no longer "assisted by social structures."

The spaces of autonomy and subordination are not fossilized; everything is not immediately fixed by the codes of work or social welfare; they are unstable, mobile, and reversible. New practices of domination and freedom grow, split, superimpose themselves, and produce and reproduce themselves together. These practices of freedom or subordination are dependent on specific, singular relations, and above all, on power relations established between the employer and the employee, and between the latter and the institutions that regulate unemployment benefits. Here more than elsewhere, laws, norms, and regulations are subject to interpretation, uses, and practices that make one or the other side of intermittence more prevalent.

We find the same ambivalence in the question of "time" that, as we have already suggested, and as the interviews show, is the real political issue of the dispute.[19] More often than not, interviewees refused to regard unemployment as a pure absence of employment, as empty time. On the contrary, they conceived it more as a "full" time, but this fullness is very ambiguous because it refers to different things: "The notion of unemployment is a bad choice of wording that embarrasses me. Unemployment does not mean doing nothing. In France, there is a system that allows you to have a little bit of time to think and create. By restraining us to timetables, they want to stop us from thinking, talking, meeting, and dreaming." Unemployment is the time emptied of employment that *intermittents* fill with things other than job seeking. But it is also possible to read a new temporality here that allows one to make the whole lifetime productive and exploit unpaid time. This is how a musician reacted to the question of unemployed time: "There is no unemployed time. When I'm at home, my hands are on the instrument, my eyes on the computer monitor, and my ears to the telephone."[20] The same "ambiguity," the same reversibility, can be equally said to apply to practices of waged laborers: on the one hand, they express the will to not be governed, to govern themselves, and the desire to escape from subordination to the wage; on the other hand, the model of the self-entrepreneur at work in these practices is the very outcome of capital as a machine of subjugation. From this perspective, the reform seems to be an apparatus destined to substitute the play of antagonistic actions, tricks, escapes, diversions, and reversible power relations, with techniques (norms, laws, and technologies) that fix and guide the conduct of *intermittents* in a constant manner, and with sufficient certainty and security. Seeing the "ambiguities," instability, reversibility, and mobility of these power relations, it is important to point out that counterconducts have really transformed the attitudes to work, employment, and life, and the subjectivity, of those who work. These transformations are under way—"subjective reconversions" that will go much further.

The "subjective reconversion" does not simply take place in the temporality of the political event, as Rancière or Badiou seem to believe. It is produced day by day in the mode of resistance to the law and existing codes that aims to push toward unwritten objectives. Despite their ambivalence, like microevents, molecular counterconducts participate in the struggle for a new subjectivity and the constitution of a new self, because they express a resistance to two actual forms of subjugation: one consisting of individuating us according to the needs of power, and "the other of attracting each individual to a known and recognized identity, fixed once and for all."[21] In practice, these counterconducts experiment with new attitudes, a new *ethos* in relation to work, employment, and unemployment that heralds new modes of existence. Molar counterconducts in the *coordination* do not function as the "consciousness" or the "politicization" of these molecular practices that, besides, can be collective in themselves. It is a question, as we will make clear, of heterogeneous levels of subjectivity, which must be coordinated even while their disparities are preserved.

Foucault's Turn to Ethics

Before analyzing the molar counterconducts expressed in the *coordination*, we will digress through Foucault and his ethical "turn," because it can help our investigation of the meaning of the molecular resistance to the effects of power in the norms of wage labor and human capital, and our understanding of how and why the "transformation of the self" and processes of subjectification have become the main modes of resistance and the very space of political confrontation.[22] According to Foucault, technologies of "pastoral power" (the government of the souls) have been integrated into the educational, medical, or psychological practices of the modern era, and finally, the apparatuses of the welfare state. But the metamorphoses of (moral) norms of the government of conducts is not what interests Foucault as much as the *use* that one makes of the governed, and their ability to give themselves their own rules in order to not be governed and to self-govern. These studies on the relation to the self and the practices of construction and transformation of the self concentrate on the moral schools of antiquity, and yet they speak to a current question.

Starting from the 1960 and 1970s, the subjective "conversion,"[23] invention, and transformation of the self (at the individual and collective level) have become inseparable from the practices of political movements. These movements have "no programs"; their projects do not aim for "global" and "universal" change but on the contrary, precise transformations concerning "our modes of being and thinking" that bear on a new relation between ethics and politics. This new *ethos*, a new subjective attitude, a new mode of thinking and living, acting and conducting oneself, first blossomed in these movements, and then contaminated the whole of society.[24] It is from the same period that it becomes impossible to think and act on the basis of a "universal ethical rule," because the "ethical multiplicity" affirmed corresponds to the explosion of different "modes of life," and the heterogeneity of existential and political choices made by the movements. We place Foucault's statement back in this political context, where he affirms that the great changes that occurred in "morals" and conducts are not produced by norms and codes but beneath them, in the relations to the self and the practices of transformation of the self.[25] Ethics, viewed from the standpoint of power or that of the movements, is at the center of political struggle.

From the end of the 1970s on, Foucault began what he called a "third displacement" of his inquiry, to find out what happened and what is happening in the realm of political subjectivity, whose theoretical and political instruments are terribly flawed.[26]

In order to clearly move away from the critiques that reduce the "relation to the self" to a variation of dandyism or the affirmation of Foucault's disinterest in political subjectification,[27] one needs to recall the reconstruction of practices of the "care of the self and others" in ancient Greece largely documented in the courses at the Collège de France, notably in the last year of 1984. Cynical militancy takes on a "lifestyle" and practices self-government while demanding to "change the world" and attack "conventions, laws, and institutions." The Cynics' coupling of conversion of subjectivity and change of institutions constitutes the matrix of the "militantism" of the West.

What makes the Cynics' activity historically relevant is also the series in which it inserts itself: the activism of Christianity that is both a spiritual and a worldly struggle; other movements that come with Christianity, for instance, the beggars, preachers, and orders that preceded it and would later reform it. In all these movements one clearly finds the principle of militantism, the revolutionary militantism of the nineteenth century, true life as another life, as a life of struggle for a changed world.[28]

Before its organization into a (Communist) party started defining "true life by a flawless uniformity to norms, a uniformity that is both social and cultural," the political project was inseparable from a lifestyle: revolutionary life, or life as revolutionary activity. The "care of the self" and the "relation to the self" are at the core of a "new definition" of politics that emerged with 1968, but their roots go deeper into the "revolutionary" history of the West. Therefore, after the analysis of power relations and discursive practices, Foucault interrogates the "modes of relation to the self by which the individual is constituted and recognizes itself as a subject." In this last displacement, the "games of truth" are not concerned with coercive practices but with the practices of formation, self-development, and determination of the subject. The relation to the self is an activity that can determine a rupture, and acquire independence and autonomy, from apparatuses of subjugation and servitude. For the Foucault of this third displacement, the problem is not to know how moral norms have been interiorized by the "subject";[29] it is not a question of "morals" or their prescriptive side. As he remarks, "By morals we also understand the behavior of real individuals, their relation to rules and values that are imposed on them." What Foucault calls the "morality of behaviors," or the morals of the governed, is separate from the injunctions and prescriptions of the morality of the apparatuses of power.

Here Foucault is interested in the study of "the manner in which the subject is *actively* constituted,"[30] how the subject behaves in relation to the norms imposed on them, their attitudes to rules and codes that are already instituted, but also how the subject invents, creates, and combines other rules, norms, and codes in order not to be governed, be governed differently, and self-govern. Studying the active dimension of the subject,

the action they can carry out on themselves, entails an interrogation of the possible *swerve* between "codes" and "modes of
subjectification." One must unveil their "relative autonomy" in
order to determine "how, and with what margin of variations or
transgressions, individuals or groups conduct themselves with
reference to a prescriptive system that is explicitly or implicitly
given."[31] According to Foucault, each action of the norm must
be understood as a power *relation*, or more precisely, a "strategic
power relation." In a strategic relation, one must distinguish the
terms of the relation from the relation itself, and the latter can
either be internal or external to them. Following historian Paul
Veyne's suggestion, it is possible to see in Foucault's theory a
theory of power as relation.[32]

Furthermore, when it comes to the analysis of the situation
of the *intermittents*, the norms that regulate employment or
access to unemployment benefits are written by the apparatuses
of power, but they are also relations that involve elements (the
ASSEDIC—Association for Employment in Industry and Trade—
and the claimant) that have their own "freedom," possibility
of action, and a specific power to act (though it is evidently
very asymmetrical). These elements activate relations in which
each (ASSEDIC or the claimant) tries to structure or de-structure
the "possible" actions of the other (with very unequal means).
Among the relations weaved into this process, some are exterior to the elements; that is to say, they are new relations that
are added to the world and thus not contained in it. Also, the
uses of unemployment benefit that *intermittents* practice are not
contained in the code of social security or work. The norms of
the apparatuses of power are actions on possible actions, *strate-*
gies that try to determine the conduct of others, structure their
field of possible action, and constitute it as a subject, to mold its

subjectivity. But it is possible that the norms of the code of work and social security fail to manage these conducts because they develop new relations to employment, unemployment, work, and the self that current norms and codes do not involve at all. The norm acts on a subject who not only can reuse, divert, or escape from it but also "bend" relations in unpredictable ways. This new "fold" of the subject builds and models a relation that is not contained in the norm and through which they expresse their "autopoietic" activity (as Guattari would say)—that is, their activity of self-constitution.

Therefore, the action of the norm must be understood as an action on a subject with the possibility to act. The norm opens up the possibility of a multiplicity of relations (obedience, conformity, and consent, but also refusal, diversion, open conflict, etc.), and this multiplicity can be "folded" in unpredictable ways through the action that the subject exercises on themselves.[33]

In addition to this, both those who govern and those who are governed are always invested by a "partial" subjectification (Guattari) that mobilizes this or that element of subjectivity so that there is always something "outside," something that eludes it. As Foucault put it: "A rule of conduct is one thing; the conduct that can be measured against the rule is another. But the manner in which one must behave oneself is altogether different."[34] In other words, a code of conduct is given, but there are different ways to conduct oneself, and different ways to "determine the ethical substance," or how the individual must constitute *this* or *this other* part of their subjectivity as a "primary matter" of the labor of the self. In this case, it is possible to relate to the norms written by unemployment benefits in different ways: by conforming to them because one respects legality, because one is conscious of participating in a national community, because one believes in solidarity among the governed, or because one has no other choice. But it is also possible to use the norms by deviating from their objectives, by advancing a whole series of different motives to give rise to different processes of subjectification. In the modes of functioning of a morality or a normative system, there is a "play," the possible, something undetermined whereby and through which the action of an "active" subject, counterconduct, can take shape.

Therefore, power has neither the capacity nor the possibility to determine, produce, and control all the relations that constitute a subject (subjugation is always partial). What is the meaning of Foucault's idea whereby "morality," as the whole of relations of power, requires the subjects on which it is exercised to be "free," if we have established that "free" does not mean that subjects are emancipated from all power relations but rather can always act otherwise?[35]

Saying it with James's pragmatism, this means that the relation is exterior to its elements, and these elements are independent. Sociologist Gabriel Tarde, perhaps, has explained this device of pragmatism in the clearest fashion: "Elements that make up" social mechanisms are the "temporary embodiment of their laws"—that is, the power relation that invests the elements is contingent, temporary. The elements, "on the one hand, only partly belong to themselves, [and] on the other hand, they elude the world they constitute." These terms are also composites of relations: "The attributes that each element gives to its incorporation in its regiment do not form its whole nature; other dispositions and instincts come to regiment it differently."[36] This means that the attributes of each element are neither deducible nor reducible to the nature of the power relation, because these elements are a multiplicity of relations (with the world, others, and oneself), only partly produced by norms.

These considerations allow us to eliminate, to a certain extent, a deep misunderstanding that often characterizes the reading of Foucault's work: to say that power "produces" the subject does not mean that it can mold the totality of the subject, or format the world completely. This reading would suggest that all relations—and the subject itself—are produced by power, while American pragmatism, the philosophy of difference, as well as the work of Foucault rightly demonstrate that there is no *one* power relation that can produce, contain, and dominate everyone. Domination must not be made into an ontological foundation of power; on the contrary, the state of domination is the result of a struggle, a battle, and a strategic relation that *momentarily* and never necessarily presents itself in the form of a totality. The pragmatism of James can be used in this sense. As the American philosopher of the subject says: when it comes to any totality whatsoever, although the apparatuses of power can always deploy some elements to try to create unity and stability, "other parts remain autonomous, and the unity in question remain absent from them."[37] The relation always lags behind them, and the "and" that prolongs it; there is always something that eludes, that can rely on other relations, and can act with other actual or virtual forces while "bending" it in unpredictable ways through the relation to the self (which can also take on an unknown direction in the meantime).[38] The "exterior" relation James discusses contains some power: to add to the world, to escape power. And the "and," while adding a relation to the elements, also makes them "flee," and effectuates a detachment from their identity. This is where we situate the example of the *coordination* (which we will analyze in more detail) and its denomination: the "and" between "*intermittents*" and "precarious workers" adds to the reality of intermittence another relation that is "external" to the elements: precariousness and its politicization. Deleuze has undoubtedly foregrounded this question of the relation to the self even more radically than Foucault. With Guattari, he has effectively clarified the main problem of contemporary capitalism, because on the one hand, "world capitalism today is a producer of subjectivity and this is its main production; material productions are nothing but mediations toward the mastery of the production of subjectivity," and on the other hand, "the production of a new subjectivity must be read against the emergence of new forms of struggle."[39] According to Deleuze, Foucault's discovery of the "relation to the self" was the discovery of a "new realm," irreducible to power and knowledge relations.[40] The self is not a knowledge formation or the product of power but "a process of individuation that bears on groups and persons, and escapes the power relations established as constituted knowledge."[41] To say that the "self" is reduced neither to knowledge nor power means that it expresses a subjective transformation that is not discursive but existential and affective. The "relation to the self" does not primarily define a knowledge or a power, because it expresses a change in the way of feeling that constitutes the support for a process of production of subjectivity from which new knowledge, new relations of power, and new discursive abilities can result.

For Deleuze, the fact that power is "individualizing," invests and produces "our everyday life and interiority," is not in contradiction with the subject's power to act, or the form of flight, refusal, deviation, and open conflict, where its form of autonomous and independent subjectification shapes its own norms.

Deleuze asks, What is left of our subjectivity once the individualizing apparatus acts on the subject? "There is nothing left to the subject, because the subject is to be made, like an empty pocket of resistance, in each instance."[42] The analysis of counterconducts and their modes of subjectification shows that the world of the microphysics of power is deeply political, because the disengagement, the detachment from roles, functions, subjugations, and servitudes that we are driven into, the desire to not be governed and subject ourselves to norms, already acts at this level, and raises the question not of the relation between the political and the nonpolitical but rather how to think the political as an action that transversally operates on molecular and molar subjectification. Power relations are not exclusively *contained* in the political realm, as they are no longer primarily in the economy; they are transversally given in realms that are traditionally kept distinct, forcing us to rethink the relation between politics and ethics.

The Actualization of the Event and Molar Counterconducts (1): The Battle of Acts

The actualization of the political event, which is at the origin of what we have called the process of molar subjectification, began to be deployed by two battles that were strictly articulated with one another: the battle of acts, and the battle of words. The whole of summer 2003 was characterized by a very high level of mobilization, which was manifested through an abundance of actions: occupations, blockades, and acts of sensibilization as well as a proliferation of words—two processes that seemed to feed off and relaunch each other incessantly. However, the discursive and nondiscursive apparatuses of power tried to countereffectuate the event; they tried to intervene to revise, adapt, and rethink—by relying on conditions that the event itself had created—a strategy and a tactic that always aimed at the same objective: to succeed in "reforming" the cultural labor market.

In opposing the reform, the nascent *coordination* was immediately confronted with a highly codified and highly consensual political space, where even the conflicts and modalities of expression had to conform to procedures that were preestablished and normalized by the state. Unions constitute the essential subjects of this consensus, as they guarantee both the representation of (class) divisions inside institutions and the possibility of a reconciliation in the "common world" of the wage relation, the configuration of which, in these fundamental traits, goes back to the postwar period (full employment, social welfare indexed to permanent employment, division of the gains of industrial productivity, and representation of wage earners). Faced with these consolidated relations, the *intermittents'* conflict made a cartography of inequalities, tracing out new divisions that were not represented in any way in the institutional frame in place (*"paritarisme,"* or social partnership), and for which reconciliation and the common world founded on "full employment" don't really mean anything.

The first months of the movement showed that on the one hand, a "floating population" like that of the *intermittents* had the opportunity of "creating a bloc," as used to be said in the nineteenth century apropos of the power of interdiction and nuisance of workers, yet without being assigned to any place of production in a stable manner. It is even the most effective manner of constructing a relationship of force in the framework of flexible production and discontinuous employment. To the trade unions' monumental and normalized mobilizations, concentrated in time and space (the demonstration-rally-demonstration ritual), the *coordination* added a diversification of actions (in terms of the number of participants and variation of objectives), conceived as "just-in-time" (in terms of the frequency and speed of their setting up and execution), allowing a glimpse of the form that actions can take in order to be effective when faced with the flexible, mobile, and deregulated organization of contemporary capitalist production. The preparation for the intervention at the Cannes Film Festival in 2004 had produced the slogans "occupy the city" and "block society." If the political forces present in Cannes were incapable of realizing these objectives, on the other hand, the movement against the CPE successfully experimented with them in certain cities in the provinces, demonstrating that these new modalities of conflict were henceforth "ripe/mature."[43] They also represent an alternative to the classic forms of mobilization of unions and leftist parties, as ineffective as they are today. The movement of the *intermittents*, taking a step alongside the codified and conventional forms of union struggle, expressed itself by the invention of new forms of action, the intensity and extension of which had more and more recourse to tactics of exposure and harassment vis-à-vis the networks of command of the flexible cycle of production, and the different apparatuses of power inherent in the enterprise society. The deregulation of the economy, work, and welfare rights put to work by liberal politics/policies was responded to with a "deregulation" of conflict, a harassing of the organization of power, not only in its territorial dimension but also in its communication networks and machines of expression (the interruption of television broadcasts, the taking

over of space of publicity, interventions in the editing of newspapers, etc.)—dimensions that classic union struggles habitually
ignore.

The Actualization of the Event and Molar Counterconducts (2): The Battle of Words

In the first place, the battle of words consisted in a struggle to
name the possibilities that the event created and define the
problems that it made emerge. It was set off notably by the
proposition to add the word "precarious" to the full name of
the *coordination*: *coordination of intermittents and precarious workers*. This name crystallized the first political battle inside the *coordination* and posed the conditions for those that followed. As we
have recalled, an individual is not a substance but a multiplicity
of relations, which are so many aspects, qualities, and identities whose assemblage constitutes the singularity of each and
every one. The individual who is caught up in the cultural labor
market is simultaneously "*intermittent*," "artist," "technician,"
"wage earner," "professional," and "unemployed" (to stick to
the vocabulary of the organization of work and social security).
Each one of its definitions opens up a specific semantic field
and heterogeneous manners of relating to the world, others, and
oneself. The choice of one of these words so as to name a political mode of organization is not at all anodyne, as it in fact organizes a "power takeover " by one relation over others—a part
and partial totalization of the situation.

By imposing themselves in a domain where the words "artist,"
"wage earner," "professional," "technician," and "unemployed"
divide up the situation, define functions, and distribute welfare
rights, the conjunction "and" along with the name "precarious"

shook up the certainties and the identities that they conveyed. The word "precarious" allowed the effects of the power of words to be seen: by introducing a relation external to the term "*intermittent*," and the consensual and codified space of norms that regulate the organization of work and unemployment benefits, it opened up the possibility of vindicating new rights and making conflicts that the apparatuses of power work to isolate instead resonate together. To say and bring the expression "and precarious workers" into the conflict was possible thanks to the event, but in turn, such a name orients actualization in a direction that opens new spaces and dynamics. What had for a long time worked away under codes, laws, and regulations not only acquires a visibility and becomes utterable but is brought into public space by the activities of the *coordination*, calling into question the power of the "standard wage earner–entrepreneur" relation that pretends to cover and totalize the whole of what is customarily called "industrial" and "contractual" relations.

For their part, the unions divide up the set of relations that constitute intermittence on the basis of the expression "wage earner" or the word "professsional," following two different "corporatist" logics. The first corporatism refers to the separation between standard and precarious wage earners. The second refers to the corporatism of trades. The Ministry of Culture, for its part, divides up this same set on the basis of the name "artist" and—from the inside of the conflict—seeks to displace the confrontation by making it slip from the terrain of social rights to that of "culture" and "cultural policy." The *coordinations* refused to limit their perspective solely to the question of cultural policy or corporatist problematics of the standard wage earner and trades, while traversing and problematizing the relations that these names designate, as they had to confront what was already there, what was already named, codified, and instituted by these names. The fact that a word—"precarious"—was added to the instituted functions and roles, making them vacillate, does not, however, signify that the other relations have disappeared. These words are still there and do still represent a part of the reality of intermittence.

Names are not, we can say, simple "copies" of the real. They can be events that supplement the real, that agitate and produce effects by affecting the world and subjectivity. The dynamic of words, ideas, and opinions is that of the event: words emerge from situations, from history, and fall back into it eventually. When they supplement what is (the situation of intermittence), as was the case with the name "precarious," they "partly redetermine the existent"[44]—first in subjectivity, and then in the real. The new determination (nomination) of what exists is a question of political struggle because it entails a displacement of classifications, places, and functions. We can thus understand why the naming of the *coordination* gave rise to very animated discussions, and why at each political turn, the battle over the name always resurfaced. In the moments of tension, the temptation to drop the "and" and fall back on the identities of the artist, the *intermittent*, or the precarious worker was strong. The words "wage earner" and "professional" were experienced as consensual words, because the reform aimed precisely to reestablish the "normality" of the artistic function, the "normality" of the wage earner function, the "normality" of the professional function, and the "normality" of unemployment benefit, following different logics and interests. The "and precarious workers" was thus played against the will to enclose the event within an instituted and conventional framework.

In the work of elaboration and the action of the *coordination*, the "and precarious workers" functioned as a veritable operator of infraction, distancing, letting go, displacement, and opening, as it interrogated what was already there on the basis of new problems. If the new model of unemployment compensation proposed by the *intermittents* was thought starting from their conditions of employment, work, and unemployment, it could be extended to every wage earner with discontinuous employment (to the precarious in catering, research, industrial temping, seasonal workers, etc.). This is because the word "precarious" is also one of the names available to designate the new inequalities that traverse contemporary society, and the tripartite management consensus of unions-bosses-state cannot represent it. In security societies, the difficulty resides precisely in the fact of naming, of designating, these new divisions; the old partitions, notably those that rely on the notions of the working class and the wage earner have lost a good part of the power of infraction, distance, and rupture.

The Battle of Knowledges

Discourse, words and ideas are not only a surface of inscription for the relation of force, but they are themselves forces, they are operators."
—Michel Foucault, *Society Must Be Defended*

It is only possible to express the sense of a situation as a function of an action undertaken to transform it.
—Michel de Certeau, *The Practice of Everyday Life*

The different political parties and the different unions—without distinction—no longer manage to problematize what is happening in our society, or to social groups. Intervening according to modalities inherited from the nineteenth century (notably the division/contradiction between economics and politics), they have lost all capacity to politicize problems, they have lost all instituting power, and confine themselves to the defense and management of the existing, the instituted. There are forces that are outside the game of representative politics (associations, movements, collectives of all sorts, and regroupings of citizens), that make new questions (unemployment, housing, ecology, health, poverty, new social rights, new rights linked to communication, etc.), and new subjects that enter the public space of conflict, confrontation, and interlocution. This enlargement of democratic action and the power of problematization goes together with the diffusion of the capacity for expertise and counterexpertise: no longer having confidence in the impartiality and objectivity of scientists or experts,[45] "users" vindicate the right to problematization and experimentation—a right hitherto monopolized by the figure of the expert or the scholar. From questions that concern AIDS to those that concern unemployment, and in politicizing what did not initially appear to be "political," these movements—from Act Up to AC![46]— produce new knowledges and experiment with new assemblages of "profane" and "learned" knowledges.

The elaboration of the new model of unemployment compensation for workers with discontinuous employment is thus a part of the informal "expertise" about modes of employment, work, and unemployment that the *intermittents* possess. This work was naturally pursued in the form of "citizen expertise" undertaken jointly with the university laboratory of Matisse-Isys.[47] This and the ensemble of multiplying practices of counterexpertise are the—occasionally caricatured—inheritors of the "battle of discourses and knowledges"[48] that unfolded in the 1960s and 1970s. "The immense and proliferating criticizability of things, institutions, practices, [and] discourses" of this epoch was at once both the product and the cause of what Foucault calls an "insurrection of subjugated knowledges" against the centralization and hierarchization of knowledges exercised by academic institutions. In Foucauldian methodology, the process of production of knowledges is an integral part of the processes of political subjectification, and has a role to play against the effects of a formally universalist conception of knowledge and power. During the realization of this expertise, what we experienced was the "holding together," the cooperation, between disparate knowledges ("erudite" and "disqualified" knowledges). To the universal references of the market and the wage earner ("permanent"), the *intermittents* seem to oppose a point of view that with Foucault, we could qualify as "naive" their practices, behavior, and forms of life refer to local, particular, specific knowledges. If contemporary "citizen expertise" has surely lost a large part of the subversive charge that it had in the 1960s and 1970s, it hasn't stopped proliferating and continues to produce an effect of delegitimation of the expert. It thus contributes to engendering a certain defiance with regard to the system of representation.

The *coordination of the intermittents and precarious workers* has a relationship that is at once both continuous and discontinuous with these post-Foucauldian struggles bearing on knowledges. If one confronts its practices with those of the majority of forms of citizen expertise, one notices that they are characterized by remarkable specificities. The formal and informal types of expertise produced by the *coordination* are distinct from the experience of the majority of forms of citizen expertise, because even if the latter continue to produce effects of delegitimation on representation-politics, most often they confine themselves to playing a role of control, vigilance, and surveillance of the apparatuses of power. They claim to be forces of denunciation, interpellation, and the solicitation of power, or organize themselves into pressure groups and lobbies, whereas the expertise of the *coordination* is conceived as one of the dimensions of the struggle and an instrument in the process of constitution of a collective "self." From this point of view, it enters into resonance with the tradition of a "knowledge of struggle" that Foucault speaks of: it is a matter of an apparatus at the heart of which knowledge is not limited to interpellating power or public opinion, but where it serves to structure and bear a demand and a collective action. Expertise thus tends to form part of the process of the construction and transformation of the collective subject in struggle. But it also expresses a "knowledge in struggle" *against* the knowledges of the unions, the media, scholars, and experts. It therefore arises from the construction of a "memory of conflicts." That is to say, on the basis of current divisions (between specialists and the profane) that it makes emerge, it rediscovers the thread of past struggles that "dominant" knowledges work to efface.

The CGT (General Confederation of Labor) was very harshly opposed to the "expertise" of the *coordination*, not only because it considered itself the sole legitimate and institutional representative of intermittent wage earners, but also, and above all, because it had one of the most reactionary visions of "objectivity" in the social sciences, conceptualizing knowledge as a copy of reality: to ensure its simple unveiling, what is already there requires professionals in research—which leaves one to suppose the impartiality and objectivity of their results. It still dreams of an "objective science of society." By means of the investigation that we carried out, we were, on the contrary, able to verify that the world is relatively "plastic," malleable, and constituted from a multiplicity of points of view and a multiplicity of heterogeneous relations, and that knowledge of it implies the carrying out of a *sectioning* of these relations and not a copying, thereby determining a singular point of view from which the multiplicity can be partially and provisionally grasped. The social sciences, like the experts, make wide use of this plasticity, and for them its exploitation can go—beyond what is habitually tolerated by the social sciences—as far as manipulation, "understandings," and scheming (of which the Guillot report is a particularly striking example).

The different ways of sectioning the "real" express heterogeneous "points of view" and thus are the matrices of heterogeneous knowledges. They operate on the multiplicity of relations that make up intermittence. One can therefore have as many "objective" and "scientific" knowledges as there are ways of sectioning, and choices made possible by these different points of view. If, for example, the ensemble of relations of power that define intermittence is sectioned on the basis of the point of view–word "wage earner" (and notably "full-time wage earner," as with the unions), the researcher will not pose the same questions, will not look for the same things, and will certainly not obtain the same results as when this ensemble of relations is sectioned on the basis of the point of view–word "precarious," "artist," or "professional." This doesn't signify that the sectionings all have the same value but rather that they are all *polemical*. There are, between them, differences of potential. Or to put it differently, certain among them express the virtualities and potentialities proper to a situation, and are opposed to and enter into conflict with current power relations, where other section-ings are restricted to legitimizing and reproducing them.

Thus the employer–wage earner function really exists, since it concerns 30 percent of the *intermittents* and 40 percent of those who work in the performing arts. But it only exists in public space, debate, and the taking of political decisions, because the *intermittents* imposed it on the debate. For reasons that have nothing to do with "science," it doesn't exist among the experts and scholars who concern themselves with intermittence; it is not an object of study, it is not measured by statistics, unless negatively. It is only within the scope of the expert knowledge that we produced with the *intermittents* that it became a problem, an object for study and discussion, because there was at the same time both a material necessity and the political will to constitute it as an object of litigation and polemic. By defining the prob-lem, the point of view adopts, delimits, and fixes possibilities. It thus sketches out the contours and boundaries of action and knowledge. Points of view, like values, refer to evaluations, and these latter to modes of life. The "desire" of/for intermittence—"intermittence my love," as an eight-page booklet declaimed in 2003—or the desire of/for full-time wage earning refer to het-erogeneous modes of thinking and acting, heterogeneous forms of existence. The "point of view" is an existential nondiscursive element, irreducible to knowledges or words, but on the basis of which a knowledge and a discourse unfolds.

But in this case, where is one to find criteria for the true and the false, surrounded by this multiplicity of points of view that all, in different ways, are anchored in "reality," and seem to secrete the truth in an immanent manner? "The truth of an idea is not a stagnant property inherent in it. Truth *happens* to an idea. It *becomes* true, is *made* true by events. Its verity *is* in fact

an event, a process, the process namely of its verifying itself"[49]
This conception of truth, formulated by James, seems perfectly
suited to political truths, and notably for characterizing the
springing up of truths that enter into the tournament of public
space, that challenges other truths, interpellating them, and that
quite simply want the "skin" of their political competitors. This
"raw" and "warrior" language ought not to upset or make scholars, experts, or journalists indignant, as it accounts for their real
practices; the hatred and contempt of the MEDEF and the CFDT,
which refused to make the statistical data of UNEDIC—public in
principle—available to us, the incompetence and bad faith of
the greater part of the journalists who talked about the conflict,
the arrogance of scholars, and the games of deception put in
place by ministers and the experts who operated with a supposedly objective expertise are all so many reasons to attach great
value to such a conception of truth. It was also Foucault's conception; he opposed "battle truth" to "reflection truth," which
is another way of affirming that words, opinions, and ideas are
not "pure" copies of reality. The truth of words, of ideas, is thus
a truth that is made and constructed in a "strategic" process at
the heart of which it is verified. The truth, with its functioning
and effects ("games of truth," to speak like Foucault), is part of
the political battle, and it is one of the instruments for the fabrication of opinion, one of the techniques for the production of
subjectivity, but also one of the modalities of combat.

The truth of the word and the idea of the "precarious" is thus
first of all produced—verified—by the event of the movement
of *intermittents*, by the subjectivity that vindicates and assumes
it. But this vindication and this taking into charge are the result
of a political battle carried out on the inside of the *coordination,*

where it confronted other points of view (those of the unions, Trotskyists, Maoists, and the words they are the bearers of—full-time wage earner, artist, and professional)—and over which it had the upper hand. The word "precarious" was imposed in this situation, but it was still only a local, specific, partial truth, strongly contested by other points of view. To be able to think this word as a "universal" truth (universals, like everything else in this lower world, are constructed by connection and in a strategic relation to other truths), it is necessary for this word, little by little, to spread and undergo other processes of verification and validation, to be put to the test in other situations and be confronted with other points of view. The diffusion of a word, an idea, or an opinion is at the same time both a conquest and an adaptation that imposes and integrates other "truths," which sketch out a discontinuous, nonlinear trajectory.

Besides, to follow the path that the word "precarious" traversed since the movement of *intermittents* made it enter into public debate, permits the observation that it underwent transformations, at first being taken in hand by the university researchers' movement in winter 2004, and then by being borne by the movement against the CPE in spring 2006. Now, one may remark that the *coordination*, which was the first to make this word a political stake, played no role in the debate about the CPE. The reason for this is that in the framework of this latter debate, the word "precarious" only had a pejorative connotation: it only expressed a lack, which ought to be met by employment. This was because the word had been caught up in other assemblages and discursive apparatuses, worked over by other politics, and adapted to other ends than those sought by the *coordination*. And if it is always a matter of extracting and imposing what is important and worthy of attention for an epoch, we can say that for the largest part of the forces at work in the movement against the CPE, it was *employment* that was important and worthy of attention, and this is certainly not, as we have seen, a point of view that allows all the potential and the virtualities of the situation of contemporary capitalism to be extracted. Besides, we can see in the inability of the *coordination* to play a role in the propagation and circulation of the word "precarious," a manifestation of the major limitation of its political activity: the forces against which it had fought in the *intermittents'* conflict (parties, unions, Trostskyists, etc.) regained the upper hand in the movement against the CPE. In this sense, knowledge is radically power, because "to speak the truth" is only possible by the imposition of rules through a fight, a struggle.

Strategies: Molar and Molecular, Macro and Micro

We might ask ourselves if political parties are not the most sterile political invention since the nineteenth century. Intellectual political sterility seems to me to be one of the major facts of our epoch.

—Michel Foucault, interview with Catherine Baker, 1984[50]

In quantum physics, it was one day necessary for physicists to admit that matter is both constituted by both waves and particles at the same time. In the same manner, social struggles are at the same time both molar and molecular. ... It is true that we have not managed to invent a political structure that is capable of developing these two types of struggle at the same time; that is why, in my opinion, political movements are essentially exhausted.

—Félix Guattari, *Molecular Revolution in Brazil*

The political action of the *coordination*, as much in its *being-against* (the intensity and the form of opposition to what it contests: the will not to be governed), as in its *being-together* (the intensity and the form of the links between those who struggle: the desire to govern oneself), is constructed *transversally* to the apparatuses of power and what Foucault calls "counterconducts." What does "transversally" mean? Political action is deployed transversally to the apparatuses that produce and reproduce both dualisms and differences. "Neoliberal governmentality" operates a dualist molar polarization, and inversely, it undoes the political crystallizations that threaten to transform themselves into irreducible antagonisms, through a molecular politics. We have seen that neoliberal politics promotes a mass unemployment and a mass poverty that—in Germany—reached the levels of the Weimar Republic, and—in the United States—creates an income distribution that has fallen back to the levels seen prior to the New Deal. It does this while—through a molecular differentiation and individualization of social, economic, communicational, cultural, gender, and other politics—it operates a neutralization of the political polarizations that these situations could set off. It is this new logic of power that the concepts of microphysics and micropolitics try to grasp.

The techniques of the differential subjection of the governed are first of all apparatuses for neutralization and depoliticization. Under what conditions is there a politicization of these new relations of power? By assembling together the point of view of Foucault with those of Deleuze and Guattari, we can say that everything is political, in the sense that every relation of power (economic, social, aesthetic, sexual, etc.) is *politicizable*.[51] It was in order to grasp the conditions for the politicization of power relations that the Western tradition defines as nonpolitical what Deleuze and Guattari introduced the categories of molar and molecular. Nevertheless, according to Guattari, one must be wary of the categories that he and Deleuze established, since these oppositions can "represent a formidable trap."[52] To avoid all the misunderstandings that these notions have given rise to, the couple molar/molecular must be crossed with another opposition that we have already encountered: macro/ micro.

Struggles against the Molar and Molecular Techniques of the Apparatuses of Power

The strategy adopted by the *coordination* was organized in the first place on one (macropolitical) level, by intervening in both the molar and the molecular aspects of power relations. The ensemble of molar and molecular techniques of governmental- ity is not given as a totality but as a heterogeneous multiplicity of apparatuses of power (economic, political, communicational, cultural, social, gender, etc.). The putting into place of the reform of the cultural labor market is not the work of a single appara- tus. Certainly, the reform had UNEDIC as its starting point, but in order to impose itself, it had to be taken up and prolonged by the discursive practices of the media, experts, and scholars, relaunched and reworked by the state and the cultural institu- tions, and integrated by union organizations, institutions for the control and activation of the unemployed, the sponsors of the cultural market, and so on. If there is a nucleus from which it proliferates, it solicits the intervention of other apparatuses with which it arranges itself and in which it is imbricated, so much so that we can say that the reform acts transversally: it is exer- cised as the potential of an assemblage that sometimes mobi- lizes now one apparatus (economic, political, social, mediatic, cultural, etc.), and now another. Following Foucault's invaluable methodological instructions, to be able to grasp a political object such as this reform, one does not have to pose the question of *what* power *is* but to ask oneself *how* it functions, where it passes, and through which techniques it is exercised. The reform has to be thought of as a strategy, and this amounts to considering power on the basis of the multiplicity of apparatuses and the forces that subtend them, constantly assembled and reassembled by political tactics.

Now, if one takes note of the heterogeneity of these apparatuses inherent to power and their dynamic, one must introduce a major change in order to understand the political action of the latter: strategy must take the place previously occupied by dialectics. The former effectuates the possible connections of disparate terms; it makes politics, the economy, the social, and every other apparatus hold together, in their double molar and molecular dimensions, without dissolving them into a unity. The second, in defining differences as contradictions, resolves them into a homogeneous element that promotes their reconciliation in a unity. The apparatuses of power of contemporary capital (and notably the relation between "economy" and "politics") do not contradict each other; they "strategize" each other. Power (in the same manner as counterconducts and their processes of subjectification) is constructed and evolves as a transversal assemblage that is both molar and molecular. It is in relation to this transversal functioning of governmentality that the *coordination* tried, more or less successfully, to construct its own strategy and deploy its own action. It operated on the socioeconomic terrain of unemployment benefits and its techniques of subjection, on the modality of control of the unemployed and the techniques of individuation that accompany them, but it also intervened in the domain of representational

politics (it was the starting point of the committee to monitor *intermittents'* unemployment insurance, which led to the
drafting of a parliamentary bill), and it engaged in the battle of
discourses, knowledges, and signs, taking up positions in newspapers, intervening directly in news programs, and producing
its own analyses (the critique of the protocol of UNEDIC, and
a socioeconomic investigation, for example), signs (tracts, web-
sites, a paper, etc.), and discourse (the "new model for indemnifying against unemployment").

The efficacy of being-against, or—in other words—the will
not to be governed, resides in its capacity to assemble its actions
against different apparatuses and intervene in their connections. When the *coordination* intervenes in the molar space of
institutions, it simultaneously bears and transforms the viewpoint of practices of molecular counterconducts. Its practices
mobilize molecular dynamics so as to undo dualist oppositions
(work/unemployment or scholar/layperson); it makes a play
of new figures of subjectivity so as to break the dichotomies of
employment/unemployement, working time/time for living,
in order to open up new ways of working and living, the possibility of new rights and equally new institutions—contained in
the state of possibility in the molecular. Unlike molecular counterconducts (which get around what exists through cunning),
the action of the *coordinations*, while aiming in the first place
at an immediate objective (the abrogation of a protocol of the
reform), carried in it implicitly, very early on, the general justifi-
cation for a new system of unemployment compensation for all
wage earners in discontinuous employment.

This demand for transformation shows that to extract oneself
from exploitation in a business and the government of conduct—
that is to say, to impose new rights—molecular practices need to

pass via macropolitics: to confront—by positioning themselves in relation to—existing union and political forces, in relation to the simultaneously dualist and differential logic of the apparatuses of power. The *coordination* makes visible and vindicates molecular uses of the norms of compensation that are not contained in the regulations for unemployment insurance, and puts into effect their capacity to de-structure subjections and enslavements. It thus opens up *another domain of action* (new rights or new institutions) that is thought to give these counterconducts the "social supports" (according to Robert Castell's definition) that are indispensable to their deployment, constitution, and subjectification. The passage via macropolitics is therefore necessary; the molecularity of counterconducts has to pass into "rigid segments," on pain of powerlessness. Organizing this passage signifies making "new objects and new subjects" emerge,[53] which exceed the molar divisions of macropolitics, and imply the imposition of socioeconomic (a new distribution of income), institutional (a new democracy), and legal (new rights) conditions, which open up new political possibilities.

It is thus the *coordination* that ensures both the continuity and the discontinuity between the molecular and the molar, between different levels of subjectification, without limiting itself to an attitude of flight, *détournement*, or ruse, but without, for all that, getting stuck at the level of representation. This passage in no way signifies a dialectical going beyond the molecularity of counterconducts into the molarity of social rights, because the two planes, while modifying each other in the action of an overt confrontation with power, continue to exist in their heterogeneity. Furthermore, even a "revolution" would not be able to operate a synthesis of the molar and the molecular; it is precisely the illusion of the synthesis and reconciliation of these different planes that signed the "death sentence" of the revolutionary strategy of the Communist movement.

Political action necessarily unfolds on heterogeneous planes that answer to heterogeneous logics that may seem contradictory. When the *coordination* calls for "new (social) rights," when it fights for the "continuity of income" and a place in the institutions that regulate unemployment insurance, it indeed enters into a dialectical dynamic of the recognition and identification of itself and its adversary. It's inevitable. In this configuration of power and possible politicization, there isn't one dimension that would be good (the molecular) and another that would be bad (the molar); *social struggles are indissociably molecular and molar.* Each of these levels contains dangers and specific potentialities, in such a way that the *coordination* has to intervene on the plane of the big binary groupings without neglecting to problematize the dangers that every logic of recognition and identity makes arise. Because it is engaged on a terrain of protest, the *coordination* is continually confronted with a threat of the blockage and paralysis of processuality, of micropolitical experimentation in representation. On pain of being imprisoned in the trap of action on the macropolitical terrain alone, it is obliged to continually call into question its modalities of action.

But the protest doesn't just have a social, economic, or corporative content. It also expresses something completely different. Struggles at the macropolitical level are of great importance, as "however modest the demand, it always constitutes a point that the axiomatic cannot tolerate." All the economic and social demands of the movement are accompanied by a deeper and more general "democratic" demand that it is a matter of unfolding: "when people demand to formulate their problems themselves, and determine at least the particular conditions under which they can receive a more general solution (hold to the *particular* as an innovative form)."[54] Struggle around macropolitical questions (unemployment insurance, organization of time, continuity of income, etc.), then, hollows out a gap between two types of politics: a politics of representation, and a politics of problematization and experimentation. The *coordination* is not the institution that would represent molecular counterconducts in a public space.[55] It is much more an "institution" that constitutes these molecular behaviors as a political problem. To problematize means introducing new objects for action and thought (precarity, discontinuous employment, social protection within flexibility, the temporalities of this discontinuity, etc.), and new subjects (precarious workers, wage earners with multiple employers, wage earner–employers, etc.) in the space of politics.

The Molar and the Molecular in Micropolitics

To characterize its strategy, the *coordination* utilized the motto "neither inside nor outside"[56] in its relation to molar institutions. This translates the fact that the struggle was conducted at the limit of the inside and outside, starting from the place where power is in the making, but also where it is in the process of being unmade because, as we will discover when analyzing molecular counterconducts, if certain power relations are in the process of being fixed into relations of domination by institutions, others escape it: there are processes of subjection that are sketched out or reinforced, but there are also processes of subjectification (of counterconducts) that emerge and become widespread. "Neither inside nor outside"—that is to say, "at the limit"—signifies that the *coordination* attacks the connections, the links, between apparatuses, that it considers what it fights to be an assemblage of assemblages (economic, social, political, mediatic, cultural, etc.), and that it attacks the places where its articulations are made. The action of the *coordinations* doesn't aim at "taking" or occupying (state) power, and as a consequence, it doesn't model organization (hierarchy, centralization, or totalization) and "militant" subjectivity (subordination, obedience, etc.) with this task in view. It doesn't distinguish between, and it doesn't hierarchize its union and political modalities of action, and thus it is not obsessed by the question, which has preoccupied and preoccupies several generations of leftist and Communist militants, of the "political outcome" of "social" movements.

What one sees emerging is an articulation between different functions of the collective assemblage *"coordination"* that overturns the principles around which the workers' movement had organized itself from the end of the nineteenth century. If in this tradition, being-together and the subjectivity that emerged from it were functions of being-against, the manner of fighting, and the way of conceiving the enemy and power, in the experiences of contemporary struggles, this relation effectively seems to reverse itself: the efficacy of being-against, its duration and even its possibility, now depend on the modalities of constitution of being-together.[57]

The *coordinations* experiment with practices in which action in the macropolitical space is indissociable from practices of the individuation and transformation of subjectivity. The efficacy and force/strength that they can exercise to impose the objectives that they pursue in the political domain, depend on the construction of common experience, the modalities of constitution, and expression of collective assemblages of enunciation and action. Being-together can be characterized by what Guattari defines as autopoietic (autoproductive) processes of subjectivity. The unions are put off their stride by these modalities of action, but also by the content of these struggles, engaged in by "wage earners" whose principal demands do not concern their wages, as with the traditional workers movement, but unemployment insurance, and do not bear on employment but concern the improvement and extension of intermittence. The *intermittents* do not perceive themselves as "cognitive workers," as theories of cognitive capitalism would like, either. As we have said, they prefer to put the accent on the word "precarious," not in order to vindicate precarity as such, but in order to name the general conditions of governmentality (for which precarity constitutes one of the techniques that are transverse to the whole of the social), and in order to look for the connections and assemblages that this transversality implies.

The *coordination* is not a collective but a distributive whole. It is an architectonic, a cartography of singularities, composed of networks and individualities, a plurality of committees and initiatives, places for discussion and elaboration, militants, political and union groups, networks of "cultural and artistic" affinities, friends, and so on, which make and unmake themselves at different speeds and to different ends. The action of the *coordination* corresponds to an experimentation with apparatuses of being-together and being-against, which simultaneously takes up the already-codified procedures of politics again and invents others. In both cases, it is always a matter of favoring the encounters of singularities and the assemblage of heterogeneous elements. Diverse manners of doing and saying are expressed in the *coordination*, and develop as apprenticeships or "collective expertises" that as soon as they start functioning, make problems, rather than solutions, proliferate.[58]

For what remains of the workers' movement (in its leftist or institutional form), its political action is, as always, dominated by a logic of representation and totalization that plays the game of hegemony with the movement. The deployment of the *coordination* thus requires, in the first place, the neutralization of its manners of saying and doing politics. Where there is a hegemony of forms of organization inherited from the workers' movement, there is no *coordination*. Where there is *coordination*, these organizations can constitute one of its components, but by abandoning their pretentions to hegemony, and adapting to the constitutive rules that are instituted in and by the movement.

As an experiment with a new social practice and a new activism, the *coordination* originates in a double—molar and molecular—dimension. There "will always necessarily be a certain functionality that is molar," says Guattari, even in the micropolitical. In other words, the action of self-organization must pass via the molar procedures of participation, confrontation, and decision making in meetings, committees, and working groups. On this matter we can say that deliberation, speaking up, and decision making seem to be structured according to the political criteria stated by Rancière[59] (declarative speech, equality, theatrical form, etc.). Let us note, however, that in the case of the *coordination*,[60] the actions of occupation, intervention, committee work, and so on, their semiotics and particular modes of expression (which are far from being solely linguistic) have without a doubt constituted a more significant vector of subjectification than "public" speech. Besides, speaking up often corresponds to having power over one's peers (differences of elocution, knowledge, political know-how, personality, etc.). In the *coordination*'s process of self-organization, the molar is constituted by techniques that *make* speak yet equally silence the vast majority of activists. The criticisms of the circulation of speech and modes of enunciation (elaborated in the 1960s and 1970s by "minorities" who attacked the representational model shared as much by institutions as by the organizations of the workers' movement) remain valid still. Even in an experiment like that of the *coordination*, "theatrical" techniques are codified and institutionalized; they "ooze" the official and the serious, and exclude as much as they include. The molar of organization and democratic procedures thus has to pass through the filter of the molecular, on pain of crystallizing in a bureaucratic (or "microfascist") modeling that reproduces the dominant modes of subjectification (separation between the specialists and the laypersons of politics, knowledge, and the division of labor, genders, etc.)

The activity of the *coordination* is transversal to heterogeneous territories—the general assembly, the activity of different committees, informal little affinity groups, and spaces of circulation between the different "instances" of the institution (the bar, the corridors, electronic discussion lists, the kitchen, the time before and after meetings, etc.)—and also and above all everything that arises from outside the *coordination*—everyday life, experiences at work, unemployment, empty time, life experiences, and so forth.

In these different territories, one speaks, thinks, and expresses oneself in different modes; one organizes according to heterogeneous modalities. But the molar dualisms, subjections (the division between experts and laypersons, political specialists and nonspecialists, between those who know and those who don't know, gender differences, etc.) tend to be reproduced, even in a micropolitical situation. But they are not, on the contrary, "gone beyond" simply by the fact of the situation of struggle in which they appear. It is therefore imperative that these dualisms be problematized as such. They demand a specific work—a work that in principle finds in the *coordination* a most favorable terrain for their being discussed and their transformation.

The molecular level and the relation that it entertains with the molar level can and must be specifically maintained and attended to. Lacking sufficient attention to these heterogeneous dimensions, the dynamic of the *coordination* would be paralyzed in a functioning attached simply to performance and the virtuosity of public speech, and its reproduction in closed and insular circles. And to return to our analysis of time, this attention requires much of it. Time is, perhaps, the most important thing that the struggle manages to extract from the subjections and enslavements of the capitalist machine. And it is also what gets lost most rapidly when the movement runs out of breath ("to no longer have time," as there must be time for work, looking for work, and the diverse subjected times of "life").

Micropolitics is a pragmatism of the "institution," the institution in action, and the institution in the process of doing what a "care of the self" that is not individual but collective requires. By "collective" must be understood not only a grouping of individuals but also the *coordination* "machine" and the milieu that supports it, the procedures of functioning and decision making, the techniques for managing activity and speaking up, the organization of places, the definition of roles, the assemblage of temporalities, the ambiance, and so on, that literally "produce" the "collective."[61]

In order that the "theatrical" dimension of speech and the codified practices of politics not get the upper hand over the circulation of multiple semiotic components of expression and subjectification, the *coordination* tried to develop a series of techniques that Guattari might have defined as "analytic." The weight of the molar is sometimes so crushing and inhibiting that one has to suspend it, for example, as the *coordination* did by declaring the "political action strike" in summer 2006. It was then necessary to reactivate the molecular level so that the entirety of the assemblage "*coordination*" would continue to function. In other words, it was necessary to once again take into account—and differently—the entirety of the territories of the *coordination* and its outside, by assuming an *internal* blockage, and one not determined by the adversary and its apparatuses— that is, finally, to reconstruct the assemblage of different modes of existence and processes of subjectification, so that desire could once again arise and circulate.

Thus, at the start of this chapter, we posed the question, How is the relation between the molar and the molecular to be articulated at the heart of the macropolitical and the micropolitical, when revolutionary action no longer aims at taking power (peacefully or violently)? Only experimentation with new social practices and new forms of activism can provide the response. Without seeking to compartmentalize or specialize, they have instead to establish a continuum between political, social, and economic questions, between practices and technoscientific transformations, artistic practices, and modalities of production of knowledges. Political action should not aim to reconcile and unify the at once independent and inseparable elements of the micro and macro, the molar and molecular. The strategy and political tactics of the *coordination* did not consist in a subordination of these different dimensions to one, specifically political plane alone, but in the fact of passing— and sometimes leaping—from one plane to another, of acting transversally on the different levels according to logics that remain heterogeneous.

Micropolitics Is a Constructivism

The process of constituting a *coordination* is not organic but polemical and conflictual; with Philippe Zarifian, who summarizes very well the political import of Deleuze's philosophical concept, we can call it a "disjunctive synthesis": "it shows the double movement of open convergence and separation when there is a position to be taken on events. No struggle, no engagement can avoid divergences and separations being produced in the very camp of those who seek to struggle together, even while proposing new unifying recompositions, openings to unforeseen compositions."[62] "Disjunctive synthesis" refers us to the movements of the 1960s and 1970s that by integrating the question of the production of subjectivity and the transformation of the self into their actions, operated a radical displacement in relation to the Marxist method of struggle, for which secondary power relations (men/women, nationals/immigrants, etc.) have to be subordinated to the principal relation (capital/labor). Minoritarian movements reverse this point of view: instead of containing the other relations, the capital/labor relation is, in reality, a specific, partial, singular relation that can only function when assembled, and by way of relations of sexual, racial, and cultural domination. The contribution of micropolitics to political action has given rise to numerous misunderstandings, although it restricts itself to affirming that if one wants to attack the principal relation, one must also attack the secondary relations. Disjunctive synthesis is the method for "politicizing" the multiplicity of power relations that are entangled with one another. It is necessary to disarticulate the "common world" in which the relations of exploitation and racial, sexual, and cultural domination, and so on, fit together, and assert the singularity of each one.

Disjunctive synthesis is equally of great use in apprehending the problem that is immediately posed to every political movement: the recomposition of struggles and the circulation/communication of "order-words." In the tradition of the workers' movement, the terms "recomposition," "generalization," "common," and "universal" evade the problem by anticipating that which has to be explained and constructed: the assemblage of singularities. Circulation cannot be achieved solely through leaps, ruptures, and discontinuities, and what circulates is always a difference that bears the singular mark of a situation. Recomposition can only be a differentiation, as the positive affirmation of singularities. Disjunctive synthesis invites us to think and practice this generalization, which is not a simple enlargement or a linear progression but a proliferation that functions by differentiation and singularization. In the same manner that in being-against one must not hierarchize the different apparatuses of power by seeking a center for them, in the process of construction of being-together one must not hierarchize the different modalities of subjectification and the different assemblages, milieus, and environments that sustain them, by seeking a political subjectivity that recomposes and universalizes them. The collective assemblage cannot be a form of political organization without at the same time and in parallel being an apparatus for the problematization of existence, the constitution and transformation of the self, and the creation of possibilities. These practices cannot be referred to an improbable "after."

Rancière's willingness to isolate the political act as such—so as to measure its "effects"—ends up by reestablishing the classical separations of political philosophy (economic, political, and social) that he elsewhere claims to write against. Trying to sketch a solitary plane by arguing for its "isolation," its "specificity," means that the dynamic opened up between heterogeneous processes, indivisible planes, and unreconcilable levels is once again confined to the solitary "political" dimension. The weakness of this position consists in the evacuation of the historicity of politics that it carries out; in its lack of any analysis of the specific characteristics of the subjections and enslavements of contemporary capitalism. Now, in the latter, it is strictly impossible for politics to hold up by and legitimate itself. The distribution and redistribution of places and functions, like the distribution and redistribution of the possible and the impossible, take place transversally to the economic, the political, the social, and the cultural, and their molar and molecular dimensions.

Far from being a "spontaneism," a "movementism," or a simple affirmation of "forms of life" (a "vitalism," as Rancière and Badiou say, with a hint of contempt), micropolitics requires a very high level of organization, a forceful differentiation of functions and political action, a multiplicity of initiatives, and a certain intellectual and organizational discipline. It demands a rigor and a great capacity to read conjunctures in their specificity, and intervene in very different and always singular situations. Instead of deducing a "depreciation" of organization from Deleuze and Guattari's theory, as does Badiou, micropolitics and its methodology are fundamental instruments for rethinking politics and organization, and making the latter effective under the conditions of contemporary capitalism. Micropolitics is a constructivism that is at the same time struggle, refusal, revolt, and problematization, experimentation, invention, organization, and reconversion of subjectivity.

Micropolitics is not a "politics of the little," the micro, the convivial, or the festive (although it is also that); it consists in the capacity to count on and move from out of the heterogeneous. It is on this condition, by holding together the different bits of political action, that one can construct the strength and the relations of force that are missing from contemporary radical politics.

Micropolitics requires a "pragmatics" of activity in order to evaluate case by case the dangers and potentialities of each of the planes on which one is engaged (as in the case of the constant and often very lively debates that accompanied the constitution of the committee of inquiry with parliamentarians—that is to say, the engagement of the *coordination* on the plane of representative politics), because what is true at a given moment, during a specific political sequence, is not so at another. If there are very certainly "classic" methods of political work that can and should be recuperated and integrated in this new dynamic, this recuperation of the political trade or "professionalism" can only be achieved starting from a different *ethos* to that of the revolutionaries of the nineteenth and twentieth centuries.

Politics is not considered the privileged instance for the constitution of the current community or the community to come, nor as a level to which the conflict would need to be raised up so as to deploy it in all its significance. In the activity of the *coordination*, neither does the political represent the privileged point of view from which to gain a "global" overview of all particularities, so as to raise them up to the level of the universal.

For the Western tradition, only political action is virtuous and noble, only politics is concerned with the universal, and it is only in politics that one can find man [*sic*] divested of his economic garb. It is only through politics that action and speech are freed from instrumental ends, and are able to encounter others. By criticizing this conception of politics and relieving it of its sacred aura, the *coordinations*, like the movements of the 1970s, well and truly practice a politics of a new type, worthy of the contemporary situation.

The Experience of *Coordinations* in France

The *coordinations* represent experiments in rupture and political subjectification that have been unfolding in France for the last twenty-five years. With the emergence of post-1968 capitalism, the conditions and possibilities for action and political subjectification changed—because the separation of the economy and politics is no longer operative; because the "social" is configured as a proliferation of apparatuses for social subjection and machinic enslavements; because the "working class" has been fragmented into a multiplicity of forms of work and activities where the division between productive and unproductive no longer makes any sense (if it ever did); and because the division between "labor time" and the time of life has exploded into a multiplicity of "temporalities."

Each *coordination* (nurses, students, railway workers, *intermittents*, etc.) carried out a singular experiment, which sedimented procedures, protocols for action, and specific modalities of organization that nevertheless circulate, communicate, and tend to be prolonged and connect with other, equally singular experiments. We have just exited (an exit that started in the 1960s) a "revolutionary" sequence inherited from the nineteenth century, and the new political sequence is seeking itself, and demands as much, if not more, time than that which was necessary to the constitution of the first sequence.

During the financial crisis, a struggle unfolded in Guadeloupe that even if it is not the mirror of our metropolitan situation, can, in its singularity, contribute to problematizing the question of politics in contemporary capitalism. Starting from its "nucleus of non-Western subjectification," as Guattari might say, it participates in this sequence of experimentation and reconstruction of a revolutionary radicalness, and it does this in several ways.

1. The heterogeneity of the "economy" and "politics" no longer defines the conditions of possibility of a politics of emancipation, as was the case in the tradition of the workers' movement. Action, which was traditionally divided between economic action (union) and political action (party), is taken transversally to what is normally defined as the economic, the political, or the cultural—that is to say, on the social and to society in its entirety—producing a multiplicity of partial ruptures. It is taken transversally to the ensemble of segmentations that decide between those who monopolizes power and those who submit to it, in the domain of work, knowledge, and culture (divisions that intersect those of sex, race, age, etc.), and transversally to machinic enslavements (based on "production," media, the welfare state, etc.).

2. The movement has no need of a "political outlet" in the state or the institutional framework of either a party or a vanguard, as it invents a new "politics" and new political subjects. The union (like every other modality of organization) indeed has to play a "political" role. That doesn't mean that it must transform itself into a party but rather that it must work at not closing in on

itself, restricting itself to its traditional functions of protecting purchasing power and the power of work, to work at taking on, like every other component of the movement, the composition of different ruptures and—finally—assembling together the singularity of movements. In their classical forms, the party and the union are structurally incapable of deploying the transversality and conjunction of differences and singularities.

3. The struggle is expressed as a struggle for independence from the state and its institutions. In an epoch in which every New Deal has become impossible, it is on the basis of this independence that at the social level, demands have to be articulated in relation to incomes, social services, production, culture, and everyday life. Negotiation and dialogue over social demands, effectuated by an autonomous movement, doesn't prevent but on the contrary reinforces the process of secession from the state. Independence is not the problem of an ex-colony but a political condition to be won back, even in colonizing countries. The conquest of this "autonomy" is perhaps the most important thing that has been lost in relation to the nineteenth century, and the most difficult to establish in the West, caught as we are in the multiplicity of apparatuses of subjection and enslavement that produce generalized subordination and dependency.

4. In contemporary capitalism, a political movement presupposes a radical democracy that distinguishes and separates itself from the democracy of oligarchies. The democracy of the movement in Guadeloupe neutralized the traditional political apparatus and the intervention of the administration (of the welfare state), and opened up a constitutive process, the effectiveness and success of which depends on the capacity to hold together heterogeneities and differences. It is the motor of a process of

constitution of a "community" that is the exact contrary of communitarianism.

5. Coordination, transversality, democracy, and autonomy are the conditions for new forms of struggle, the outcome of which is the "blocking of society." The blocking of networks of communication, distribution, transport, and enterprises plays the role that the strike had in the previous political sequence, because it corresponds to the level of socialization of "production" of current capitalism. The conditions for blocking society are not the same as those for the strike (even if the strike is one of the elements of blocking), precisely because they require a mobilization of the "social" in its entirety. Coordination, transversality, and democratic radicalness can then articulate different forms of struggle and forces, going from peaceful demonstration to "insurrectional" riots. The modalities of these forms of struggle do not have as their end the taking of "power" but a process of "reconversion" of subjectivity that has to confirm, extend, and reinforce autonomy and independence in relation to the state, and reconfigure assemblages of "production."

6. If, to speak like Vladimir Lenin, the "dualisms of power" are always brief and intense, they require a political work of construction of *coordinations* and situations of confrontation that that is completed before (the unions were working for six years with cultural, musical groups, etc.), during and after the emergence of the struggle. This work is very different from that of the vanguards and parties, because the problem is not that of taking power but that of the constitution of new institutions and the "conversion of subjectivity."

7. The exit from the workerist logic of the unions and leftist politics (the reduction of politics to full employment) is

possible, to use the terms that emerged from the struggle itself, by articulating the "prosaic" (questions of wages, incomes, and social services) with the "poetic" (the contents and the meaning of life and activity, the conversion of subjectivity on the basis of another type of "production" and another type of activity). The question of property and the appropriation of wealth (salary and income) is posed *with* that of the refusal to be governed, the "exit" from capitalism, and the meaning and content of activity.

Thus there are evident continuities between the experiences of the metropolitan *coordinations* and the experience of the collective that undertook the struggle in Guadeloupe, as much as there are discontinuities. Continuity and discontinuity, transversality and singularity, are, in any case, the political conditions for this new revolutionary sequence that is seeking and constructing itself.

3 Economic and Subjective Impoverishment under Neoliberalism

Think about the ready-mades so dear to the Dadaists, to the pop artists, etc., what did they mean if not that art is already on every street corner and in every shed? It is enough to make the decision to harvest them! It is not necessary to have special talents! It is enough to have the strength to make up your mind to pick them and art will be born in the hands of anyone, merely by means of an act of mental liberation. ... But this naive creativity, this operational choice for liberty, as soon as it was proposed and before it became the model for a more general practice, was castrated, intellectualized, relegated to a cultural ghetto.

—Manfredo Massironi

What amazes me is that, in our societies, art no longer has any connection with anything except objects, not with individuals or with life; and also that art is a specialized domain, a domain belonging to the experts we call artists. Can't the life of every individual be a work of art? Why is a canvas or a house considered an art object, but not our life?

—Michel Foucault, "On the Genealogy of Ethics"[1]

In parallel with economic impoverishment, liberalism has produced an impoverishment of subjectivity, a reduction in its existential intensity. If economic impoverishment has affected the population in a differential manner, creating profound hierarchies and polarities of revenue and status, subjective impoverishment concerns the population as a whole across its entire horizon. In security societies, in contrast with disciplinary societies, the rich and the poor inhabit the "same world" in the sense that they are exposed to the same semiotics of information, publicity, television, and art and culture. The production of this common semiotic is a new and defining element of the government of conduct that had been put into place between the end of the nineteenth century and the beginning of the twentieth century, but that truly took off beginning with the New Deal. We are able to problematize the effects of these semiotics on subjectivity in the twentieth century by interrogating the transformation concerning the place and function of art and the artist in both the economy and society by using Marcel Duchamp's concept of "anart"[2] and the aesthetic paradigm of Guattari.

Duchamp describes a double expansion of the concept of art and the artist—an expansion that required the invention of neologisms ("anart" and "anartist") in order to make sense of the new function and the new roles that such an expansion entails. First, art, which was once an activity reserved for economic elites like the pursuit of intellectual and scientific knowledge, has extended and expanded its presence among those classes that were once excluded from its practice. As Plato commented long ago, these classes did not have the time to worry about art since they were entirely occupied by work for their masters and lords ("work never waits"). Second, access to the "products" of art (like the products of intellectual and scientific "knowledge") is no longer restricted to an elite of spectators as had always been the case in aristocratic and bourgeois society; it touches an ever-growing public that continues to develop its part in and capacities for coproduction. This first "sociological" expansion entails another expansion, ontological in nature, that is perhaps even more important: Duchamp liberates art from its restricted meaning as a specialized activity conducted by a guild of professionals; according to him, art is primarily a coefficient that is present in every human activity to differing degrees.

Duchamp, always very attentive to the material conditions of art objects, described in the 1960s the changes affecting art and artists since the beginning of the twentieth century: "The position of the artist today has no connection with that of the artist fifty years ago. ... Today, there are one hundred times more painters than fifty years ago." At the beginning of the century, art was still a marginal phenomenon: "There were a few painters, a few dealers, a few collectors, art was an esoteric activity, those people spoke their own language that the general public didn't understand." The few artists, collectors, and dealers spoke a "language of initiates." When we think about the avant-gardes of the early twentieth century in light of the place that art and culture occupy today in the economy and society, we fall victim to an optical illusion that Duchamp corrects for us. "Hardly anyone spoke about cubism in the general public, there was a small scandal, but it was momentary and was only of interest to Le Figaro. Since then, everything has entered into the public domain. The esotericism of art has become exo-terism; the public has something to say and it says it. Add to that the fact that art now brings in money. There wasn't the public interest then that there is now, which is becoming worrisome." Art has raised the political and economic stakes by introducing new subjects (from new publics) and new "objects" (artistic techniques and practices) into society.

The expansion of art not only allowed for its entry into public space but also (and above all) into the market. Contrary to the lamentations of those who uphold the "cultural exception," there is no longer any difference between merchandise and artistic products: "The visual arts, due to their close connection to the law of supply and demand, have become commodities. ... Art is a product like beans, we buy art in the same way we buy spaghetti." Painters "don't make paintings, they write cheques." Art is completely "integrated" into the market in the same way that the artist is completely integrated into society. "We are not the pariahs we were at the beginning of the century. ... [T]he artist has come to pursue, little by little, a fundamentally economic venture."

Duchamp can himself be considered an indicator of the transformation in the material conditions of the artist's existence; his life (1887–1968) coincides with these major shifts. Child of a notary, he received a small annuity from his father and long lived off the "patronage" of his wealthy friends. Duchamp practiced an economy of the "gift," offering his works as gifts or exchanging them for services such as lodgings. Not wanting to be involved in the art market that was in the process of developing in the United States during the 1920s, he lived a modest life. He once turned down a contract to sell his entire year's work to a dealer for $10,000. He refused to give over to the "mass" production inherent in all commodified production, which according to him, characterized the vast majority of work done by painters.[3] He died in 1968, at the precise moment when that which he had foreseen made another important development as art expanded again in relation to both artists and the public.

The annuity, the patronage, and even the art market: in spite of its highly speculative growth, art was still limited to a very small elite, and was not large enough to support the lives and activities of the thousands of artists who turned toward salaried and independent labor. By 1968, we were already living in our present. The boom in art and culture would have amazed Duchamp. Transformed into an economic sector that employs 2 percent of the active European population, it has become one of the apparatuses for governing publics that have multiplied at an insane pace, but also it has become a terrain of conflict and collective resistance, as was shown in the movement of the *intermittents* between 2003 and 2007.

Duchamp gives two different accounts of the "ontological" expansion of the activity of creation, understanding art both as making and acting. But in each case, he is interested in leading art—or artistic practices, to be more precise—away from being narrowly understood as "fine arts."

Like all authors and artists who worked with art in its expanded sense, Duchamp was suspicious of the concept of creation.[4] "In the social, ordinary meaning of the word, creation seems very nice, but ultimately I don't believe in the creative function of the artist. The artist is a man like any other, that's that. ... [T]he word art means 'to make' (*faire*). Yet the whole world makes things and those that make things on a canvas are called artists. ... But at the end of the day, what is an artist? Somebody who makes furniture is also an artist such that somebody might be said to own 'a Boulle.' Boulle's reputation is made of the admiration we give to him."[5]

The second version of the expansion of art he offers is more coherent with Duchamp's thought and actions. Radically detached from the idea of the artist as homo faber making objects, he was closer here to a conception of art as a "technique of the soul," a technology of subjectification, a technique of the self, or even as a system of signs that compels thinking and

feeling. He was also drawn to the idea of the function of the artist as a "medium" of subjectification.

After all the word "art," etymologically, means "to act," not "to make"
but "to act." The moment when you act, you are an artist. You are really
one, you don't sell a work, but you make an action. In other words, art
means action, activities of all kinds. For everyone. But in our society,
we have decided to distinguish between a group called "artists," a group
called "doctors," and so on, which is completely artificial. ... Art, rather
than being a singular entity that fits in a little box with many artists
each with their own little works, it could be universal; it could be a
human factor in the lives of people. Each person could be an artist, even
if not understood as an artist. Do you see what I'm saying?[6]

Every activity is equal to all others; all people are equal to
all others. Duchamp is expressing a radically democratic point
of view where the problem is not one of how to give the public
access to art, or how to educate these publics. The problem is
the constitution and the enrichment of a capacity to act that is
universally shared, even if in a differential manner. Duchamp
is among the first to understand that in the security societies
that begin to evolve at the beginning of the century, art as an
institution, "art" in the "social meaning of the word," does not
represent the promise of emancipation but on the contrary constitutes a new technique for the government of subjectivity.

Art is involved, to use Marx's language, in the social division
of labor, or to borrow from Rancière, in the division of the sensible. From this point of view, to be an artist is a profession or
a specialization like any other, and it is precisely this command
to occupy a place, a role, and an identity with one's body and
soul that is the object of Duchamp's permanent and categorical
refusal. He refuses the title of "artist" and claims the existential constitution of "breather." In an interview from 1962, art
critic Pierre Cabanne, either intrigued or annoyed by this denial

of identity (a denial that Duchamp continued to play with; hesitating between a becoming-jew and a becoming-woman, he finally chose the latter, becoming "Rrose Sélavy"), tries to squeeze Duchamp into a corner: "You refuse the title of painter, as well as man of letters. ... What, then, is your profession?" To which Duchamp responds, "Why do you want to classify people at all costs? What am I, do I know? A man, quite simply a 'breather.'"

"To be obliged to work in order to survive, that, that is obscene!" declared Duchamp when he encountered those who saw a profession, a job, a salaried position as the goal of political action because it assured identity, integration, socialization. His friend and accomplice Picabia was even more extreme in his views against learning skills and "professionalization"; he claimed amateurism for himself (a claim which, it is worth highlighting, was the object of attacks from the Ministry of Culture according to whose logic "everyone had their place"): "I go beyond the amateurs, I am a 'sur-amateur'; the professionals are shit pumps. ... My paintings aren't taken for serious works because they are made without the afterthought of speculation and because I work on them in order to entertain my self, in the same way one would engage in sport."

While Duchamp refuses the injunction to be an artist (he defined himself as a castoff from art), he does not abandon in any way artistic practices, protocols, and procedures. But as we will see, this desire to be seen as an "anartist" asks for a redeployment of artistic functions and techniques. This would involve a subtle positioning that would place him neither outside nor inside art as an institution, but at its limit, at its borders. From this position at the limit, at the borders, one could "cut loose (to borrow an expression from Deleuze and Guattari) the dialectical opposition art/nonart.

The New Division of the Sensible

The social and ontological expansion of the concept of art marks a paradigm shift that concerns society in its entirety. In order to grasp the political consequences of these changes, it is necessary to make explicit the "new division of the sensible" that it implies. By means of this idea, Rancière describes the division between ways of doing and ways of saying that determines who has the power to name the possible, the sayable, and the thinkable in an epoch and a society. This "division of the sensible" thus allows us to grasp in a particularly profound manner the distribution of roles and functions that were proper to industrial capitalism during the nineteenth century, marked as it was by the dualisms active/passive, culture/nature, and sensibility/ understanding. These dualisms are political: they separate and hierarchize society according to relations of domination that organize the powers held by people of "refined culture" (activity) over people with "simple natures" (passivity), the power of people of leisure (freedom) over working people (necessity), and the powers of the class of intellectual labor (autonomy) over the class of manual labor (subordination). This distribution of the sensible corresponds to a dualist divide within the population between the "cultivated classes who have access to the totality of lived experience," on the one hand, and "the savage classes, mired in the fragmentation of work and sensible experience," on the other.[7]

Yet it seems to me[8] that this division of the sensible represents the politico-cultural and semiotic conditions from which Duchamp marks the exit, with his conception of art as coefficient to different degrees in each human activity. While the disciplinary model poses a difference of kind between art and nonart, nature and culture, and material and intellectual labor, the new division of the sensible that Duchamp intuited is no longer marked by dualisms but by a chain, a series, a continuum that expresses differences in the power to act.

The disciplinary division of functions, roles, and identities intersects perfectly with the divisions between the dominant (capitalists) and the dominated (proletariat): refined culture, art, mastery of speech, developed sensibilities, and intellectual labor fall to the dominant class while nature, a poor facility with language, rough sensibilities, and manual labor fall to the dominated. Rancière's "division of the sensible" also presents us with another opposition: the "two humanities." Yet in our society today, there is but one population that engages in activities all of which contain "coefficients" of creativity, speech, developed sensibilities, intellect, and refined culture—in other words, all that once constituted the exclusive "heritage" of the bourgeoisie (or the aristocracy). Salaried workers, the unemployed, and welfare recipients represent a continuum that encompasses and mixes manual and intellectual labor, which were once separated between different classes, in the same way that cultivated and rough sensibilities are no longer distributed between "bourgeoisie" and "proletariat," but are distributed in a differential fashion within a single population. Moreover, we are living through a veritable reversal in relation to the old division of the sensible as there is today an injunction to "equip" oneself (in the way one once spoke of equipping a machine) for that which the dominated were once excluded from: speech, autonomy, intellectual work, refined culture, art, and educated sensibilities. In the new division of the sensible, the problem is less the divide between activity and passivity than the requirement to become "autonomous," and assume the responsibility and the risks that these behaviors carry. The issue resides less in the division between mastery of "speech" by the bourgeoisie and the inarticulate "cry" (of pain) from workers and the proletariat than in the inciting of everyone to expression; it is less in the separation between the cultured people and the uncivilized than in the continuous training and acculturation that we are obliged to undergo throughout our lives. This new "division" of the sensible, in the form of a continuum, reconfigures the field of possible experiences. Thus, we are able to describe *another continuum than that of power*—one along which are distributed a multiplicity of activities that express variations of the same power (*puissance*) to act.[9] This plane does not trace those distinctions that neoliberalism transforms into competing inequalities but the differential distribution of "creativity" and the potential to act, and therefore a multiplicity of sources of partial subjectification.

Equality of Kind, Equality of Power

Starting from an understanding of the differential distribution of the potential to act, Duchamp proposes a new concept of equality that might be able to stand up to the differential logic of neoliberalism (inequality and competition), saving equality from its transformation into market exchangeability. That "anybody at all" is able to declare themselves "an artist," and that any object whatsoever can be the object of artistic practice is what Duchamp claims as "anart." The logic of "anybody at all" is also at the core of Rancière's renewal of the concepts of democracy and equality. For Rancière, the scandal of Athenian democracy is precisely its "natural" equality—that is, the supposition that anybody at all is equal to anybody else. Whether cobbler or blacksmith, anyone can give their opinion regarding the management of a common good regardless of whether or not they hold a "title" (whether acquired through birth or wealth) that authorizes them. Belonging to the demos (the people) is determined by the "simple fact of being born in this city, specifically the city of Athens." Beyond the fact of being born in Athens, the Athenian demos possesses no title, not one recognizing the wealth of the few (the *oligoi*), or those who have the virtue or excellence of the "greats" (the *aristoi*.) Thus we understand that the dualisms inherent in the division of the sensible discussed by Rancière are the product of the inequality of property between the dominant and dominated classes, through which the wrong suffered refers back to natural equality (we are "all equal in nature," as Ranciere would say).

Through the "anybody at all" of Duchamp, we can see the outlines of another concept of equality, an "equality of power" (according to the definition that Deleuze gives in *Difference and Repetition*), that is better adapted to the new division of the sensible. If it's true that anybody at all is equal to anybody else, what matters is the singularity and the power for differential change and metamorphosis of all that becomes apparent in the light of the equality of all. The expanded notion of art, as suppressing the differences in degrees of creativity, introduces a concept of quality where "the being equal is immediately present to all things ... even though things participate unequally in this equality." Here, equality resides in the fact that things and beings go to the limit of what they are about to do, even if they express a different ability to act. Things are at once different and equal, the smallest action equal to the greatest, because all of them go to the limit of what they are capable of, since all things being equal, they each have their own "coefficient of art" and participate in the same ability to act.

Art and Culture as Techniques for Governing Subjectivity

Contemporary societies provide us with a good example of how techniques of government intervene into the double expansion of art and culture outlined by Duchamp. Art and culture, as Duchamp sensed at the beginning of the last century, can be used as two techniques, heterogeneous yet complementary, which enable the impoverishment of subjectivity and limit governed subjects' capacity to act.

As we already noted in the French context, the *economic* impoverishment of artists and technicians is produced through the organization of a cultural labor market that accentuates competition and the difference in revenues between employees in order to construct human capital as precarious, flexible, and subject to the production of content in the cultural industries. At the same time, the *subjective* impoverishment of artists and technicians (but also publics) develops according to two logics that appear contradictory at times: first, industry incorporates and "de-potentiates" the critique of the division between art and nonart initially raised by avant-garde movements while, second, reestablishing this distinction.

With regard to the first logic, televisual "culture"—the paradigm and model of contemporary mass culture—plays with the essential differences between art and nonart through the production of a nihilism for the people whose order-word is "Everything is worthwhile!" Television, advertising, and marketing are the most fully developed forms of *banalization* and *degradation* along the democratic continuum. They are produced by a section of contemporary art that no longer hierarchizes subjects (the high, the low, the common, and the noble), events, or genres, and that brings together anything with anything else in

order to reach anyone at all. We find in most television programs the use of these artistic techniques of democratization,
but purged of any depth. The artist, the athlete, the writer, the
cook, the philosopher, the rock star, and the man on the street
all confront one another on the same plain of "equality" that has
been constructed and is managed by journalists, a group whose
powers continue to expand. The equality between all people and
all things was originally the subversive program of contemporary art.[10] When all is said and done, it is this subversion that is
transformed into the commodified translatability and exchangeability of all differences, semiotics, and forms of subjectivity by
television, marketing, and advertising.

At the same time, the second logic—the subjective impoverishment that is at work in most cultural policies—tends
to reconstruct differences of kind as well as the opposition
between art and nonart, artist and nonartist. This reconstruction of differences aims to reestablish those criteria of evaluation (Who is an artist? What are the best cultural policies?)
that escaped the state and cultural institutions over the course
of the twentieth century, initially within closed artistic circles,
and later, after 1968, in circles that were much larger (and of
which the *intermittents du spectacle* are only the most clearly visible fraction). Along these lines, Sarkozy announced in Janu-
ary 2009, among his other promises to the cultural world, that
he would create a "council for artistic creation" over which he
and the minister of culture would preside, and that would be
lead by the film producer Marin Karmitz. The mandate of this
council notably includes the "refocusing of support on artistic
excellence." Karmitz, in an interview the day after Sarkozy's
announcement, declared the necessity of reconstructing a culture of the state. The state must, in other words, reestablish

the criteria of evaluation that divide the good artist from the bad (something that was already the aim of the former minister of culture, Jean-Jacque Aillagon, who was "let go" by the *intermittents'* movement). Thus, Sarkozy's proposition found a milieu that was already favorable to its realization. Thinkers like Pierre-Michel Menger or Badiou along with all the major trade unions seemed nostalgic for "great art and artists," "high culture and intellectuals," and were aiming for the reconstruction of "excellence" and a "reprofessionalization"[11] designed to seal the breach through which "anyone at all" was allowed to proclaim themselves "artists."[12]

Therefore we have, on the one side, the hypermodernity of television and the cultural industries that no longer distinguishes between culture and commodities, art and nonart, and on the other side, the neoarchaism of the Ministry of Culture and the cultural institutions that are reestablishing criteria of excellence, professionalization, and the culture of the state, through which art and nonart will once again be separated.

Art, Market, Institution, and the Government of Publics

Any attempt to understand the operations of the systems for governing the population and publics through art (and culture) must distinguish between art as an institution (its molar dimension) and art as practice and technique (its molecular dimension). The molar dimension of art is organization by a distribution of functions and specific roles (the artist, the work, the public, the critic, the curator, etc.) into systems (the museum, the festival, the theater, the exhibition, etc.), and criteria of evaluation that show and explain art as a distinct activity conducted by experts and specialists who guide a public in need of "cultivation." The molar dimension of art defines the modalities of enunciation and the visibility of these functions, roles, and systems.

The modes of enunciation and visibility of modern art were instituted by the American and French revolutions, which defined all at once the status of the artist and the public, their property rights, and the spaces where art is displayed (museums) and pondered (aesthetics).[13] The French Revolution established a division and a classification that still grounds our contemporary institutions. The revolution transformed the multiplicity of "handicrafts" (*arts de faire*) into the specific disciplines of modernity: art, craft, and science. Each one of these had its own institutions: the Academy of Fine Arts, the Conservatory of Arts and Crafts, and the Polytechnical Institute, respectively.

On the other hand, the molecular dimension of art is constituted through the practices and techniques of artists and publics that evade (*déjouent*) these divisions and codifications, these modes of enunciation and systems (*dispostifs*) of visibility, opening up spaces of experimentation, of the molecular transformation of the sensible, perception, and ways of feeling. The molecular dimension of art introduces a suspension of, and discontinuities in, ways of feeling and perceiving as well as the distribution of places and social functions for both the artist and the public. Starting from this molecular dimension, artists and publics have continuously used the molar norms and systems in order to work through them, alongside them, or against them. In sum, the molar dimension is assimilable to the disciplinary assignation that distributes roles. It functions according to dialectical logic (art/nonart, artist/nonartist, and work of art/commodity); the molecular dimension, on the other hand, is assimilable to the differential management of liberties, heterogeneities, and subjectifications.

A large number of those artistic practices that "activate and make use" of these microliberties, microruptures, and micro-heterogeneities as their zone of intervention and action are represented by "relational aesthetics." This aesthetic involves a "sliding" (*glisser*) across "all the cultural codes, all the forms of everyday life, and all works of global patrimony, making them function,"[14] without any pretense of negation or overcoming, in order to "inhabit" them. In this way, the work of art approaches its traditional role as a "receptacle of the artist's vision" in order to become an "active agent" of the relation with the spectator, with whom the artist negotiates the meaning and function of the work. This culture of "use" and negotiation with the public as well as institutions opens up to what Nicolas Bourriard— the theorist of relational aesthetics—has called a "formal communism."[15]

Since Duchamp and his readymades—institutionalized from the 1960s as "artist" and "works of art," respectively, to be contemplated and consumed in museums—lost their capacity to call art into question with their passage into the molar world of institutions, the micropractices, their processes and dynamics, were no longer able to overhaul and transform the modalities of enunciation and visibility of art as an institution. We continually come up against the translation of the multiplicity of these innovations, experimentations, liberties, and heterogeneities in the figure of the artist, the work, the museum, and the public, and their enclosure within these classifications. Indeed, if the molecular level clearly confirms the fact that "creation comes from more than its author, the supposed subject, and spills out from their works, objects whose closure is a fiction,"[16] then the molar level systematically re-centers (or closes off) this overflow, these openings and spaces of the possible within the logic of property (or patrimony) of the "author," the "creator," or the "work," or even the museum and other institutions.

Therefore, it is not just that molecular practices are unable to overhaul and transform the disciplinary categorizations of art and the artist but that they are equally engaged in the processes of capitalist valorization and the "cultural" government of populations and publics. Enterprise and the state use them to feed the industries of tourism, "free" time, and leisure without even making an effort to counter the critical potentials contained within these practices, or their potential to suspend the established codes and values and transform subjectivities. They use them to build museum territories (Bilbao), museum cities (Venice), museum districts (Vienna),[17] city shows (Kassel), or city festivals (Avignon) that monetize and capitalize the artistic and cultural desires of publics and the population. These practices also constitute the motor of the luxury industry, which exploits their outputs (in the same way that industry exploits the outputs of basic research) in order to sell "lifestyles" to the new millionaires of globalization along with the upper tiers of the middle class. Capitalist valorization has the capacity to integrate these "counterconducts," these semantic innovations, the experimentations with new materials of expression and unknown modalities of enunciation, within the production of an entire series of material and immaterial goods.

This policy does not prevent the molecular level from having a real effect—an effect in which an encounter with an artwork, film, theatrical or dance performance, or installation might open to the one who experiences an unimagined world, new possibilities that put in movement a transformation in the relationship to themselves, others, and the world. But at the same time (and inversely), a "monochrome blue," a piece of theater or dance, a film or performance, or something else, can serve as a kind of "special offer" that motivates the "spectator/tourist" to circulate around the territory or city, inciting them to consume. Capitalists in the "creative industries" are not ready to pass over these sources of innovation—sources that they have, on the contrary, the tendency to encourage. Here, publics are very much coproducers of the work, just as Duchamp wanted, but from within the cultural industry and the art market. The same conclusions might be made about the artistic practices of precarious cultural workers, who at the same time as they experiment with spaces and coefficients of freedom for themselves and the public, enjoy the creativity and inventiveness of their activity while feeding the culture industry.

In this context, the concept of differentials of freedom and creativity and that of Deleuze and Guattari's "undecidable propositions and movements"[18] are more effective instruments than totalizing oppositions (liberty/domination, creativity/passivity, etc.) for making sense of the systems of capture and control as well as the modalities of escape and rupture that are inherent in such systems. Undecidability and indetermination do not point toward a systemic incertitude (as is preached by the theoreticians of the risk society) but the possible political actions that flow from the intersection and confrontation of the "freedom" of governing systems to act and the freedom of action of the governed. The undecidable is the "germ and place *par excellence* of revolutionary decisions."[19] It is the place of activation for the transformations of subjectivity, but it is also the place where the possibility for new relations of domination is outlined, the germ and place of a new capitalist valorization.

Art and Industry: The Case of "Crossed Values"

In order to describe the contribution of art and culture to capitalist valorization and its modeling of subjectivity, the biennial of contemporary art in Rennes (Les Ateliers de Rennes, first held in 2008), financed by the industrial "patrons" of the region, provides a great experimental laboratory. The title of the debut festival was Crossed Values, referring to the confrontation, juxtaposition, or even opposition between the values of business and the values of contemporary art. In the construction and operation of this biennial, we can see the molar and molecular dimensions of governmental action and artistic action. In the most interesting artistic residencies in businesses that were organized under the rubric of "crossed values," the artists seemed to act as anartists, multiplying the "micropolitical" techniques and procedures in order to introduce an uncertainty, a discontinuity, and a heterogeneity into the habits, norms, and codifications that govern the protocols and policies (*dispositifs*) of labor, commercialization, and marketing. The salaried workers, employees, and entrepreneurs that participated in these experiments opened themselves to "processes" that unsettled routine perceptions and habits, and produced an atmosphere of indeterminacy in situations where finalized and instrumental action normally constituted the principal criterion of evaluation for activity. The nonfunctional use of machines and tools, for example, or the repetition of work activities (*gestes du travail*) by white-collar workers in an expressive context that is no longer that of the organization of production, or even the transformation of a small number of temporary workers into art critics, allowed for the vacillation or suspension, if only for a brief moment, of the distribution of roles and functions inside these businesses as well as within art as an institution. Business did not try to submit artistic endeavor to its logic. It did not try to instrumentalize it but let it function according to its own principles and protocols. The molecular perturbations that affected subjectivity and power relations (the "sensible" of the business) did not displease some kinds of businesses. The market imperative had pushed them to put in place protocols of permanent innovation and adaptation for a continuously evolving economic situation. Businesses are obliged to invent new strategies of commercialization and marketing as well as (and above all) "pastoral" techniques for transforming and guiding the subjectivity of its permanent workforce. This is the hypermodern aspect of relations with capital.

This is not to say that artistic practices are in a functional relation with the interests of businesses, since artists are playing with the constraints of the business, and some of the workers immerse themselves in the micropossibilities opened by the artistic interventions. Indetermination and undecidabilty can, at a microlevel, be quite real for both entrepreneurs and workers, who with evident differences in power, each play at their own strategies. How, then, is it possible for a business to govern these microruptures in routine behaviors? How is it possible to control these waves of molecular indetermination and undecidability? First, by using techniques proper to the business itself, but also (and more fundamental in nature) through an intervention in the social assemblage (*agencement*) constituted through the continuum of business/town/territory/political system/welfare state/cultural policies.

In contemporary capitalism, the permanent employee is caught between the hypermodern and neoarchaic actions of the business. According to a modulation that follows different hierarchical levels, the permanent employee must implicate themselves subjectively, invest their sensibility, become "human capital" that is autonomous and performs while always staying within the structures of hierarchical subordination. The injunction to be creative and perform at a high level is a paradox. First, this is because the autonomy that the salaried employee must acquire does not change the conditions of their heteronomy within the organization of labor. Furthermore, this is because creativity and performativity must be transformed, directly or indirectly, into an increase in productivity and efficiency (the transformation of a nonfinalized action into an instrumental action). And finally, because the injunction to be creative corresponds neither to new revenues nor new rights, but to a taking in hand of risks and responsibilities by salaried workers themselves, when such risks and responsibilities should fall on the lone entrepreneur.

The artist is also caught between hypermodernity and neoarchaism. On the one hand, their activity is no longer concerned with the production of "beautiful works," aesthetic objects, or virtuosic exercises, but with intervening in social situations as an agent of perturbation in order to open and allow the emergence of processes that interrogate the modalities of perception, affect, and action as well as the power relations on which these modalities rest. The artist experiments with, invents, and indicates what it means to be an anartist today. On the other hand, the institutions, territorial collectivities, and patrons neutralize the micropolitical roles and functions of the anartist by reconstructing the roles and functions of the institutional artist. The biennial at Rennes can, in this sense, be seen as a neoarchaic system where the roles and functions of the artist and the public are reconstituted to allow for it to be legible without limits or ambiguities. The creative "processes" deployed during the artist residencies in the business world efface themselves within the work (*oeuvre*); with their signature, the artist appropriates the labor of coproduction carried out with the workers, who come to form a part of the public for the exhibition. The plurivocity and multiplicity of components and active elements in the process are channeled into individual creativity. Thus the artist, who interrogates, problematizes, and refuses predetermined social categories (their own as well as those of the public) as well as experiments with other assemblages that no longer find themselves linked to the function of the author in molecular situations, finds themselves "codified" once more in the canons of aesthetics. In the "creative process," the artist and the salaried employee still act beneath and beyond the disciplinary division of autonomy (of the artist) and subordination (of the employee.) Even while at the molar level, the functions of subordination (of the employee) and autonomy (of art) are reconstructed, recodified, and even, we might say, magnified.

The point here is not to criticize the development of the biennial in Rennes. There is no autonomy or liberty for art that is given a priori; neither the artist nor the salaried employee is situated outside power relations. This outside, just like autonomy and freedom, are not already given. It is necessary to construct them from microruptures, from partial freedoms and the bifurcations and local discontinuities that we are able to locate. Nor is the point here to reclaim for artists those solutions that politics is not able to imagine. It is just the opposite, because the present moment seems to me to be best problematized through the arts and culture rather than in social or union milieus. This is why it seems relevant to me to interrogate the system of the biennial at Rennes.

The neutralization of the anartist's micropolitical activities is effectuated through an assemblage of systems of power transversal to society—an assemblage in which the institutions of art and culture are nothing but articulations. As Foucault says, summing up, governmentality and capitalist valorization are produced through the articulation of "plural powers" (businesses, the state, territorial collectivities, and artistic institutions) and the "social." If it is true that we are unable to imagine radical political changes that are brought about little by little by means of molecular behaviors, it is also true that the possibility of such radical change is unimaginable without these same behaviors. How is it that these partial freedoms, these coefficients of heterogeneity introduced into the "banal" and the "ordinary" of routine activity, these microdiscontinuities that we might call "anartists" that mark the emergence of subjectivity and possibility, might extend and resonate in other situations, affecting other subjectivities? Beginning from these emergent partial subjectivities, how do they contribute to the constitution of a macropolitical assemblage capable of bringing together collective action (in order to win new rights for all) and distributive action (such as the taking into account the "singularity" and creativity of all)?

Resistance and Creation

We find an initial problematization of these questions through an interrogation of the practices of resistance and creation found in the movement of the *intermittants*, the anartistic work of Duchamp, and the more conceptual practices of Guattari. Artists and technicians in struggle have pointed to three fundamental questions beyond those we have already considered: the new figure of the artist/intellectual, the relationship between time and money, and property rights in neoliberal societies. The *intermittants'* movement is one expression of a double expansion of art ("sociological" and "ontological"), which transforms the figure and functions of the artist and the intellectual. The transcendent intellectual, the organic intellectual of Gramsci, and even the specific intellectual of Foucault, along with the image of the artist found in the romantic tradition, is here substituted with what Guattari called "a collective intellectuality"; this collective intellectuality was called "mass intellectuality" in Italy as early as the 1970s.

Under the conditions of contemporary capitalism, "it is necessary to speak of the intellectual function and not of intellectuals with a capital 'I.' This function is called to inhabit social and productive practices of all sorts."[20] Similarly, it is necessary to speak of "creative functions" rather than of art and artists. We return to the intuitions of Duchamp, but on a much larger scale. The intellectual and creative functions are no longer assigned to a specific social group but are massified and distributed across the population according to differential coefficients. Nonetheless, these functions, constituted as "professions," are one of the components of the assemblage of contemporary capitalism. Guattari invites us to take into account both the singularity and the transversality of collective intellectuality within social assemblages. If the creative and intellectual functions are not the monopoly of either the artist or the intellectual, it is still necessary to "organize, work, and reinvent the capacity for self-affirmation and expression" of these activities that play a fundamental role in the new modalities of the semiotic governance of populations carried out by the cultural industry.[21] This is not about making "collective intellectuality" the hegemonic form of these activities, as in theories of cognitive capitalism, but to reflect on the conditions under which these "professions" might recover, expand, reinvent, and transpose the individual experience of anart and the anartist to the level of the collectivity. For Duchamp, the figure of the anartist does not replace the professional artist, who continues to reproduce themselves, but opens up a new manner of sensing, making, and expressing as well as a new finality for artistic techniques "detached from the author-function."[22]

At the beginning of the 1970s, de Certeau observed the degree to which something of anart and the anartist influenced the behaviors of "artists" and the public. The techniques of expression as well as part of the collective intellectuality and the public witnessed a transition from a "problematic concerned with representations, cultural products and the exceptional character of the expression being 'cultivated' towards a perspective centered on practices, on human relations and on the transformation of the structures of social life."[23] In the practices that developed during the 1960s and 1970s, the "operative" (making something) was opposed to representation, the "illocutionary" (making something with somebody) to cultural products, and the "trivial" ("changing the quotidian reality and way of life") to the exceptional. These three constituted "the axes of the cultural revolution that took shape starting at the bottom."[24] It is precisely the expansion of practices emerging during these years that pose a problem to neoliberal governmentality and must be "regulated" in the manner we have just described.

The principal regulation that traverses both the welfare state and the world of art and culture concerns time. Time is regulated in order to homogenize and make uniform subjectivity. The impoverishment of subjectivity is first and foremost an impoverishment of time as a source of change, metamorphosis, and the creation of the possible. As we have seen, the conflict over employment insurance for *intermittants* is a conflict over time. The affirmation of an *intermittent*—"employment insurance doesn't just give us a subsidy, it gives us time"—is the reversal of the capitalist formula "time is money" into "money is time." This resonates with Duchamp's motto: "My capital is time not money."

We require time as the initial primary material needed to create something, whether a theatrical piece, a film, a way of life, or a political action. Empty time, time suspended and ruptured, open time, and time for hesitations, which are the conditions of all artistic, social, and political production, are the kinds of time that neoliberal policies empty of their power of metamorphosis. The only temporality known and recognized by such policies are work time and the time spent searching for work, transforming so-called free time into a market for the cultural and tourism industries.

Cultural policies aim for the normalization of the time for artistic production (the professionalization of crafts and the professionalization of production), while social policies aim for the normalization of "unemployed" time by reducing it to the search for work or training to find work. This normalization occurs by means of a double acceleration: an acceleration of the rhythms of production, and an acceleration of time working, which results in the disappearance of "dead time." What the logic of capital calls "dead time" is, in reality, "living time": the time of the creation of something new. This conception of time is the fundamental contradiction inherent in so-called cognitive capitalism, the "knowledge society," or "cultural capitalism," since by considering "living time" as "dead time," it eliminates that which is the source of its value: creation. Cognitive capitalism is strictly speaking a system of "antiproduction," because, as Kafka explained in a synthetically poetic manner, "The most sublime part of creation, and most difficult to grasp even by trial and error, is time, which is imprisoned within the net of sordid market interests."

The hunt for all this "dead time," this time of suspensions, empty time, open time, leads to the realization that "we are never in the present" (in the words of another *intermittant*!). This is to say that we are never at the time when something can be produced or done, or anything happens. If the movement of *intermittants* was the source of new political divisions, and new forms of creation and resistance, this is because it discovered a way to bring the conflict to the interior of the "expression/property" relation.

Since the 1980s, corporate management and the government of the social have turned to techniques of expression in order to encourage the implication of subjectivity and an incitement to activity and "performance." The neoliberal motto "express yourself, be creative" has taken its place alongside the liberal motto "make yourself rich!" Expression is not only solicited but has become the condition of employability. But the incitement to creativity has no corresponding social right. On the contrary! Neoliberal governmentality reinvents new "copyrights" and new rights for intellectual property, and imposes a massive reduction in "social property" and collective rights. However, this strategy isn't new to the history of capitalism; Walter Benjamin, who discussed this process in the period between the two world wars, describes this as one of the origins of fascism.

In Benjamin's writing, we discover the problem of the sociological and ontological expansion of art and expression anticipated by Duchamp described in a different modality. For the German philosopher, cinema, the press, and sports give direction to the transformation of cultural consumption by the masses, by means of which the difference between author and public becomes simply *functional*. In effect, it is as a "connoisseur" or an "expert" that a person attends cultural exhibitions.[25] The competences and know-how of workers and publics is not based on an individual "specialization" or "professionalization" (such as is described by theories human capital). Rather, they constitute a "polytechnic formation" and "become by means of this formation a common good." Accordingly, the figures of the "specialist" or the "expert" are not individual qualities but refer to collective assemblages within which they constitute "intellectual and creative functions."

When criticizing the conclusions of his essay on "The Work of Art in the Age of Mechanical Reproduction," we often forget the direct and fundamental relationship that Benjamin establishes between transformations in regimes of expression and transformations in property regimes. According to Benjamin, it is the desire to organize mass expression without changing the property regime that characterizes fascism. "Fascism attempts to organize the newly created proletarian masses without affecting the property structure which the masses strive to eliminate." Liberal governance, in a different framework from that of the totalitarian state, seeks the same objective: to allow "the masses to express their 'nature,' but certainly not their rights."[26] The slogan of the *intermittants'* movement is "no culture without social rights," which means that neither action, creation, labor, nor expression are possible without the possibility of having a certain mastery over time (such as the ability to say "no" to the market, withdraw from work and the search for work for even a brief time, waste time, etc.) and breaking out of the "monetary constraint." The limits that capitalism put in place for those who are governed are, on the one hand, a reversal of the differentials of heterogeneity and inventiveness that it calls for within the system of modulated inequalities, and on the other hand, the reterritorialization of creativity within the neoarchaic forms of art, the artist, and the "value of work." But the insurmountable limit that capitalism imposes on the majority of humanity is that of private property.

The Artistic Act as a Process of Subjectification and the Artist as Medium

We can find in Duchamp other methods of problematizing the relationship between art and capitalism, and with this other practices of resistance and creation. In order to resist the impoverishment and uniformity of subjectivity, Duchamp asks us to think the act of creation as a process of subjectification and the artist as a medium. "A work in itself does not exist. It is the viewers who make the picture": this is the well-known aspect of Duchamp's position. The work is a coproduction, "a product of two poles; there is the pole of the one who makes the work and the pole of the one who looks at it. I give the ones who look at it as much importance as the one who makes it."[27] The public, as the actual or future viewer, introduces the work in the real and bestows its "social value."[28] The artist is not the only one to complete the act of creation, because the spectator establishes the contact with the external world by deciphering and interpreting the work, and thus adds their specific contribution to the creative process.

However, perhaps the most interesting thing in Duchamp resides in the description that he gives of the creative act as a process of subjectification, produced through time, and that is a metamorphosis of the artist as well as the viewer. The creative act is not exclusive to artistic creation; it indicates a creative path of possible subjectification for each domain of activity. Duchamp describes more than the production of the artistic object; he tries to "describe the subjective mechanism which produces a work of art." That the work of art could be "good, bad, or indifferent" is of little importance, since Duchampian art's principle of measure is not the beautiful but the "disposition to act" in order to transform subjectivity. In order to speak of the activity of the artist, he utilizes a metaphor not generally used, which profoundly redefines its function: "The artist acts like a mediumistic being"[29] (or a shaman, as Joseph Beuys would say, continuing this tradition), which returns to the point of emergence of subjectivity. The techniques of the artistic medium are techniques of spirit, or techniques of the emergence of the production of the self, which produce outbreaks of mutant subjectification, and work, from their emergence, for its construction. The activity of the artist as medium must then be deployed before subjectivity congeals in repetition, before the potential mutations of subjectivity crystallize into habit. In order to reach this point, to arrive at forces, intensities, and mutant and process temporalities, it must interrupt the functions assigned to both subjects and objects. The rupture of ordinary experience thus opens up to another dimension of experience, a "labyrinth beyond time and space"[30]—that is to say, a time that is generative, a proliferation of possibilities. This rupture of the ordinary spatiotemporal coordinates of sensible experience does not give us an "originary" subject, which would blossom forth, free of subjections and enslavements. It merely gives us the point of emergence, which opens onto the immanent process that constitutes its rules and procedures, its techniques, by which subjectivity can metamorphose itself.

The task of the construction of the work of the sensible that produces this metamorphosis goes beyond the artist and the viewer. According to Duchamp, the artist is never "fully conscious" of their activity; there is always a distance between what is intentionally planned and what is effectively realized, and it is never possible to control the effects that are produced on the viewer, because the viewer is actively involved in the process of deciphering and interpreting the activity of the artist and what it produces. Critical art that would intend to make the viewer aware simply makes no sense for Duchamp: "awareness," thought, and the sensible emerge from and are produced in the creative act itself. The transfer of subjectification between artist and viewer operates through an osmosis, a transubstantiation, a transmutation, of the utilized material (objects, but also ideas, signs, etc.), deployed in the universe, and weaves a world. The artist-medium connects itself and connects us to forces that exceed us; it does not produce an object but a series of relations, intensities, and affects, which constitute vectors of subjectification. More than the object or the work, what interests Duchamp is these "incorporeal" transformations operated by the creative work (the transubstantiation of utilized inert materials), which affects both the subjectivity of the artist and that of the public. The creative act is an aesthetic act in that it displaces and reconfigures the field of possible experience, and constitutes an apparatus of the fabrication of a new sensibility and a new thought.

Nondialectical Techniques of Rupture and Subjectification

The artistic techniques of Duchamp constitute procedures that make possible the permanent undoing of all established values (including aesthetic values) in order to finally undertake a "transvaluation of all values." The Duchampian method is radically antidialectical and invites us to insert a third term between binary oppositions (art/nonart, activity/passivity, play/work, etc.); this third term acts neither as a mediation nor as an agent of sublation but as an operator of a disjunction. Duchamp explains quite clearly that there is a false heterogeneity in these dialectical oppositions: in reality, if two things are opposed, it is to benefit their shared homogeneity.

Thus, in the dialectical opposition between the work of art and the industrial object, Duchamp introduces his well-known invention, the readymade, which interrogates the use value of the industrial object (its utility, its functionality) as much as that of the work of art (its nonutility that has a function, a nonfinality that has its place in society and capitalist valorization). The readymade puts into question the production of the worker as much as the virtuosity of the artist. The readymade does not involve any virtuosity, any specific know-how.[31] Through this claim of nonvirtuosity, it "desacralizes" and deprofessionalizes the function of the artist in society, "reducing his status in society."

Play and work constitute another dialectical couple in which we can insert a choice: the readymade is not made, it is chosen. For Duchamp, the choice is however not intentional or conscious; it express neither the interiority nor the good taste of the artist. He chooses to choose, instead of manufacturing with his own hands, and even says: "One does not choose a ready-made, but is chosen by it," so that this choice does not oppose determinism and free will.

Following Duchamp, we can thus place the possibility of "doing nothing" between activity and passivity. That possibility refuses to do what is expected of you, whether it is the passivity of the worker or the activity of the artist (or the immaterial laborer or cognitive worker). We are "acting to the minimum" rather than being stuck between the alternative of artistic creation and wage labor (the one and the other are, for Duchamp, functions to which we are assigned). "Doing nothing," "acting to the minimum," is to evade the distribution of competences of contemporary capitalism and open a nonteleogical space-time, a condition of any creation. The readymade is used to put in check the dialectical logic of exclusive disjunctions of the *either-or* variety, and put in place a logic of inclusive disjunctions of the *and*: "I lived in a tiny apartment in Paris. In order to use this small space to the maximum, I imagined using a single leaf door that would shut alternately in two frames placed at right angles. I would demonstrate this to my friends, and tell them that the proverb 'A door must be opened or closed' is found to be completely inexact." The door at Rue Larrey, opened and closed at the same time, is an example of the "cointelligence of contraries," of which the idea of the disjunctive synthesis is the best equivalent in the field of philosophy.

Duchamp deploys a thought and a practice of the infinitesimal, the smallest differences, the micro, and the "hypophysics," which he calls the "infra-thin," and which interrogates and examines the role and function of art in the age of mechanical reproduction. Seizing the different in the same, finding the infra-thin interval in the identical, resingularizing serial production, implies in every case a methodology of difference and repetition that wards off the illusions, the generalities and divisions that operate by language. Duchamp's play on words, which accompanies all his works and apparatuses, expresses the break with the imperialism of signifying semiotics, which limits the ability to seize the prediscursive and impersonal forces, and the power of time. "It would be better to try to pass the infra-thin interval which separates two 'identicals' than to easily accept the verbal generalization which makes two binoculars resemble two drops of water," we say. Identity and language represents a neutralization of time, because "in time, the same object is not the same in the second interval." It is solely at the molar level, at the level of the verbal generalization, that there is identity. At the level of the molecular level, time makes a difference: the infra-thin is not a special dimension but a temporal dimension. Time is the infra-thin that differentiates, alters, and widens the gap, even if two objects are absolutely identical.

By disjuncting the dialectical oppositions, Duchamp opens up an undecidable process to ambiguous possibles. For Duchamp, the shock, the short circuit produced by the readymade, has not only the critical function of revealing the world of commodities, and it does not represent simply the opportunity of realization. If it opens on undecidable propositions, it is the sense that the destiny of the latter depends solely on immanent becoming, since there is no model, be it positive (art) or negative (domination and exploitation in work), which they refer to in order to combat or realize. Becoming, the movement of undetermined or undecidable propositions, is identified with a production of subjectivity, the production of an ethos, and a modus vivendi.

Subjectivity and Belief

The practice and thought of the anartist make possible a problematization from a new point of view: belief/confidence, which we have described as a process of subjectification. Duchamp is interested in "gray matter" rather than in "retinal" sensation, but this does not refer to the intellect ("too dry, too devoid of expression") but to belief—in other words, to the spiritual or mental dimension of subjectivity. "I like the word 'to believe.' Generally, when one says, 'I know,' one does not know, one believes. To live is to believe; at least that is what I believe."[32] Duchamp puts to work in art the same transformation that modern philosophy underwent by substituting the system of knowledge with the system of belief.

According to Duchamp, the intellect is not a good tool to capture the effects of artistic practice, the latter being "traversed with emotions which resemble more religious belief or sexual attraction." Duchamp introduces a distinction between affect (the "aesthetic echo" or aesthetic emotion) as a generative force that is constitutive of subjectivity, and the affections (tastes), which are content to repeat the habits of "aesthetics," which carry established authority.[33] The dissociation of the aesthetic echo from taste permits us to think the belief-affect as a force of existential self-positioning, which emerges, affirms, and acts in any process of the production of subjectivity, and not solely in the artistic act. The nature of the aesthetic emotion (existential affect, intensive, and not accompanied by representation or images) is expressed as much in the confidence of the "idiot" who falls in love as in the innocence and the faith of the "idiot" who believes in God (as in the Dadaist "idiot"). In suspending tastes and constituted sensations, the readymade returns us to "the point of the emergence of subjectivity" to the point of departure of a new process of subjectification, as seen in the convert, the lover, the militant, and so on—and that is, according to Guattari, the proper task of the artist.

Straddling the nineteenth and twentieth centuries and both sides of the Atlantic, a profound theoretical elaboration developed (we cite here only the names of James and Tarde), which aimed to define the nature of belief and its conversion to immanence. Religion and politics are two great "mines" or "funds" that mobilize, nourish, and stock this "motor force," this "disposition to action,"[34] this power of affirmation and subjective investment that one calls "belief." According to James, in the religious phenomenon, our experience is not limited to the "visible" and "tangible" world; it also integrates an "invisible world," animated by forces (soul or spirit), which exceed perception and knowledge, and make the visible world "incomplete," a world not entirely determined. The indetermination and incompleteness of the visible call on belief, whose principle and measure is action. The essence of faith consists in affirming and believing in the invisible world, and risking our power to act on this possibility. Religion addresses these most intimate forces, the nature of which is at the one time "emotional and active" (James) and unreasonable.[35] These forces are less psychological or personal than forces that we can define, thanks to contemporary concepts, as preindividual, subconscious, and intensive. Moreover, these forces do not belong to us; they traverse us and constitute what Duchamp has called "the mysterious and agreeable constraint," and the ecstasy to which we are abandoned in belief and love. They produce at the same time an enlargement of our states of consciousness and therefore an augmentation of our power to act.

The Duchampian "emotion" (the aesthetic echo) corresponds to the encounter with these forces that place us outside ourselves, outside the "me," and thus outside the codified and instituted "taste' and sense, outside aesthetic habits and prejudices, but also outside the social and political prejudices that make up our customary modes of life. These forces render us both "humble," since *belief exceeds knowledge*,[36] and "perceptive," since they overflow the contours of the self and its modalities of perception limited by the imperatives of routine action.

Belief ("disposition to action") is at the same time a productive and expansive force, a "generative power" that believes in the future and its "ambiguous possibilities," and an ethical force, since these possibilities harbor our relation to the world and others. It engages the subject in a risky action whose success is not assured in advance. It is thus the condition of all transformation and all creation. Belief establishes a connection with the world and with others that neither *knowledge* nor the *senses* are capable of instituting, since they always give us a closed world, without exteriority. In the moral world, this force refers to courage and generosity—virtues that risk themselves in the unknown, gamble on the future, and correspond to taking charge of one's own destiny.

The secularization of religious belief in the invisible world and its forces can be described in the manner of Tarde: "The real is only intelligible as a case of the possible," "the actual is only an infinitesimal part of the real." The real is not entirely actualized, in a way that our action "is exercised on possibilities and not on 'brutal and actual' facts." Knowledge of the invisible world escapes us, "since the elements of the world harbor unknown and profoundly unknowable virtualities, even to an infinite intelligence." This invisible world no longer constitutes a beyond, but the "outside" immanent to the world. It is a world, as that of the art of Duchamp, that is not "ruled by space or time"[37] but by the logic of the event, which is at one and the same time immanent and heterogeneous to chronological time, which breaks its linear progression, and by so doing, opens a new chronology and nourishes the world of possibilities, while calling on our power to act. From this leap into indetermination, experience transforms itself into experimentation, risk taking and wagering, and the will to test oneself, others, and the world.

But if the principle of belief is action, if belief is the measure of the power to act that it releases, what kind of action is it? And what sort of subjectivity does this power to act engage? To believe in that tradition of thought that from James to Tarde, is extended through Deleuze and Guattari, the forces and the action in question would be neither psychological, social, nor organic; the energy that animates them is "nonenergetic and noninformational." According to Guattari, these forces belong to a world that while entirely immanent to the real, is situated "outside spatiotemporal coordinates"; it consists, then, of an energy that "does not engage a quantity of movement," and operates by "infinite speed" and not according to a finite speed, not even the speed of light. This nonorganic action is different from organic or sensory motor action, which works on facts, operating on "a particular matter: an optional matter." Its objects, according to Guattari, are "rhizomes of choice." Acting then means choosing, as when Duchamp "produces" his readymades.[38] Deleuze and Guattari distinguish between action and act, where action (sensory motor) is exercised on the "brute facts" or what is entirely given, while the act is always exercised on possibles. With the act we make a kind of a jump in place:

"We pass from physical space to spiritual space, which gives us a physics."[39] Belief is an affective force that founds, supports, and qualifies the act. It is comparable to the "existential function" of Guattari because, on the one hand, it acts as an intensive, intentional force,[40] which affirms, marks, and indicates the emergence of an existential territory, and therefore a force of existential autopositioning, taking a position in relationship to the world and others. And on the other hand, it is a force that gives, that "recharges" worlds in possibilities and constitutes an "opening to the future," as James puts it. It is in this sense that belief/confidence establishes an "ethical" link with the world and others. The force and the inescapable role of confidence can be measured by the social and political devastation that can be produced by its contrary: distrust and fear with respect to self, others, and the world. Neoliberal government is precisely a government that destroys all confidence and industrially produces its opposite: distrust and fear.

In this new "mental or spiritual" dimension introduced by belief, subjectivity, as Deleuze observes, takes on a new sense that is no longer "motor or material, but temporal or spiritual."[41] The relationship between sensory motor action and nonorganic action, between material subjectivity and spiritual subjectivity, is given by the dynamic of the event. Temporal or spiritual subjectivity and the anorganic forces intervene in the social, the psychological, and the organic through "incorporeal" affects. When Duchamp speaks—in a polemic with "retinal painting"—of the gray matter, he is referring to this temporal or mental universe, and what he wants to achieve, through a new form of production of works that are not art, are forces that found and render perception possible, forces that found and make enunciation possible, and that constitute their implicit and nonexplicable presuppositions.[42] It is therefore easier to understand the reasons that compel Duchamp to speak of the "mediumistic role" of the artist, which operates a transfer of subjectification[43] toward the public by acting on these impersonal forces. Beuys himself follows suit in playing the "shaman," the pagan and animistic way of acting with nonorganic forces.

Deleuze has developed the differences between organic and anorganic in his two books on the cinema, and speaks of the "actor-mediums" and spectators as "visionaries."[44] With postwar cinema, we reach this "spiritual or temporal" dimension without passing through religious techniques and beliefs. His analysis is developed as follows: our customary perception always captures less than there is to see in the image, an object, a relation, or a situation. We perceive only what interests us—that is to say, we only see that which is a function of our economic interests, ideological beliefs, and psychological exigencies. We perceive the world through clichés, habits, and tastes that permit us to act in a world that is entirely given and customary. In these conditions, vision is only a simple identification and thought a simple recognition. When the force (belief) of habit through which we recognize things, roles, and functions is dissipated, when the spatiotemporal coordinates of the actual (visible) world are suspended, the aberrant movements of the cinematographic images cause to surge forth what Deleuze calls the time image—the image at once actual and virtual. We see at one and the same time "the actual state of things and the possibility, the virtuality that exceeds it." With this idea, Deleuze begins a diagnostic of our present: we see the "invisible" and its forces, but because we lack belief in the "ambiguous possibilities" that this world envelops, the capacity to see beyond the actual does not correspond to an increase in our power to act.

Why then must we, along with Duchamp, insert belief between the intelligible and the sensible, between knowledge and the affects? Because neither knowledge nor the senses permits us to form an existential link with the world and other people. Neither knowledge nor sensations gives us the force to act from the void—that from which the operation of the readymade is proclaimed. The readymade does not simply testify to the simple passage of the prosaic world of merchandise to the world of art, nor the blurring of the frontier between art and nonart, and it does not constitute a simple mixture (or shock) of heterogeneous elements, as contemporary aesthetics claims. On the contrary, the readymade introduces us to a "completely void domain, if you would, void of everything to the point that I could speak of a complete anesthesia," which is the condition of the emergence of the process of subjectification. The void created by the choice of the readymade makes direct reference to the radicality of Guattarian ruptures of a signification, for which, when there is a change of referent, or a new signification emerges, new processes of subjectification are put into process/effect, and there is "almost by definition, this kind of passage in/to the void, an a-signifying point, a blind spot." And it is from this point of the void, from this point of non-sense, "that we no longer see the same thing, no longer hear the same thing."[45] The void of Guattari, as the anesthesia of Duchamp, is a void full of "passional and active," transindividual and pre-discursive forces, of forces that push one to risk and test oneself in an undetermined world, a "new work/oeuvre," and new possibles/possibilities. The readymade must first make a rupture (polemic) with what exists, in neutralizing the use and meaning of the object, in suspending the beliefs/habits (taste) and the beliefs/prejudices (meaning) that make us act and think in a predetermined world, where everything is always already given. In these cases, the figure, the belief that is adhered and fixed to an object, an idea, a relation, and a function, Duchamp calls, rightly, authority.

After all, the problem of apparatuses (*dispositifs*) of power is to make it possible to capture and control this "disposition to action" and fix it in/as authority. Neoliberalism "fabricates" belief[46] as it produces "freedom." Subjection is in fact not just a question of disciplinary apparatuses and incentives and solicitations that are financial, legislative, or related to security. Subjection implies, first and foremost, belief, which the contemporary economy, with its injunction to autonomy, responsibility, and risk taking, is more than avid for.[47] Subjection to the logic of the entrepreneurship of the self requires the institution or the displacement of the force to believe. But capitalism today requires "belief without believers": hence the cynicism that it creates, which makes it necessary for politicians to have recourse to all sorts of neoarchaisms, notably religious neoarchaisms (the expected reservoir of belief and believers), in order to fix/set belief. Once the break with belief/habits or belief/authority has been made, the readymade must free and organize the conditions of action in an undetermined and unknown world, where the possibilities are not "already there," crystallized in established tastes that establish authority, in habits and meaning that guide our actions, in a world where the possibilities are sometimes (the points of) unknown bifurcations. At the edge of the void and anesthesia, belief is called *confidence*, since it acts without any adherence to an idea or a meaning, which would conform it to a habit, but since it creates a new idea and a new meaning, which implies the availability, the generosity, and the will to put the world and others to the test, to experiment as much on the side of the artist as on that of the public.

The majority of our conducts, as Duchamp has correctly indicated, do not relate to making, to fabrication, but to "acting." Our behaviors and our modes of life can be described as an accumulation of choices whose alternatives are predetermined, and the risks to which these choices expose us have nothing of the "tragic," since the alternatives consist in the choice between different yogurts, different politicians, different television channels, different clothes, different vacation destinations, and so on. Economic or political marketing has only one end: the production of "alternatives" where one exercises the "freedom of action" of the democratic man. Art, as practiced by Duchamp and described by Guattari, "resides in the capacity to promote actions and processes that become ruptures, at the heart of the signifying tissues and the semiotically structured denotations, that open onto processes of subjectification."

Art does not pass completely into life, nor does it hold itself in a superb autonomy, as claimed by the avant-garde: between life and art, there always exists a gap that one cannot fill. But it is from this interval between art and life, by settling within this interval, that a production of subjectivity becomes possible.

I wanted to use the process of painting, to use art to establish a modus vivendi, a sort of a way to understand life—that is to say, probably to try to make my life itself a work of art—instead of spending my life making works of art in the shape of paintings. ... The important thing, it is to live and have a way of conducting oneself. This way of conducting myself orders the paintings that I made, the play of words that I made, and all that I have made, at least in the public point of view.Using art to establish a modus vivendi, making one's life a work of art, as

Foucault would like, implies the capacity to seize time and its intensity. This means living in the present instant, where "all future and past fractions of time ... reproduce themselves and coexist" as a "kind of present with multiple extensions."[48] Robert Lebel, in his biography of Duchamp, speaks of "a hold over time where Marcel would like to reunite the during, the after, and the before." The art of time is the art of "the present with multiple extensions."[49] Reducing these techniques of subjectification to the individualism of Max Stirner, of whom Duchamp was an avid reader, would also be as reductive as reducing the theoretical and practical ethos of Foucault to dandyism. It is more interesting to see this modus vivendi as a political problem: the impossibility of separating the political revolution from the revolution of the sensible, the macropolitical revolution from the micropolitical revolution, the political question from the ethical question.

The Aesthetic Paradigm

My concern, after all, has been to detach subjectivity from human individuation and therefore to work on a line of partial subjectification. Subjectivity is always partial, polyphonic, collective, and machinic. ... [S]ubjectivity is at the crossroads of heterogeneous compositions. ... [T]he individual is the endpoint of partial and heterogeneous compositions.

—Félix Guattari, interview with Uno Kuniichi[50]

Guattari's aesthetic paradigm extends the Duchampian gesture of enlarging art. It is a remarkable innovation in relation to the Foucauldian concept of subjectification, since it is no longer religious practices and techniques, or those of the schools of philosophy, that are examined as technologies of the self, but artistic techniques and practices. Guattari believes that these are better able to respond to the two main challenges that define our epoch: "Subjectivity has become the number one target of capitalist societies," and this "subjective mutation" is not primarily discursive. It affects the nondiscursive, affective, existential focus of subjectivity: capitalism thus attaches itself to modes of existence and forms of life.

It is important to mention that the "aesthetic paradigm" does not express a will to aestheticize the social; it does not proceed from art insofar as it is an institution but rather seizes the techniques of art, its processes of creation, and its practices in order to make them evolve in other domains, putting them to work outside, at the limit of, or transversally to the space designated by art as an institution. It is necessary to speak of "artistic" techniques and practices, since art, like "culture," is integrated into the apparatuses of valorization and the government of publics[51] and populations. The powers of art can set themselves up with those of other apparatuses (economic, social, and political) for the worst: constructing the market, favoring the becoming-tourist—consumer and communicator of subjectivity—and contributing thus to its uniformization; or for the better: permitting the bifurcation and singularization of subjectivity.

In order to dispel any misunderstanding, it is perhaps better to speak "of the proto-aesthetic paradigm, to emphasize that we are not referring to institutionalized art, to its works manifested in the social field, but to a dimension of creation in a nascent state, perpetually in advance of itself, its power of emergence." Moreover, the promotion of this new paradigm, in harmony with anart, "involves overthrowing current forms of art as much as social life." The basis of this new paradigm is, as with Duchamp, "an effort to seize the creative potential 'before' it is applied to works, philosophical concepts, scientific functions, [and] mental and social objects."[52] The ethical aesthetic paradigm aims at seizing in art a "creative potential" transversal to all domains[53] and thus also concerned with "political" experience. It does not consist in any specialized knowledge or some kind of virtuosity.

It is in order to activate and put to work this creative potentiality that Guattari calls for artistic practices insofar as they are techniques of "rupture" and "suture," de-subjectification and subjectification, abandoning roles and functions that we are assigned, and seizing new realities and subjectivities. In what senses is the turn toward these techniques useful for the process of subjectification in general? In the tradition of the workers movement, the rupture was overdetermined by a dualism (worker/capital) that delimited its possibilities. It acted as a totalizing and predetermined break, the outlines of which were, in a certain way, already traced. History had always been that of class struggle and it would have been abolished by that same class struggle. The question of "suture" (organization or composition/ constitution) followed from this rupture. It was also already traced, since class struggle not only defined the conditions of rupture but also the conditions of its composition, evolution, and development, and the passage from class-in-itself to class-for-itself, to sum up using the terms of the original formulation. Besides dualistic divisions, contemporary capitalism produces fractal and differential ruptures and sutures that open onto partial liberties and subjectifications that are not predetermined by any "structures." Artistic practices can help us in understanding the unpredictable developments of these ruptures and working on always-partial compositions.

The aesthetic paradigm refers to the artist, but affirms that creativity is always the result of a collective assemblage.[54] Subjectivity and the processes of self-transformation always result from a collective assemblage of enunciation and action that destroy the unity of the individual subject and the political subject, and return it to a complex "multiple individual-group-exchange machine." Subjectivity is not confined to the subject and language. It is disseminated, in an almost animistic manner, in a multiplicity of objects, relations, and materials, and it produces itself in the intersection of prelinguistic,[55] preindividual, and transindividual multiplicities (social, political, cultural, and machinic). This "nonhuman" part of subjectivity, beside and beyond the individual, is essential, since it is from it that one can put to work its transformation, its "heterogenesis." Artists interest Guattari because with their materials and techniques, they explore and experiment with processes of subjectification beyond the subject, the language, and the conscience within which modernity has enclosed them.

The assertion that subjectivity is first of all a collective assemblage, even when it is expressed through an individual, is essential to the dismantling of the neoliberal ideology of the "creative class" or the theory of the "cognitive worker," which maintains belief in the creativity of individuals or social groups defined by certain socioanthropological characteristics. However, if the artist is only an "end point" of compositions of subjectivity that for the most part, as in the creative act of Duchamp, escape their conscience, they have the capacity to single out these compositions and make of them vectors of subjectification. The artist is thus an agent or an operator of the reconversion of subjectivity, since they provoke its emergence, and invent the techniques that put to work its becoming and constitution. Artistic practices produce, starting out from the molecular dimension, a gap, a displacement, or a de-centering of the ordinary spatiotemporal coordinates, which suspends social divisions and functions, and disrupts the preexisting organization and classifications. As in the texts of Duchamp, often cited in the final works of Guattari, they "disconnect" our perception and customary way of feeling in order to "reconnect" them to other universes, other possibilities.

At the molecular level, as we have seen, art extracts the "affects" and "percepts" from empty signs and the pollution of signification, cognition, and culture within which we bathe, and gives them the role of "partial enunciations" and new "existential coordinates." In artistic work, certain semiotic segments (images, materials, relations, words, objects, etc.) are selected from the "mesh of the everyday," detaching themselves from dominant significations and thus start working on their own, synthesizing new fields of reference and new universes of values. Images, sounds, objects, and in fact everything and anything (Duchamp) can then become, in the same manner as words, vectors of subjectification; even if they do not speak, even if they do not express signification, they state something. They are the place of proto-enunciation in the sense that they constitute the nondiscursive kernel that is at the heart of all discursivity. Guattari refers to artistic practices as the nonverbal techniques of semiotization. While in the beginning of the twentieth century, social sciences and analytic philosophy concentrated on language and signifying semiotics, art effectively put to work a remarkable valorization of nonverbal modes of subjectification (and enunciation).

Guattari does not refer to art as a technique of the production of objects—that is to say, as "images passively represented"—but as a technique that puts to work three types of problems that concern the entire being of political action: the polyphony of enunciation, or in other words, the taking into account of the heterogeneity of voices and semiotics that constitute it; processual creativity, or in other words, the permanent placing into question of the identity of object and subject; and autopoeisis, or autoproduction, or that is to say, the capacity of apparatuses of subjectification to produce their proper norms and coordinates. The "work" does not have the function of carrying or transmitting a message but that of constructing and demonstrating the process of autoproduction that constitutes it. According to this perspective, artistic practices should not be about the retelling of histories but should create the apparatuses from/through which history can be made. What interests Guattari in the practice of the artist is not a search for "mythical freedom" but the construction of liberties and partial heterogeneities, going beyond the opposition between freedom and domination. The relationship between these differentials of freedom and the macropolitical dimension remains nonetheless problematic, since if these artistic practices produce molecular possibilities, the key to this problem rests with the collective capacity to enter into other ethical, aesthetic, and political paradigms.

We are thus able to say that there is a contiguity between the act of political resistance and the artistic act, when the later transforms itself into anart; that there is a transversality between the molecular action of the rupture and composition of art and the practices of rupture and composition of political action. Politics does not represent the model of subjectification, since what is constructed in the political act is not universal subjectivity. What is actually constructed is a partial mode of subjectification that must be pursued, arranged, and connected to other modes of subjectification that are also partial.

The Expansion of the Utterance

In order to grasp the construction of "collective" assemblages of enunciation, and understand its nature and dynamics, it is necessary to expand the concept of enunciation, which cannot be limited to its linguistic elements (as is the claim of linguistics) or be enclosed in the logic of representation (which is as much individual as political, conventional politics claims). This expansion of enunciation has largely been anticipated by the art of the twentieth century that considered, much before linguistics and the social sciences, that "the problem of the enunciative assemblage would no longer be specific to a semiotic register but would traverse an ensemble of heterogeneous expressive materials."[56]

Expression is not the property of linguistic domains; it also appears in extralinguistic, nonhuman, biological, technological, and aesthetic domains. The aesthetic paradigm leads us to consider enunciation as the assemblage of multiple semiotics (verbal, symbolic, machinic, etc.) and multiple compositions of subjectification (economic, ethical, social, etc.). Recognizing the autonomy and the independence of semiotic and expressive compositions is a political question, since capitalism effectuates continually their subordination and re-centering on the signifying semiotics—that is to say, on the subject, conscience, and representation. This operation of homogenization, reduction, and standardization of subjectivity and its modalities of expression becomes radicalized in what has been called "cognitive capitalism."[57]

In any collective,[58] and notably in every political collective, "multiheaded" enunciation is present, but it is never problematized as such; it is most often repressed and negated. The possibility of enunciating and putting to work the multiplicity of semiotics and the modalities of expression has been neutralized for a long time, notably in the political domain, by the takeover of other modes of semiotization by the power of speech, representation, and signification. Even the process of revolutionary subjectification was centered on the "subject" (class), "conscience" (reflexive), and "representation" (the party).

The affirmation, by Guattari, of a kind of "semiotic pluralism," the claim for a "democratization" of the components of enunciation and matters of expression, has great political purchase, since the hold of signifying semiotics over the nondiscursive semiotics corresponds to the hold of the techniques of political representation over other modes of expression and organization. The work of Guattari finds its origin and legitimacy in the critique that the movements of the 1960s and 1970s have made of the techniques of expression and procedures of representation put to work by revolutionary politics as much as by institutional politics. This critique was thus contemporaneous with the affirmation, by these same movements, of "the multiple centers" of semiotic production and the utilization of "polyvocal matters of expression" that liberate a heterogeneous process of subjectification and organization, undermining the subordination of individuals to capitalist models of subjectivity as well as socialist ones. These modalities and matters of expression are at the same time those of "minorities" (women, children, the insane, and the sick as well as sexual, linguistic, and social minorities) and "artists."

Speech that declares or claims is neither a criterion nor a measure for the definition of the political, as it is for Rancière. If
subjectivity escapes this specific modality of political action (as
in the case of the 2005 "aphasic" revolts of the *banlieues*), "it
fabricates what I call an endo-reference and it leads to a production of subjectivity before that subjectivity is aware of itself. That
is what we lived through in 1968: a subjectivity in the making
before anyone had time to realize anything."[59]

The Existential Function

The ethico-aesthetic paradigm of Guattari does not preach the
devalorization of speech, nor does it underestimate its representational and "cognitive" functions; instead, it invites us to
displace our point of view and situate it in the widening space
between the pathetic (affective, intensities, and prelinguistic)
and the discursive. It does not limit itself to "democratizing"
the process of subjectification to introduce the "molecular
populations" and the machinic or affective protosubjectivities;
it cannot be reduced to the affirmation of semiotic pluralism
and a pluralism of matters of expressions. This ethico-aesthetic
paradigm grounds itself on the apprehension of a force that first
expresses a change in the manner of sensing, in existence, before
expressing itself through knowledge and language. This affective
force of "existential self-positing," this force of construction and
formation of existential territories, is translated by Guattari into
a new enunciative function, the "existential function," which is
instituted prior to and besides "denotation and signification."
This expansion of the concept of enunciation is the condition
sine qua non for a new praxis, since it refers to the "confidence,"
to the mobilization of the disposition to act.

The aesthetic paradigm proposes in effect to construct the apparatuses that one can make use of and through which one can experiment with linguistic, political, economic, and artistic techniques, not solely to denote or signify something, but also, and especially, for "putting into play a universe of expression" and "to trigger an existential function, to engender a certain mode of life."[60] In other words, the aesthetic paradigm considers the broadened the concept of enunciation not, initially, in terms of discursive production or artistic production but in terms of the "mutant places of the production of subjectivity." At the basis of enunciation, there is not a linguistic competence, in the same way that at the foundation of art, there is not an aesthetic competence but an existential apprehension of the world. It is from this existential apprehension, this affective apprehension, that there can be discourse, knowledge, narrative, work, and so on.

According to Guattari, we live in a paradox that becomes one of the fundamental political stakes of security societies: "We find ourselves thrown into discursive systems and, at the same moment, we have to deal with centers of existential affirmation, which are not discursive. ... [W]hen an amorous machine or a machine of fear is set in motion, this is not due to the effect of discursive, cognitive, or deductive phrases. It is given immediately. And this machine will progressively develop different means of expression."[61] Speech has therefore a double function: to signify, communicate, and declare "politically," but also and above all, to produce the assemblages of enunciation able to capture, territorialize, and deploy the singularities of a situation, at the same time political and existential, and give consistency and persistence to modes of existence.[62]

The existential function is an affective and intensive force, which anchors in a determinate situation that which happens to us and singularizes "the order of things," the "expressions and the contents," making of the event an ethical material and opportunity, "a subjectivity option," which gives us back the world and the "production of self" as open processes that we are engaged in. The event of the *intermittents' movement* is a phenomenon of this order. It is at one and the same time the taking of a political position and an existential position. That which is expressed in the order word of the *intermittents* "We are no longer playing around" (*on ne joue plus*) (or in the aphasia of the "revolt" of the *banlieues*, which does not say anything and does not declare anything, but surely enounces something) is a "complex affect," a "problematic" in the sense that it is not a simple "drive." It envelopes much more than refusal, much more than the critique of the system of unemployment insurance. It contains more than the simple critique of reform.

The existential affirmation, the existential autopositioning, is not an affect that one can conceive as a "matter of brute energy": it is "hypercomplex," Guattari tells us, since it is rich with "all the fields of potentiality that it is capable of opening." Just as the affect of love is not limited to "waiting for a 'libidinal discharge'" but is "a charge of unknown worlds, at the crossroads of which it places us," the affect of revolt, indignation, the will not to be governed, does not resolve itself in the expression of these passions but envelopes possible worlds and subjective bifurcations that must be deployed. It is in this sense that one can define these acts as potentialities, as possibles, that must be put to work by the techniques that can be borrowed from artistic practices.

The production of subjectivity is the actual process of actualization, singularization, and differentiation of this complex "affect," both political and existential, the deployment of which depends on a multiplicity of favorable conditions that must be constructed and a multiplicity of unfavorable conditions that must be destroyed, bypassed, or neutralized. The emergence of the refusal to be governed and an existential insubordination is precisely the nondiscursive element that must be interrogated and worked, since it is the point of rupture, the "unnamable" that contains more than it enunciates, and that will create speech and action and give consistency to the production of subjectivity. The process of subjectification cannot consolidate itself unless it succeeds in transversalizing and reconfiguring the political, the economic, and the social. And it is this dynamic of transversalization that was blocked by the different apparatuses of power throughout the struggles of the *intermittents*.

It is here that, according to Guattari, the techniques of "artistic" composition or suture can be called on and utilized, not in place of political, social, and so on, techniques but with them. This "work" must be understood as a process, a construction, and a transformation of subjectivity. When one speaks of the production of subjectivity, it is this process of creation and the work that appears to be the paradigm. It is on what is taking place and how that our attention should be focused, and not solely on the product or the result. Considering the process and the means involves valorizing the collective agent as autopoetic, as capacity for autoproduction of subjectivity, as capacity continually to engender its own organization, its own reference points and limits.

The "existential function" is a point of bifurcation, which engenders processes of singularization, generative temporalities, and processual temporalities, which are irreversible. Approaching the production of subjectivity by way of its processual nature therefore means reconquering the present as a nonchronological time, which engenders, creates, and mobilizes the capacity for action. Time ceases to be endured; it is directed, the object of qualitative mutations. It is an "ethical" temporality allowing subjectification to position and grasp itself as "a pragmatic crossroads," and therefore, as a choice that implies confidence in self, others, and the world.

For Deleuze, "the modern fact is that we no longer believe in this world,"[63] that we have lost confidence in self, others, and the world. In the gap opened up by the collapse of confidence is installed the distrust and fear of the self, others, and the world—affects that fuel throughout the West, including Europe, the neoliberal techniques of government: competition, racism, and isolationism. The ethical and existential relationship of humans and the world, and humans with other humans, is broken. "Henceforth, this link must become an object of belief; it is the impossible that can only be restored within a faith. Belief is no longer addressed to a different or transformed world. ... We need reasons to believe in this world,"[64] as it is, and in the possibilities of action and life that it contains. Thus, our skepticism is no longer cognitive, but ethical. The political impasse is primarily an ethical impasse—an impasse that concerns our position, commitment, and ability to test the world, others, and ourselves.

Deleuze underscores, along with Guattari, the profoundly ethical nature of our collective assemblages of subjectification and creation. Since 1968, we have lived through a long sequence of the exhaustion of revolutionary political models, constructed and based on paradigms that we could define as "scientific."

Despite the important direction that the aesthetic paradigm gives us, the assemblages of being-against and being-together, the assemblage of rupture and sutures, the assemblage of techniques of not-being governed and governing oneself, have not yet found the war machine that could express them, or enunciations that could carry them. Under these conditions they can only be, as was possible in the case of this struggle, objects of experimentation.

Appendix A: Kafka and the Production of Culpability

Social insurance was born from the workers' movement. It should therefore be invested with the luminous spirit of progress. And yet, what do we see? This institution is nothing but a dark nest of bureaucrats, amongst whom I operate in my capacity as the sole and representative Jew.

—Franz Kafka

The production of culpability, the strategic affect of neoliberalism, of which Nietzsche speaks, can just as well be analyzed through the literature of Kafka. Kafka anticipates our epoch to a great extent, since his characters speak of a reality, an organization of *work*, and administration (the welfare state) that seems closer to ours than to that of the interwar period. Bürgel, the secretary of *The Castle*, expresses something that has become familiar to us: "We don't acknowledge any distinction between ordinary time and work time. Such distinctions are alien to us."[1] And K., the surveyor of the castle, lives the experience of a relation to power that we can characterize, with Foucault, as biopolitical, in the sense that it engages life as a whole. "Nowhere else had K. ever seen one's official position and one's life so intertwined as they were here, so intertwined that it sometimes seemed as though office and life had switched places."[2]

The institutions of *administration* such as RMI, unemployment insurance, and so on, express something before articulating any discourse on it whatsoever. They posit that there is a problem (unemployment, employability, and so forth, and that it will no longer be society that will be invoked to insure *the monitoring of the individual*, but ... you, "Joseph K.!" There is an elision from "there is a social problem" to "it's your problem!" This elision is embodied in the very institution, in its practices and procedures, before finding its way into the heads of social workers and benefit recipients. As in *The Trial*, the *accusation* is never clearly formulated (they try hard to insinuate that "unemployment is *your* fault!" but this is difficult, because the "fault" of unemployment has vague, indefinite, and imprecise contours. The only possible definition is political, and that causes its own problems!).

But very soon, one forgets the vagueness of the accusation. It installs, little by little, a sense of doubt and the feeling of being to blame for something, being *at fault*, since one has indeed received a document, since one has indeed been summoned by the administration, and must indeed present oneself at such an address, on such a day, at such an hour, in such an office. The *arrest* of Joseph K. changes nothing in his life; he carries on working and living as before. He is therefore at the same time arrested and free. Guilty or innocent, they have a file on *you*, "Joseph K." Somewhere there exists a file, and officials who attend to it, but *you will only ever see* the minor functionaries of the institution, and never the great magistrates. Besides, is there really a vertical organization of offices, with bosses and underlings, or does everything occur *horizontally*, between *subalterns*? It is rather both at the same time, but in any case, accurate information is always to be found in the next office along; it is always necessary to knock on the next door, to infinity.

The number 3949^3 is a telephonic platform that replaces face-to-face relationships with the agents of the institution. It's the contemporary version of the bureau. One has to call repeatedly, speaking to multiple agents, trying to verify that they are all indeed enforcing the same law, given that each of them seems to interpret it differently. Often, they simply don't know, and in any case they hang up after six minutes.[4] So one must knock on the next door, and the next. In this way, 3949 is a deterritorialization of the bureau and the agent.

Appendix B: Kafka, Art, Work, the Artist, and the Public

Kafka, in his very last story, from 1924, engages in a dialogue at a distance with Duchamp. In "Josephine the Singer, or the Mouse Folk," we encounter two poles of art production. If, with Duchamp, we had witnessed the point of view of the artist confronted with the impact of industrialization, the birth of the art market, and the transformations of the public, with Josephine and the mouse people it is the latter that is at stake: a public that coincides with the people.

The mouse folk are a "people of workers," endowed with a "certain practical cunning," fearing neither adversities nor "work." Josephine the singer, as the narrator informs us, belongs to this people; that is, she works to earn her living like every other "worker" and sings to enchant the mouse folk. In other words, she exercises two professions. The race of mice does not love music and is not musically talented. The mice, busy with their everyday worries, cannot "rise to anything so high and remote from our usual routine as music." Only Josephine knows how to elicit the love of music in the people. Where does this power of her singing to deeply affect its listeners come from? Where does the passion for this art originate? And as the narrator asks himself, what kind of art are we dealing with, since the people do not love music?

Evidently, we are not dealing with the classical principles of aesthetics, since Josephine's art is not "so great that even the most insensitive cannot be deaf to it"; her singing does not "give one an immediate and lasting feeling of being something out of the ordinary," and what the people hear is not "something that Josephine alone and no one else can enable us to hear." "Among intimates we admit freely to one another that Josephine's singing, as singing, is nothing out of the ordinary. Is it in fact singing at all?" the narrator asks. Josephine's singing "hardly rises above that of our usual piping—yet perhaps her strength is not even equal to our usual piping, whereas an ordinary farmhand can keep it up effortlessly all day long."

Piping is the "real talent of the people" of mice. "We all pipe, but of course no one dreams of making out that our piping is an art." So there's nothing exceptional, no genius, no sublimity, no technique, and no talent, in Josephine's art, since the capacity to pipe is shared by all, and requires no virtuosity. It is not just the "anyone" (even the vulgar farmhand pipes while working) and the "anything" (a piping so feeble that it is difficult to tell it apart from the silence surrounding it) that seem to define her art but also the "anywhere." Josephine's "concerts" are prey to the fortuitousness of circumstances as well as her whim. "She can do this where she likes, it need not be a place visible a long way off, any secluded corner pitched on in a moment's caprice will serve as well."

Were this true, it would certainly deny Josephine her claim to the status of artist. The fact that her status "has never been quite defined" is indeed what makes her nervous and uneasy. To resolve the enigma of this "mediocre" art, the narrator multiplies the questions and suggests several avenues. All these questions will be left unanswered, which leaves the public of readers—as well as Duchamp's "posterity, that pretty bitch"—with a total freedom of interpretation.

The readymade supplies the first avenue we encounter in the story. The effects of Josephine on the public are perhaps due to a new "form of singularity"—the fact that someone makes "a ceremonial performance out of doing the usual thing," the "usual workaday piping." Here the narrator provides an extraordinary definition of the readymade—whose existence Kafka himself almost certainly ignored—by inventing a form that Duchamp had not envisaged: readymade quotidian action—an action that like piping, everyone is able to reproduce.

To crack a nut is truly no feat, so no one would ever dare to collect an audience in order to entertain it with nut cracking. But if all the same, one does do that and succeeds in entertaining the public, then it cannot be a matter of simple nut cracking. Or it is a matter of nut cracking, but it turns out that we have overlooked the art of cracking nuts because we were too skilled in it and this newcomer to it first shows us its real nature, even finding it useful in making their effects to be rather less expert in nut cracking than most of us.

As in Duchamp, the readymade is a mental technique that forces one to think, that obliges one to interrogate the "real," since after having experienced this strange piping, the mice can affirm that "we admire in her what we do not at all admire in ourselves."

But there are numerous avenues available in order to try to grasp the sources of Josephine's art. The mouse folk are a people of workers that because of their practical spirit, basically have no childhood, since they become adults very rapidly, precisely in order to work. By suspending the space—time of everyday banality by means of techniques that are neither beautiful, extraordinary, nor sublime, Josephine's art opens onto the innocence of childhood, its prelinguistic and precognitive world, before the latter is fixed into words, tastes, opinions, and judgments.

Piping is our people's daily speech, only many a one pipes his whole life long and does not know it, where here piping is set free from the fetters of daily life and it sets us free too for a little while. We certainly should not want to do without these performances ... [since into the people's dreams] Josephine's piping drops note by note ... [and] something of our poor brief childhood is in it.

But perhaps the effects produced by Josephine's art are also due to the specific techniques she employs. Josephine's singing, "a mere nothing in voice, a mere nothing in execution," is not the product of any technique. Were she to use techniques of musical virtuosity, she would not exercise any fascination over the mouse folk: "A really trained singer, if ever such a one should be found among us, we could certainly not endure at such a time and we should unanimously turn away from the senselessness of any such performance."

The effects that she produces are thus perhaps due to the fact that "her means are so inadequate." Nonvirtuosity and the weakness of materials are "democratic" techniques to neutralize the authority of tradition, the author, and the work over the public. But perhaps the force of her singing comes from something else. Josephine does not measure herself up to the history of art and its traditions but she plugs into the outside, into what happens. She makes art as much with small events as with large ones.

Among the mouse folk, "a certain tradition of music is preserved, yet without making the slightest demand upon us." On
the contrary, "every trifle, every casual incident, every nuisance,
a creaking in the parquet, a grinding of teeth, a failure in the
lighting incites her to heighten the effectiveness of her song. ...
So all disturbance is welcome to her; whatever intervenes from
outside to hinder the purity of her song" contributes to "awaken
the masses." But Josephine "likes best to sing just when things
are most upset," in the midst of great contemporary events, and
it is here that a different politics is opened up between Josephine's art and the people. The relationship between Josephine
and the people (the community of mice is coextensive with
the public) is a problematic one, since it involves the relation
between individual and people, community and singularity,
freedom and equality (one of the main themes that also preoc-
cupy Duchamp's oeuvre).

No single individual could do what in this respect the people
as a whole are capable of doing. To be sure, the difference in
strength between the people and the individual is so enormous
that it is enough for the nursling to be drawn into the warmth
of their nearness and he is sufficiently protected. To Josephine,
certainly, one does not dare mention such ideas. "Your protection isn't worth an old song," she says, because she believes it is
she who protects the people.

When she rebels against the people's communal grip, when
she tries to evade its "stable mass," its collective "protection,"
Josephine is equated with an infant, and the people are equated
with a father. (For Foucault, patriarchy is the aspect of the regime
of sovereignty that reproduces itself within the disciplinary
regime, and without which the latter could not function.)

It is true that "whenever we get bad news ... she rises up at once" and sings, but it is not she who saves the people, "who have always somehow managed to save themselves." Boltanski and Chiapello might well share the narrator's viewpoint, since "social critique" does not need "artistic critique" in order to save itself. The events of 1968, as they say, are an "exception." The workers' movement has always saved itself. It doesn't need Josephine. Nevertheless, in emergencies we harken better than at other times to Josephine's voice. It is not so much a performance of songs as an assembly of the people, yet to be only an incidental, unnoticed performer in a corner of the assembly of the people, she would certainly not make the sacrifice of her singing.

The singer nurses other differends[1] with the people-public, and the main one concerns the economic status of her activity. She exercises two professions (working and singing) and she wages a veritable fight for recognition—even of an economic kind—of her singing-piping.

Josephine has been fighting for exemption from all daily work on account of her singing; she should be relieved of all responsibility for earning her daily bread, which—apparently—should be transferred on her behalf to the people as a whole.

She lays claim to something like a guaranteed income, or at least she would like to be assured of some continuity of income since what she demands is not a direct wage but an income drawn from the sum of the incomes of the mice. Josephine seems to be soliciting here what she refused earlier—namely, the (social) "protection" of the people, the community. Yet perhaps we should not view this as a contradiction but rather as the need to establish a new relationship between (social) "protection" and "individual freedom," community and singularity, freedom and equality.

On the basis of the singer's claim, it is the very status of work that becomes undecidable, since according to Josephine, the strain produced by singing is greater than that of the work necessary to earn her daily bread:

Josephine argues, for instance, that the strain of working is bad for her voice, that the strain of working is of course nothing to the strain of singing, but it prevents her from being able to rest sufficiently after singing and to recuperate for more singing.

We can understand, then, why Josephine's status is never clarified. If art in disciplinary societies is defined in opposition work, when Josephine struggles, in various guises, for the "recognition" of the strain of her singing, it is this very opposition that no longer makes sense. It is the status of both art and work that must be clarified. This would lead to the invention of a new system—at once economic, political, and aesthetic—whose conditions cannot even be envisaged within the theoretical framework of the present-day Left.

It is striking that the questioning of the category of work comes—as it does in France today with the *intermittents du spectacle*—from artists.

The laboring mouse folk are not ready, like the reformist and revolutionary Left, to ask what work has become today. The caricatural version of this attitude can be found in the self-styled "new radicalism" of Badiou, who wants to advocate both "great art" and the "revalorization" of the figure of the worker and the factory as a political place, while three-quarters of the workforce today (90 percent in the United States) will never cross the threshold of the factory gates. We are still within the art—work opposition, great art, and workers—that is, within a world that has been completely turned upside down both on the side of art and that of work.

In Kafka's story, Josephine's stubborn struggle and the working people's utter refusal of her claims will lead to her disappearance: "The people listen to her arguments and pay no attention. Our people, so easily moved, sometimes cannot be moved at all. Their refusal is sometimes so decided that even Josephine is taken aback." In an entirely arbitrary way, these pages of Kafka evoke for me the relationship between political and artistic avant-gardes in the Soviet Union. Josephine has come up against the "authoritatively sovereign" people, just as the futurists and constructivists hit up against the "stable mass" and "sovereignty" of the working-class-turned-state. This evocation in turn makes me think of a remark by Duchamp, according to which he does not believe in the universal and eternal "essential aspect" of art. For Duchamp, "one could create a society that would refuse art, the Russians got close. It's not funny, after all, but it's something that can be considered." For the narrator, "Josephine's road ... must go downhill," she will be "forgotten," while the "authoritatively sovereign" people "continue on their way."

Prolonging our interpretation, we could affirm that the refusal of the people/class to integrate these new aesthetic practices and their new economic and political conditions in turn leads at first to the decline and then to the disappearance of the people/class.

To conclude: there is no politics of art as such, just as, moreover, there is no politics of politics as such. The transformations of aesthetic, political, and economic practices are the elements of a single assemblage traversed by a single problem, of which work, art, and politics constitute the different facets or viewpoints. A politics capable of confronting the capitalist government and management of differences implies not only a strategy that articulates political revolution with the revolution of the sensible, the macro with the micro, but also a politics transversal to the separate orders of the economic, the political, the social, and the cultural artistic—a politics whose outlines are sketched in Kafka's story.

Notes

Introduction

1. For one of the best-informed discussions of the concept by Anglophone commentators, see Rosalind Gill and Andy Pratt, "In the Social Factory: Immaterial Labour, Precariousness, and Cultural Work," *Theory, Culture, and Society* 25, no. 7–8 (2008): 1–30.

2. *Le Bassin de Travail Immateriel (BTI) dans le Metropole Parisienne* [The zone of immaterial labor in metropolitan Paris]. Paris: L'Hammartan, 1996); Joanna Fiegiel, Stevphen Shukaitis, and Abe Walker, eds., "The Politics of Workers Inquiry," *Ephemera: Theory and Politics in Organization* 14, no. 3 (2014): 307–314, accessed December 28, 2016, http://www.ephemerajournal.org/sites/default/files/pdfs/issue/14-3ephemera-aug14.pdf.

3. Compare with Paul Willis, *Learning to Labour: How Working Class Kids Get Working* Class Jobs (London: Saxon House, 1977); Stuart Hall, Chas Critcher, Tony Jefferson, John Clarke, and Brian Roberts, *Policing the Crisis: Mugging, the State, and Law and Order* London: Macmillan, 1978).

4. See http://www.cip-idf.org.

5. Antonella Corsani and Maurizio Lazzarato, *Intermittents et Précaires* [*Intermittents* and precarious workers] (Paris: Éditions Amsterdam, 2008).

6. Maurizio Lazzarato, *The Making of Indebted Man* (New York: Semiotext[e], 2012); Maurizio Lazzarato, *Governing by Debt* (New York: Semiotext[e], 2015).

7. This is only one of a number of available terms to refer to this current, and it is not necessarily the most accurate, but it is sufficiently recognizable and distinctive to serve our purposes here.

8. Alberto Toscano, "Vital Strategies: Maurizio Lazzarato and the Metaphysics of Contemporary Capitalism," *Theory, Culture, and Society* 24, no. 6 (2007): 71–91.

9. See Nicholas Thoburn, *Deleuze, Marx, and Politics* (London: Routledge, 2003); Jason Read, *The Micro-Politics of Capital: Marx and the Prehistory of the Present* (New York: SUNY Press, 2003).

10. See Thoburn, *Deleuze, Marx, and Politics*.

11. Michael Hardt and Antonio Negri, *Empire* (Cambridge, MA: Harvard University Press, 2000; Michael Hardt and Antonio Negri, *Multitude* (Cambridge, MA: Harvard University Press, 2003); Michael Hardt and Antonio Negri, *Commonwealth* (Cambridge, MA: Harvard University Press, 2009).

12. David Harvey, *The Condition of Postmodernity: An Enquiry into the Origins of Cultural Change* (Oxford: Blackwell, 1991); David Harvey, *A Brief History of Neoliberalism* (Oxford: Oxford University Press, 2007); Frederic Jameson, *Postmodernism or the Cultural Logic of Late Capitalism* (London: Verso, 1991).

13. Hall et al., *Policing the Crisis*. See also Jeremy Gilbert, "After '68: Narratives of the New Capitalism," *New Formations* 65 (2008): 34–53.

14. See Sheila Rowbotham, *Edward Carpenter: A Life of Liberty and Love* (London: Verso, 2007).

15. See Kristin Ross, *May 1968 and Its Afterlives* (Chicago: University of Chicago Press). See Curtis's documentary series *The Century of the Self*.

16. Compare, for example, the work of Fernand Braudel with that of E. P. Thompson.

17. Some works that in fact do this include Lawrence Grossberg, *Caught in the Crossfire: Kids, Politics, and America's Future* (Abingdon, UK: Routledge, 2005); Brian Massumi, *The Power at the End of the Economy* (Durham, NC: Duke University Press, 2014); Philip Mirowski, *Never Let a Serious Crisis Go to Waste: How Neoliberalism Survived the Financial Meltdown* (London: Verso, 2014).

18. See Hall et al., *Policing the Crisis*; Raymond Williams, *Marxism and Literature* (Oxford: Oxford University Press, 1977).

19. See, for example, Ernesto Laclau and Chantal Mouffe, *Hegemony and Socialist Strategy* (London: Verso, 1985); Ernesto Laclau, ed., *The Making of Political Identities* (London: Verso, 1994); Chantal Mouffe, *The Return of the Political* (London: Verso, 2005).

Introduction to the French Edition

1. This chapter of this book was published in another form in September 2008 under the title *Le gouvernement des inégalités. Critique de l'insécurité néolibérale* (The government of inequalities: Critique of neoliberal insecurity) by Éditions Amsterdam. Most of the hypotheses that will be advanced in the first chapter have been the topic of internal discussions at the Open University organized by the Îsle-de-France coordination of casual and precarious workers, 2006–7, the title of which was "nous avons lu le néolibéralisme" (literally: we have read neoliberalism), and the guiding thread of which was Michel Foucault's *The Birth of Biopolitics*. I am solely responsible for this text.

2. Antonella Corsani and Maurizio Lazzarato, *Intermittents et Précaires* (Casual and precarious workers) (Paris: Éditions Amsterdam, 2008).

Chapter 1: The Government of Inequalities

1. UNEDIC is a joint body—that is to say, a body administered by an equal number of representatives of employers and employees. The list of those having the right to be members of it (CGT, CGT-FO, CFTC, and CGC) was fixed by a governmental decision of March 8, 1948. It was

updated by the decree of March 31, 1966, to include the CFDT (following its establishment and the split of the CFTC in 1964). The trade union structures that have been constituted subsequently do not have the right to belong to the joint bodies. This form of "comanagement" does not take account of the evolution of the salariat, the birth and the development of new unions that often more representative than those that belong to UNEDIC, do not have the right to take part in the institutions that administer social welfare, as they did not exist at the moment in the 1960s when the promulgation of the law fixed the position of the five trade union confederations benefiting from a *"présomption irréfragable"* (incontestable presumption) of recognition at UNEDIC.

2. Antonella Corsani, Maurizio Lazzarato, Yann-Moulier Boutang, and Jean-Baptiste Oliveau, *Statistical, Economic, and Sociological Study of the Unemployment Insurance Regime of Professionals in the Live Entertainment, Cinema, and Audio-Visual Industries*, 2005, accessed October 3, 2016, http://www.cip-idf.org/article.php3?id_article=2145, published in modified form in Antonella Corsani and Maurizio Lazzarato, *Intermittents et Précaires* [Casual and precarious workers] (Paris: Éditions Amsterdam, 2008).

3. The average income of a casual entertainment worker is close to that of an average worker (€22,000) in 2003. On average, such a worker declares 709 hours of work under contract and earns a monthly salary close to that of a certified teacher, who is supposed to perform before a public (students) for 18 hours per week during term time (36 weeks per year), amounting to some 648 hours per year (540 in the case of a teacher who has passed the *agrégation*, the competitive examination that assigns the most prestigious teaching posts). Contrary to what Luc Boltanski and Eve Chiapello write in *The New Spirit of Capitalism*, the "new professions" (media, fashion, culture, etc.) are not composed of homogeneous blocs of relatively privileged individuals, whose situation could be opposed to that of workers, the unemployed, and the precarious. The new professions are not analyzable in terms of the molar categories used by the authors of *The New Spirit of Capitalism*, as a very high level of internal differentiation characterizes people in these professions, as we have just seen in the case of casual entertainment workers.

4. Translators' note: In the Anglophone context, this distinction would clearly map closely onto the traditional one between the "deserving" and the "undeserving" poor, or even the Elizabethan distinction between "sturdy" beggars who were deemed capable of work and the authentically destitute.

5. Denis Kessler, "L'avenir de la protection sociale" [The Future of Social Welfare], *Commentaire* (Autumn 1999): 629.

6. Michel Foucault, *The Birth of Biopolitics: Lectures at the Collège de Francs 1978–9*, trans. Graham Burchell (London: Palgrave Macmillan, 2008), 259. In disciplinary society, the management of power is hegemonic, in the sense that it is founded, on the one hand, on the injunction to follow a highly uniform and homogenizing trajectory, following a singular and general norm (Foucault calls this "normation"), and on the other hand, on the exclusion of the nonnormalizable ("the residue, the irreducible, the unbreakable, the unassimilable"). In the society of security, the operation of "normalization," which Foucault opposes to "normation," is organized without recourse to an external norm or process, but through relying on differences (normalities) themselves, by pitting one against the other. In the society of security, it's the normal that comes first, and the norm that is derived from it; in other words, the norm is not exterior to its field of application, not only because the former produced the latter, but also because it produces itself in the process. The norm no longer acts on a content that would exist outside it, independent of its action. What "norms the norm" is its action and the process of its becoming, its effectuation. The norm does not encounter a milieu and individuals that exist prior to its intervention, and this intervention is not preordained. The action is everything, and the actor comes later, as Friedrich Nietzsche, one of Foucault's great inspirations, would say.

7. Robert Castel, *Les Métamorphoses de la question sociale: une chronique du salariat* (Paris: Fayard, 1995).

8. Gilles Deleuze and Félix Guattari, *A Thousand Plateaus: Capitalism and Schizophrenia* (London: Continuum, 1992), 215–216. Henceforth we will often mobilize the conceptual pair molar-molecular. As such,

we will give a definition here. The molar assemblage is a spatiotemporal division, a dichotomic distribution of possibles (the exclusive disjunctions work-unemployment, labor-leisure, intellectual-manual, masculine-feminine, scholarly-profane, heterosexual-homosexual, etc.). It is characterized not only by its asymmetrical and productive aspect but also by the excessive narrowness of the options that it proposes. The molar is at origin what Deleuze and Guattari call a "hard segmentarity," a dichotomic segmentarity. The molecular, by contrast, escapes from these types of segmentarity, refusing its strictures and upsetting the dualisms that organize them, opening up a new distribution of possibles. It constitutes what Deleuze and Guattari call a "supple segmentarity."

9. Kessler, "The Future of Social Welfare," 629.

10. Ernest-Antoine Seillière, president of MEDEF at the time of the "social reconstruction," press conference, June 20, 2000.

11. Foucault, *The Birth of Biopolitics*, 242.

12. Kessler, "The Future of Social Welfare," 629.

13. Ibid., 622.

14. Quoted in Richard Sennett, *Respect: The Formation of Character in an Age of Inequality* (London: Penguin, 2000), 174–180.

15. Foucault, *Birth of Biopolitics*, 262.

16. Ibid., 243.

17. See Gilles Deleuze and Félix Guattari, *Anti-Oedipus: Capitalism and Schizophrenia* (Minneapolis: University of Minnesota Press, 1994), 228.

18. Ibid., 229.

19. On this subject, we do not know how to characterize the political program of Bernard Stiegler, who claims to be able to separate industrial capitalism from financial capitalism, if not as an example of the greatest naïveté, since "it is the bank that controls the whole system and the investment of desire" (ibid., 228).

20. Ibid., 229.

21. Daniel Cohen "Desormais, le salarié est exposé, l'actionnaire protegé" [Henceforth, the wage earner is exposed, the shareholder protected], *Challenges*, October 11, 2006. http:/./www.challenges.fr/ entreprise/entretien-avec-daniel-cohen-economiste-la-remunerationet -la-protection-du-risque-sont-aberrantes_392486.

22. Theories of risk surely grasp some of the changes that affect their societies, but they completely evacuate the capitalist dimension, which nonetheless is becoming increasingly systematic. It's Ewald and Kessler who best express this tendency, in less simplistic forms than sociologist Ulrich Beck. According to them, society is no longer divided along the old lines (bosses and workers), but according to a "moral division, over ways of life, over style," which opposes "riskophiles [the new 'social entrepreneurs'] to 'riskophobes' [the dependents of the welfare state]."

23. In 2005, the 300,000 richest Americans declared an income equivalent to that of the 150,000,000 poorest. The top 0.1 percent declared an income equivalent to the bottom 50 percent. On average, each individual member of the top 0.1 percent declared an income equivalent to 440 times that of the average member of the bottom 50 percent (within companies, one can find even greater levels of inequality, while the remuneration of a Fordist manager was never supposed to exceed forty times the average salary of their company's employees). To find this level of inequality in the past, we have to go back to before the Great Depression. It's also the mythical US middle class that pays the price for this program. In 2005, total income increased by 9 percent, but that of 90 percent of the population decreased by 0.9 percent. The fruits of growth have gone to the remaining 10 percent, which appropriate almost a full half of the national cake (48.5 percent). In 1970, the richest 10 percent of Americans appropriated one-third of the wealth; in 2005, it was one half. These figures show more clearly than any words that the Fordist pact for the sharing of profits has had its day.

24. Christian Marazzi, *Capital and Language: From the New Economy to the War Economy* (New York: Semiotext(e), 2008), 37.

25. Michel Aglietta therefore writes in *Le Monde*, December 9, 1997: "If Fordism integrated the salariat by way of consumption, the emergent growth regime seeks integration through savings and investments."

26. Francois Bilger, *La Pensée économique libérale de l'Allemagne contemporaine* [The liberal economic thought of contemporary Germany] (Paris: Pichon et Durand-Auzias, 1964), 186; cited in Foucault, *The Birth of Biopolitics*, 267.

27. Deleuze and Guattari, *A Thousand Pleateaus*, 457.

28. Here we are not talking about the wage earner with access to a pension fund but about all those who are subjected, by the mutations of the system of social protections as by transformations in the organization of work, to the injunction to be entrepreneurs of the self.

29. Kessler, "The Future of Social Welfare," 630.

30. Dennis Kessler and François Ewald, "Les noces du risque et de la politique [The marriage of risk and politics], *Le Débat*, March–April 2000, 71.

31. Kessler, "The Future of Social Welfare," 626.

32. Ibid.

33. Ernest-Antoine Seillière, interviewed by François Ewald, in *Risques: Les cahiers d'assurance* (September 2000). http://revue-risques.fr/revue/risques/html/Risques_43_0003.html.

34. The system of indemnification for the *intérimaires* is also in deficit. All such regimes of indemnification are structurally and by definition in deficit, as they are founded on a system of discontinuous employment. To seek an internal, sectoral equilibrium within them is therefore absurd.

35. A student who had received his masters of law declared in *Repubblica*, an Italian daily, on August 4, 2008, "I don't think I will ever repay the debts that I ran up to pay for my studies; some days I think that when I die, I'll still be making monthly payments for my university debts. Today I have a repayment plan spread over twenty-seven and a

half years, but it's too ambitious, because the interest is variable, and I'm only paying the interest. ... I'm very careful with my spending. I note every expenditure in a notebook, from a coffee to a bus ticket ... everything has to be planned. ... The thing that preoccupies me the most is that I can't save, and my debt is always there and haunts me."

36. The "political liberties" introduced by liberalism are surely an expression of opposition to sovereign power, but throughout history they have been, without exception, limited by property. We know that the universalization of those liberties that the liberals wanted to guarantee only to the owners of property, such as universal suffrage, were not the outcome of liberal policies (if it was down to the liberals, we would still be limited to male household suffrage) but of the struggles and victories, first of the workers' movement (from 1848), and then the women's movements.

37. Translators' note: The RMI (Revenu Minimum d'Insertion, or "minimum income of inclusion") is the most basic form of welfare support for unemployed French citizens.

38. Translators' note: That is, the unions and the employers.

39. Translators' note: *Allocation du fonds transitoire*.

40. See *Spectacle, Culture et communication*, February 2007. http://www.culture.gouv.fr/culture/infos-pratiques/formations/spectacles.html.

41. The first article of the "bill for the creation of higher professional diplomas" issued by the ministry of culture states, "To be created ... national higher diplomas for musicians, dancers, actors, and circus performers. These diplomas certify the acquisition of the competences, knowledge, and skills necessary to these professions." The *coordination* remains the only organization that opposes this: "We oppose the sorting of the wheat from the chaff." Coordination des intermittents et précaires, *Synthèse des lundis de saison en Lutte* [Synthesis of the Monday meetings of "Season in Struggle"—a committee of the *coordinations*], accessed October 6, 2016, www.cip-idf.org.

42. Translators' note: It is worth bearing in mind here the important role played by the belief that neoliberalism equals laissez-faire in

convincing many former social democrats to adopt a fully neoliberal program in government since the 1980s: the belief that *any* form of government intervention constituted a legitimate extension of the social democratic tradition was crucial to the self-image of many of the key individuals responsible for political projects such as British prime minister Tony Blair's "new labor," and was grounded in the belief that what their opponents on the Right proposed was a simple return to nineteenth-century liberalism (which was clearly always an erroneous belief, yet one that those rightists themselves often rhetorically adhered to).

43. In his book on the 1990s, Joseph Stiglitz offers some hilarious insights into the politics of the Clinton administration: "If we were forced to cut back on welfare to the poor, there was an even more compelling case to eliminate welfare to the rich, and in particular to cut back on corporate welfare-subsidies and tab breaks to corporations. ... The initiative, though, proved highly divisive. The US Treasury violently opposed the whole idea, suggesting that the very vocabulary, 'corporate welfare,' smacked of class warfare" (Joseph E. Stiglitz, T*he Roaring Nineties: Why we're paying the price for the greediest decade in history*, London: Penguin, 2003, 107). In arguing for economic "necessity," all of the countries of the North have indeed created a welfare state for the rich. Stiglitz writes: that "we did manage to tighten the belts of the poor as we loosened those on the rich: not only was little done about cutting out old corporate welfare programs, left over from the Reagan/Bush administrations; new forms were developed and old forms were altered to keep them alive" (*The Roaring Nineties*, 108)

44. Translators' note: "Les caisses sont vides' was a notorious remark of Sarkozy's in 2008, justifying a lack of public spending, in response to a journalist's question about the lack of purchasing power being the most immediate concrete concern of French voters. See http://www.dailymotion.com/video/x3zjv2_sarkozy-pouvoir-d-achat-les-caisses_news. This "Court of Audit" is the French government office charged with auditing the government.

45. More generally, the political and trade union Left has labored for years under the delusion that it can safeguard the labor rights and the

social welfare of one part of the population by unloading labor market flexibility (precarity) onto another, to whom a future of full employment is always promised. In reality, this fierce defense of the standard salariat reveals itself to be one of the principle instruments for the segmentation of the labor market and its ever more intense segmentation, precisely because the strategies of the trade unions refuse to integrate the new plane of reference that, according to Foucault, enables liberal logic to govern "the social" (the social minima, the continuum that runs from the welfare recipient through to the standard wage earner).

46. Luc Boltanski and Eve Chiapello, *The New Spirit of Capitalism*, trans. Gregory Elliott (London: Verso, 2005).

47. All the quotations from Boltanski and Chiapello that follow are drawn from an interview with them: "Vers un renouveau de la critique sociale" [Toward a renewal of the social critique], *Multitudes* 3, no. 3 (2000): 129–142.

48. Translators' note: *Bobos* equals bourgeois bohemians, a term with connotations in France somewhere between "hipsters" and "yuppies" in English.

49. Translators' note: CPE is short for "*contrat première embauche*," or first employment contract. This was a new type of employment contract for employees under age twenty-six in their first positions, proposed by the French government in 2006, that would have seen costs and obligation applying to employers of young people in their first jobs significantly reduced, thus, the government claimed, improving the employment prospects of a young population suffering from very high level of unemployment. Young workers themselves as well as students and trade unionists largely perceived this as an attack on basic labor rights and an attempt to turn the young workforce into a pool of cheap labor, as had already happened notably in the United Kingdom in the preceding years. A major protest campaign against the legislation eventually saw it repealed without ever having come into full effect.

50. "L'e Nombre de musiciens 'RMIstes,'" *Culture chiffre*, 2007–2002, Départment des études, de la prospective et des statistiques (DEPS) du ministère de la Culture et de la Communication.

51. Louis Chauvel, *Les Classes moyennes à la dérive* [The middle classes adrift] (Paris: Seuil, 2006), 76, 75.53. Ibid., 61.

52. "Nearly one in three working Americans is an independent worker. That's 42 million people—and growing. We're lawyers and nannies. We're graphic designers and temps. We're the future of the economy. Freelancers Union serves the needs of this growing independent sector. We're bringing freelancers together to build smarter solutions to health care, retirement, wage security, and other broken systems. We call it New Mutualism. You can call it the future." See http://www.freelancersunion.org/about/index.html.

53. See Richard Florida, *The Rise of the Creative Class: And How It's Transforming Work, Leisure, Community, and Everyday Life* (New York: Basic Books, 2002); Richard Florida, *The Flight of the Creative Class: The New Global Competition for Talent* (New York: HarperCollins, 2005).

54. Michel Foucault, *Dits et Écrits* (Paris: Gallimard, 2001), 2:1481. For a recent English translation, see Michel Foucault, *Wrong Doing, Truth Telling: The Function of Avowal in Justice* (Chicago: University of Chicago Press, 2014, 299).

55. For a rehearsal of a critique that limits itself to this first form of dependence, as in the majority of critiques of the welfare state, see Sennett, *Respect*.

56. Foucault, *Wrong Doing, Truth Telling*, 299.

57. Translators' note: *Trente Glorieuses*, literally "Glorious thirty [years]," is the French colloquial expression for the years of the postwar boom.

58. Foucault, *Wrong Doing, Truth Telling*, 299.

59. The mobilizations of the 1960s and 1970s attacked different "power effects" of the welfare state. They criticized the health system and the medical profession because of the control that they exercised over bodies, the health of individuals, and life and death. Social expenditure on training and culture creates "knowledge elites" (the medical profession, the teaching profession, scientists, experts, etc.), who themselves

are so many "power effects" and modes of government exercised over populations of schoolchildren, the sick, and the public at large.

60. Editor's note: Some doubts must be cast on the precise chronology here, as Lazzarato appears to be referring to those measures such as the US "Patriot Act" most closely associated with the period following the commencement of the *second* Gulf War, in 2003, whereas the period following the first Gulf War, the 1990s, would normally be seen as the high-water mark for the neoliberal discourse of the "new economy," typical as it was of the rhetoric and policies of the Clinton administration in the United States and the early years of Blair's "New Labor" administration in the United Kingdom. This has no consequences for the validity of Lazzarato's argument, however.

61. Félix Guattari, "De la production de la subjectivité," *Chimères* 50 (2003): 54 (first published in issue 4 of the same journal). This essay is also collected in Félix Guattari, *Chaosmose* (Paris: Galilé, 1992). It appears in English as "On the Production of Subjectivity," in Félix Guatari, *Chaosmosis: An Ethico-Aesthetic Paradigm*, trans. Paul Bains and Julian Pefanis (Bloomington: Indiana University Press, 1995).

62. Foucault, *The Birth of Biopolitics*, 242–243.

63. Ibid., 301.

64. Disinterested interests are "neither purely economic nor purely juridical, which cannot be superimposed on the structures of the contract … and which, in their nature if not their form, are also different from the economic game." Ibid., 308.

65. Ibid., 304. Translators' note: Although this phrase appears in quotation marks in the French original of Lazzarato's text, it is not actually a direct quotation from Foucault, whose phrasing in the French original of *The Birth of Biopolitics* is slightly different from Lazzarato's in *Experimental Politics*. We have translated the phrasing here directly as it appears in the French edition of *Experimental Politics*, but readers looking for this precise quote in the English or French editions of *The Birth of Biopolitics* should be aware that the phrase does not occur in either text

precisely as given here, and that the misquotation is a faithful rendering of Lazzarato's text.

66. There is no question of a rupture, in any case, but rather of the perfection of policies begun twenty-five years ago by the Socialists and continued by every subsequent government. The only novelty of note consists in the fact that the state now takes on, without any "republican" ambiguity, both sides of the neoliberal dynamic, in making its own the program of "hypermodernization, "social reconstruction," and integrating all the neoarchaisms whose implementation it shares responsibility for with the Far Right. It is important to underline the fact that the complete conformity of the state to neoliberal principles occurs at the moment when their deployment encounters major difficulties in the government of the economy and society.

67. The feminists are surely the most creative readers of Foucault's work. Strangely, however, they systematically reduce his contribution solely to the description of disciplinary societies. For Donna Haraway, he "names a form of power at the moment of its implosion"—a judgment shared by Rosi Braidotti, author of the introduction to the Italian edition of Haraway's *Cyborg Manifesto*, as well as Judith Butler, even though Deleuze never stopped saying that for Foucault, the disciplinary institutions and mechanisms were what we were in the process of leaving behind.

68. It is impossible for an Anglophone editor to let this passage pass without comment. Lazzarato here uses the term "hegemonic" in a way that is certainly common in both English and French, but that no student of the Anglophone Gramscian tradition could easily endorse. The most celebrated exponents of that tradition, such as Stuart Hall and Raymond Williams, have *specifically* defined hegemony in terms of a process of *"differential modes of incorporating"* that does not operate according to simple binary distinctions and certainly cannot be reduced to crude mechanisms of normalization. (See Stuart Hall, "Gramsci's Relevance for the Study of Race and Ethnicity," *Journal of Communication Inquiry* 10 (1986): 5–27.) "Hegemony" in Antonio Gramsci's work and the writings of all his most intelligent commentators is *never* simply a synonym for "domination," but always, even in Gramsci's own writings

from the 1930s, implies a process of "supple segmentation" as alliances are formed between multiple class fractions to produce "historic blocs" that cannot be understood in simple class terms, and themselves must engage in constant negotiation with other social groups in order to sustain their position.

69. Michel Foucault, "La sécurité et l'État," in *Dits et Écrits*, 2:386.

70. Ibid., 46.

71. "The molecular problematic is entirely connected—as much at the level of its repressive modeling as at the level of its liberatory potentialities—with the new type of international market that is establishing itself." Félix Guattari and Solney Rolnik, *Micropolitiques* (Paris: Les Empêcheurs de Penser en Rond, 2006), 174.

72. Ibid., 29.

73. Michel de Certeau, *Culture in the Plural*, trans. Tim Conley (Minneapolis: University of Minnesota Press, 1997).75. Translators' note: In French, "la police." The etymology of the word "police" in French has, or retains, a rather different significance to that in modern English. The same word "la police" is used to designate several different but overlapping things: the public institution known in English as "the police," the act of policing, a "policy" in the sense of an "insurance policy," and, most important in this context, the general process of administering a city or region. The latter is now understood as a somewhat archaic meaning of the term, but it retains this resonance in a way that it has not retained it in modern English. The convention among translators today, especially following the translation of Jacques Rancière's work within which this old meaning of the term "police" to designate generalized administration takes on a particular significance, seems to be simply to use the English "police" wherever the French is used. This is potentially very confusing, however, and we will use the term "policy" from hereon out, because we find this less confusing and also more appropriate given that the etymology of the word "policy" in English matches much more closely the etymology of this usage of "la police" in French.

74. Michel Foucault, *Security, Territory, Population: Lectures at the Collège de France 1977–1978*, trans. Graham Burchell (London: Palgrave Macmillan, 2007), 165.

75. Ibid., 130. Foucault would have been doubly astonished by Giorgio Agamben's reading of his concept of biopower: first, because he makes of that theory a metaphysics, and second, because he seeks out the genealogy of the concept in the Roman political tradition, which is a possibility categorically excluded by Foucault.

76. Michel Foucault, "Omnes et Singulatim," in *Dits et Écrits*, 2:958.

77. The political government of men does not aim initially for "the common good." Already in the sixteenth century, government was defined as a way of organizing and conducting men and things not toward a "common good" (kingdom, city, republic, or democracy) but "appropriate ends." That implies that it pursues a plurality of particular ends (producing as much wealth as possible, increasing the population, etc.), of which the convergence, the coordination, and the synthesis are problematic.

78. Policy consists in attending at the same time to the life of the citizens and the vigor of the state. In keeping watch on health and provisioning, it applies itself to the preservation of life; as regards commerce, manufacturing, workers, the poor, and public order, it concerns itself with the commodities of life. In watching over theater, literature, and the performing arts, its object is none other than the pleasures of life." Foucault, *Dits et Écrits*, 2:978.

79. The pastor continually manages this economy of merits, "which presupposes an analysis, in discrete elements, of transfer mechanisms, inversion procedures, variable application of contradictory elements" between the pastor and the believer. Ibid., 176.

80. Ibid., 184.

81. Ibid., 173.

82. Ibid., 329.

83. Even Foucault draws inspiration, for his theories of discipline and to describe the microphysical operation of its powers, from the Marxist analysis of the factory.

84. Foucault, *The Birth of Biopolitics*, 13.

85. Translators' note: In French, "agencer"—meaning to arrange a set of elements, to assemble, or to construct. This is closely related to the word "agencement," which is normally rendered in English by translators with the now-familiar word "assemblage."

86. Gilles Deleuze, *Foucault*, trans. Seàn Hand (London: Athlone, 1999).

87. Translators' note: ANPE is short for L'Agence nationale pour l'emploi, or National Employment Agency.

88. See Foucault, *Dits et Écrits*, 2:963.

89. Foucault, *The Birth of Biopolitics*, 164.

Chapter 2: The Dynamics of the Political Event

1. Alain Badiou, *Logics of Worlds* (London: Continuum, 2009), 35.

2. On this point, see the first chapter of the present book.

3. "The force of Marx's conviction in the 19th century resides especially in the fact that it had followed its liberal-bourgeois adversary onto the economic terrain, and defeated it on the same terrain with its very weapons. This had been necessary because [of] the economic conversion which was imposed by the economic victory of the industrial revolution." Carl Schmitt, *The Concept of the Political* (Chicago: University of Chicago Press, 1996), 74. We have here directly translated the French version cited by Lazzarato, but this is the reference to the relevant passage in the English edition.

4. These changes become visible from the 1980s onward, but a careful observer could have detected them in the 1930s, following the example of Schmitt, for whom the clear and univocal distinctions of the classical age (between the economy, politics, the state, war, peace, etc.) no longer apply, since state and society have penetrated one another.

5. We repeat here the definition of "molar-molecular" offered in the previous chapter. The molar assemblage is a spatiotemporal division, a dichotomic distribution of possibles (the exclusive disjunctions work-unemployment, labor-leisure, intellectual-manual, masculine-feminine, scholarly-profane, heterosexual-homosexual, and so on). It is character-ized not only by its asymmetrical and productive aspect but also by the excessive narrowness of the options that it proposes. The molar is at origin what Deleuze and Guattari call a "hard segmentarity," a dicho-tomic segmentarity. The molecular, by contrast, escapes from these types of segmentarity, refusing its strictures and upsetting the dualisms that organize them, opening up a new distribution of possibles. It con-stitutes what Deleuze and Guattari call a "supple segmentarity." Gilles Deleuze and Félix Guattari, *A Thousand Plateaus: Capitalism and Schizo-phrenia* (London: Continuum, 1992).

6. Michel Foucault, *Le gouvernement de soi et des autres. Le courage de la vérité* (Paris: Gallimard, 2009), 169.

7. The ethics of the care of the self and others has nothing to do with the "good" life of Arendt, because in the tradition of the Cynics, Christi-anity, and revolutionary modernity, Foucault retraces the history of "a life that is scandalously other," and poses "the otherness of another life, not simply as the choice of a different life, blessed and sovereign, but as the practice of a combativeness at the threshold of which lies another world." Ibid., 264.

8. Unlike other political organized forces, the Précaires associés de Paris had the wisdom to "disband" during the *coordination*.

9. Félix Guattari, *L'inconscient machinique* (Paris: Éditions Recherches, 1979), 242.

10. Interconnections and overlaps between history and the event do not feature in Rancière's thought, because the event only comes after a "formal" analysis, where it is never a question of capitalism as it func-tions, as it changes, and as we are subject to it. The event is conceived of as a suspension that can be thought in history. It is sufficient for it to keep to the formal conditions of the "syllogism of equality" (the legality of speaking men that make demands of the presupposed power: the

major of the syllogism—and the inequality [or wrong] that the same power establishes with its statement: the minor of the syllogism). But if the event only occurs through history, it no longer returns to it, in the sense that it always guards the splendor of its nonactualizable and eternal side, and reduces the political to the glorious emergence of the act of subjectification. The "idealism" of Badiou is even more radical, because for him, "History does not exist. There are only disparate presents," in his caricaturing analysis of powers in struggle (not better described as "workers"). See Badiou, *The Logic of Worlds*.

11. For James, the (living or dead) hypothesis is confronted with the "will to act that it provokes." To say of a hypothesis that it is alive to the maximum degree is to say that it irrevocably inclines someone toward action. See William James, *The Will to Believe* (Mineola, NY: Dover Publications, 2003).

12. "When a political movement comes about, it is not sufficient to adjust the economic and political situation to respond to the effects of events. Society must be able to bring about institutional changes that correspond to this new subjectivity, and facilitate the subjective reconversion at the collective level, with the transformation of the state of things." Gilles Deleuze, *Deux régimes de fous: textes et entretiens, 1975–1995* (Paris: Les Éditions de Minuit, 2003), 217.

13. This is how Guattari formulates the question of an ethics of singularity in the interview "Vertige de l'immanence," *Chimeres* 38 (2000): 22.

14. Francis Fukuyama (*The End of History and the Last Man* [New York: Free Press, 1992]) has been a member of the policy planning staff of the State Department.

15. According the results of our socioeconomic inquiry (see Antonella Corsani and Maurizio Lazzarato, *Intermittents et Précaires* [Casual and precarious workers] (Paris: Éditions Amsterdam, 2008), nearly one-third of *intermittents* are declared waged employers. This figure is proportionally higher in the art sector than in the technical trades; 43.7 percent of *intermittents* are art workers and registered as such. Women are relatively more numerous than men, and wages are much lower among waged

employers than waged laborers: the latter earn an average of €14,367 per annum (median €11,880), against the €9,991 average (median €7,477) per annum of the waged employer. In fact, the allocation of revenue among waged employers is 55 percent versus 45 percent for waged laborers. This means that the employer-employee is a "poor worker," or on the path to proletarianization, and not an entrepreneur in the classical meaning of the term.

16. In intermittence, we found phenomena that other researchers located in more classical forms of employment. For instance, Alain Supiot brought to light a double process that blurs the classical definitions of employee and freelance worker. He speaks of a gray area where waged laborers, while formally remaining in a subordinate position to the employer, are called to take on the characters of freelancers: autonomy, flexibility, decision making, initiative, project management, and responsibility. Inversely, freelance workers, while formally remaining in a position of autonomy and independence, are really subordinated to an employer in situations of "parasubordination," following a neologism forged in research led by other European countries, notably Italy and England, where the phenomenon is much more widespread. See Alan Supiot, *Au-delá de l'emploi. Rapport pour la Commission européenne* (Paris: Flammarion, 1999).

17. Bernard Latarjet (2004) "Pour un débat national sur l'avenir du spectacle vivant" (French government report: http://www.culture.gouv. fr/culture/actualites/rapports/latarjet/rapport_7mai2004.pdf), 33.

18. Michel Foucault, "The Subject and Power," in *Beyond Structuralism and Hermeneutics*, ed. Hubert Dreyfus and Paul Rabinow (Hertfordshire, UK: Harvester Press, 1982), 208–226.

19. An interviewee remarks: "What benefits give to people is not money but time, and this poses a political problem."

20. For more details of the interview and research process conducted by Lazzarato and his colleagues, see Antonella Corsani and Maurizio Lazzarato, *Intermittents et Précaires* (Paris: Éditions Amsterdam, 2008).

21. Gilles Deleuze, *Foucault* (London: Athlone Press, 1988), 87.

22. We can only fully understand the meaning of the concept of the government of conduct, and fully describe the "pastoral" and institutional technologies that this government entails, starting from these processes of "reconversion of subjectivity." In societies of security, the problem of the "mode of conduct" becomes a primary concern. For the apparatus of power of security, the "morals," the government of conducts, is a technique that aims to reduce the uncertainty of the "self-transformations" of the governed that undermine it. James has described this function of "morality" well: "What must one recognize as virtue? What is good conduct? That is to say, what must be produced?' James, *The Will to Believe.*

23. Deleuze, as we have seen, prefers the less religious term "reconversion."

24. Like the majority of people who were activists or simply witnesses to the epoch, Foucault, starting from his own experience, was able to measure the power of "self-transformation' of these new political practices: "It is a fact, that the everyday life of people has changed between the 1960s and now, and my own life is certainly a testimony of this. This change, clearly, we do not owe to political parties, but to a number of movements. These social movements have really changed our lives, our mentality and our attitudes, as well as the attitudes of other people, people who do not belong to these movements." Michel Foucault, *Dits et Écrits* (Paris: Gallimard, 2001), 2:1565.

25. "What I tried to show in this series of studies is that these transformations are produced beneath codes and rules, in the forms of the relation to the self and the practices of the self that are linked to them. A history, not of morality, but of the moral subject." Ibid., 2:1440.

26. Michel Foucault, *L'Usage des plaisirs* (Paris: Gallimard, 1984), 12. English translation available as Michel Foucault, *The Uses of Pleasure* (London: Penguin, 1985). According to Foucault, neither Marxism nor psychoanalysis "have clearly and courageously faced the question of 'the conversion of the subject.' The idea of a class position, the effects of the party, belonging to a group or a code, initiation, the training of analysts, etc.—all of these point to the question of the formation of the

subject with the purpose of accessing truth, and yet they have been thought in social terms, in terms of organization." Michel Foucault, *L'Hermeneutique du sujet* (Paris: Gallimard, 2001), 31. English translation available as Michel Foucault, *Hermeneutics of the Subject* (London: Palgrave Macmillan, 2005).

27. "If Foucault has spoken differently of biopower and biopolitics, it is because his thought on politics is built on the question of power, and he has never been interested, theoretically, in the question of political subjectification." Jacques Rancière, "Interview," *Multitudes* 1 (March 2000): 23–30. The reduction of the ethics of the "care of the self" (Foucault) and "processes of subjectification" (Deleuze and Guattari) to a "vitalism of life forms," the opposition of "artifacts of equality" and "*bios*," lead Rancière (and Badiou) to theorize a mode of "political subjectification" that is formal and empty. Once again, they reproduce the politics that they wish to critique when separating politics from the reconversion of subjectivity.

28. Michel Foucault, *Le Gouvernment de soi et des autres II. Le courage de la vérité* (Paris: Gallimard, 2008), 279. The English translation of this text is available as Michel Foucault, *The Courage of the Truth* (London: Palgrave Macmillan, 2011).

29. Or to put it in the language of analytic philosophy, Foucault's problem is not to know what it means to "follow a rule" but to know under which conditions one can state something new. The statement as conformity to "grammar" can be substituted by the statement as event.

30. Foucault, *Dits et Écrits*, 2:1538. For a recent English translation, see Michel Foucault, *Wrong Doing, Truth Telling: The Function of Avowal in Justice* (Chicago: University of Chicago Press, 2014), 299.

31. Foucault, *L'Usage des plaisirs*, 33.

32. "Foucault's philosophy is not a philosophy of 'discourse" but a philosophy of the relation. This is because 'relation' is the name of what is designated as 'structure.' Instead of a world made of subjects and objects or their dialectic, a world where consciousness knows its objects in advance, sees them, or is itself what the objects make of it, we have a

world where relation is primary. ... One must try to study power, not from the primitive terms of the relation, legal subject, state, law, sovereign, and so on, but starting from the relation itself, because it is the relation that determines the elements on which it bears." Paul Veyne, *Comment on écrit l'histoire* (Paris: Seuil, 1996), 236.

33. Foucault also insists on the fact that all action "entails a relation to the reality in which it is carried out, and a relation to the code to which it refers; but the action also entails a certain relation to the self, an 'ethical' labor that is carried out on the self." Foucault, *L'Usage des plaisirs*, 34.

34. Ibid., 33.

35. Gabriel Tarde strongly defends the view that this notion of "freedom" is ambiguous and suggests replacing it with the notion of "difference." Thus we could say that the individual does not always have the possibility to act freely but always the possibility to act differently.

36. Gabriel Tarde, *Monologie et Sociologie* (Paris: Les empêcheurs de penser en rond, 1999), 80.

37. William James, *Pragmatism* (Cambridge MA: Harvard University Press, 1979).

38. Hence the imperative of the society of security: to anticipate, intervene in the event, in the process of the unfolding and *self-making* of the relation.

39. Félix Guattari, "Félix Guattari et l'art contemporaine," *Chimères* 23 (1995): 49.

40. Deleuze, *Foucault*, 103.

41. Gilles Deleuze, "What Is a *Apparatus*?" in *Michel Foucault: Philosopher*, ed. Timothy J. Armstrong (Hemel Hempstead, UK: Harvester Wheatsheaf, 1992).

42. Deleuze, *Foucault*, 113.

43. The CPE (as noted in chapter 1, "*contrat première embauche*") was the first employment contract introduced under Jacques Chirac to make it

easier to fire workers under age twenty-six in their first two years of employment.

44. The phrase continues: "so that reality as a whole appears incompletely definable unless ideas also are kept account of." William James, *The Meaning of Truth* (New York: Longman Green and Co., 1911), 185–186.

45. This separation between politics and economics is also the basis of the theories of Rancière and Badiou.

46. "AC" is a reference to "Agir contre Chomage" [Action against Unemployment], an anarchist-influenced protest group active in the 1990s.

47. For the results, see Lazzarato and Corsani, *Intermittents et Précaires*.

48. See Michel Foucault, *"Society Must Be Defended"*: *Lectures at the Collège de France, 1975–1976* (London: Palgrave, 1997). Foucault gives a very clear account of the stakes of this battle.

49. James, *The Meaning of Truth*, x.

50. http://1libertaire.free.fr/MFoucault163.html.

51. Guattari anticipated Rancière's critique of microphysics and micropolitics. To the assertion "if politics is everywhere, then it is nowhere," Guattari responded that it is "not everywhere, but it must be put everywhere, in the stereotyped relations of our personal lives, married lives, love and professional lives." We have made our own translation of the French here, but the English equivalent of this passage can be found in Félix Guattari and Suely Rolnik, *Molecular Revolution in Brazil* (New York: Semiotext(e), 2007), 190.

52. Guattari and Rolnik, *Molecular Revolution in Brazil*, 91ff.

53. "Molecular escapes and movements would be nothing if they did not return to the molar organisations to reshuffle their segments, their binary distributions of sexes, classes and parties." Gilles Deleuze and Félix Guattari, *A Thousand Plateaus* (Minneapolis: University of Minnesota Press, 1987), 216. "If the processes of molecular revolution are not

taken up on the level of the real power relations (social, economic, and material power relations), they may begin to revolve around themselves as imploding processes of subjectification." Guattari and Rolnik, *Molecular Revolution in Brazil*, 186.

54. Deleuze and Guattari, *A Thousand Plateaus*, 471.

55. Ibid.

56. In this "little" experience of self-organization, there are two clearly different phases. There is a first phase, which corresponds to the brief time of the springing up of the movement, in which the principal problem was that of the coordination of heterogeneous "points of view" (the unions, organized political groups, and different sensibilities that traverse the large mass of participants in the assemblies and the work of committees). The second phase corresponds to the lengthy time of the continuation of procedures and protocols of a new social practice, which no longer takes place inside a coordination, but instead within a collective that the *coordination* sedimented.

57. The enemy on the molecular plane is not easy to identify, because it is not incarnated in the exteriority of the exploiter or dominator but in the processes of reproduction of the dominant models of subjectivity among the dominated. In the molar and the molecular, the enemy is not the same, which implies a different definition of politics.

58. The opening up of this instituting space feeds a tension between the affirmation of equality proclaimed by politics (we are by rights equal) and the power relations between singularities, which are always asymmetrical (inside an assembly, a discussion, the taking of a decision, the circulation of speech and "power," places and functions, is not egalitarian). One *refuses* the differences imposed by power, but one *composes* the differences between singularities. One refuses the hierarchy of power, but one composes the asymmetrical relations between singularities.

59. Guattari and Rolnik, *Molecular Revolution in Brazil*, 183. "This transversality character of new social practices—the refusal of authoritarian disciplines, formal hierarchies, orders of priority decreed from

on high, obligatory ideological references, etc.—must not be held as contradictory with the evidently inevitable putting into place of *decision-making centers.*" Félix Guattari, *Les Années d'hiver, 1980–1985* (Paris: Les Prairies ordinaires, 1986), 66.

60. See Jacques Rancière, *On the Shores of Politics* (London: Verso, 1995).

61. The care of the self (Foucault) is indissociable from the care for "the machine," the collective assemblage of enunciation. To have a care for the collective means caring for a multiplicity of assemblages: interpersonal, infrapersonal, semiotic, material, machinic, institutional assemblages, and so on. Guattari inherits a theory of the institution of the work of caring for the mentally ill practiced by François Tosquelles. To care for the ill one must first care for the institution; to open the institution to the outside, one must first open it on the inside (the condition of transversality). There is a double care: a care for the institution in action, and a care for the instituted institution, but also a care for their relationship and discrepancy.

62. See Philippe Zarifian's website, http://philippe.zarifian.pagesperso -orange.fr.

Chapter 3: Economic and Subjective Impoverishment under Neoliberalism

1. Michel Foucault, "On the Genealogy of Ethics: An Overview of Work in Progress," in *The Foucault Reader*, ed. Paul Rabinow (Harmondsworth, Middlesex: Penguin, 1991), 350.

2. "I am against the word 'anti,' because it's a little like 'atheist' compared to 'believer.' An atheist is nearly as religious as a believer, and an 'anti-artist' is almost as much of an artist as an artist. ... 'Anartist' would be much better than 'anti-artist,' if I were able to change the term." Anart and anartist play against the dialectic oppositions between art and nonart, between artist and nonartist. All the citations from Duchamp that are not clearly referenced are taken from Bernard Marcadé, *Marcel Duchamp: La vie à crédit* (Paris: Flammarion, 2007).

3. Andy Warhol exploited Duchamp's intuitions and made reproduction/repetition central to his trade.

4. The incessant call to creativity " is an obsessive call to order, since creativity has been extinguished everywhere ... except this desperate call to creativity. ... You can conjure pockets of creativity in industry: the lamination of subjectivity is such in research, among the employees, and so on, that there is a vital urgency for advanced industries to resingularize subjectivity a small amount." Felix Guattari, "La Vertige de l'immanance" [The vertigo of immanence], *Chimères* 50 (2003): 55.

5. Pierre Cabanne, *Entretiens avec Marcel Duchamp* (Paris: Belfond, 1967). The English equivalent of this passage can be found in Pierre Cabanne, *Dialogues with Marcel Duchamp* (London: Thames & Hudson, 1971), 70.

6. See, among others, Jacques Rancière, *On the Shores of Politics* (London: Verso, 1995); Jacques Rancière, *Aesthetics and Its Discontents* (Cambridge, UK: Polity Press, 2009).

7. Elsewhere in this volume, Lazzarato uses the plural personal pronoun, alluding to the fact that his analysis of the *intermittents'* political struggles has emerged from a collective process of research. Here he uses the singular pronoun. We have chosen to reproduce this distinction in the translation by using "we," "us," and "me" accordingly.

8. Inspired by an Aristotelian definition of politics, there is clearly a "continuum" along which are distributed in a differential manner political positions and functions in Rancière's work. But this continuum only concerns the "police" who organize this distribution and says nothing about the potential to act of the dominated. In both Aristotle and Rancière, this continuum is a technique of domination and cannot express the will of the dominated not to be governed. Therefore, we never understand how the "division of the sensible" is itself "produced" and how it reproduces itself, while the "government of conduct" (the Foucauldian police) is obliged to multiply and singularize the techniques of subjection in the economic, the social, and the arts. This is something that Massironi, visual artist and militant in Potere Operaio, had already explained in the 1970s: "The artist elaborates and produces ideas, discoveries, projects, and provocations that are inherent to the

aesthetic field, and presents them all as artistic objects of one kind or another. Art dealers negate this immediately in order to take them and allow them to circulate as commodities, as money, through processes of control and privatization. The art critic transforms the ideas made material in an overly emotive manner in these objects into the rationalization of verbal exposition. ... The historian of art verifies the artist's product, correcting the conclusions of the critics, and ignores the market entirely. He conjures up the depth of the ideas that the work itself produces and ignores the materiality of the process. The art collector is the art dealer's reason for being. He is the negation of the task of the artist because, through privatization, he slows the circulation of ideas that he doesn't understand anyway. He see art as nothing but an object, like money, like shit, which he holds on to without letting any go." Manfredo Massironi, "Solo lo amor," in *Lea Vergine: Attraverso L'arte* (Rome: Arcana Edizioni, 1976).

9. "There is, therefore, no difference (neither of kind nor degree) between spirits, nor is there between their products or things. For the Pataphysician Total, the most banal *graffito* is equal to the most fully realized book and the simplest mass-produced pot with the Nativity of Altdorfer. Such is the postulate of the 'Pataphysic Equivalence.' ... [T]he Pataphysician is without a doubt the only absolutely reliable supporter of democracy: without any effort, he surpasses the egalitarians in their own backyard." "Testament de sa Feue Manificance le Docteur I. L. Sandomir de son vivant Fondateur du collège de Pataphysique." Cited in Marc Decimo, *Le Duchamp Facile* (Dijon: Les presses du réel, 2005).

10. These logics are far from being applied in the artistic/cultural sector exclusively. In France, in research and at universities, the same processes of "reform" as in culture are developing, with the same objectives: the reduction of space for researchers/instructors, the introduction of competition between researchers and universities, and the recentralization of institutional control over evaluation and measurement of performance in order to create centers of academic excellence. The French government has done nothing but apply the "Lisbon strategy" to the letter. The European Commission considers research as a site for the production of intellectual property and innovation that can be pat-

ented. The "time when the knowledge acquired in the world of Academic science constituted an open patrimony, available to all, has apparently passed." The "ultimate goal of public research is no longer simply to produce scientific knowledge, but also to promote the concrete exploitation of the scientific advantages they develop. And this exploitation has an intrinsically economic nature in a market economy." European Commission, "Vers un marché de connaissances" [Towards a knowledge market], *RDT Info* 34 (July 2002): 16. In the same way that, in culture, the adaptation of economic logic to the cultural industries required the transformation of the artist and the technician into "research-entrepreneurs." European Commission, "Le temps de chercheurs-entrepreneurs" [The age of research-entrepreneurs], *RDT Info* 35 (October 2006): 6.

11. But might we restore the subjects and procedures of the old ways of cultural production, as is the desire of the supporters of the cultural exception? Must we, as Walter Benjamin was already asking in the 1930s, wait for the Wilhelm Meister of our age? "The author who has fully reflected on the contemporary conditions of cultural production would never dream of waiting for, or evening wishing for, such works."

12. Duchamp reminds us of this in a general way when writes that "before the French Revolution, there were no artists from a social point of view, there were only artisans." Marcel Duchamp, *Rencontre avec Marcel Duchamp* (Paris: L'Échoppe, 1996), 12).

13. Nicolas Bourriad, *Relational Aesthetics* (Dijon: La Presses du reel, 1998). In reality, art must participate in the consensual recovery of the social relation to the working of negation promoted by the avant-gardes.

14. Ibid., 13.

15. Michel de Certeau, *Culture in the Plural*, (Minneapolis: University of Minnesota Press, 1997), 11.

16. An advertisement for Austria published in French newspapers reads, "Where culture feels at home—it's Austria, naturally." And continues to say, "In one of the largest cultural areas in the world, you will find

masterpieces from every age and art lovers from every continent. Between Klimt, Schiele, [and] Nitsch, visitors regain their energy for the next exhibition while relaxing on innovative urban furniture. Surrounded by baroque and modern architecture, they will feel immediately at home in the Museumsquartier of Vienna."

17. There is undecidability because there is "the co-existence and inseparability of that which the system conjugates and that which continuously escapes it following the lined of flight." Gilles Deleuze and Félix Guattari, *A Thousand Plateaus: Capitalism and Schizophrenia*, trans. Brian Massumi (Minneapolis: University of Minnesota Press, 1987), 590.

18. Ibid.

19. Guattari, "La Vertige de l'immanance," 151.

20. Ibid.

21. Gilles Deleuze, "On the New Philosophers (Plus a More General Problem)," *Two Regimes of Madness: Texts and Interviews, 1975–1995* (Cambridge, MA: MIT Press, 2007), 146.

22. de Certeau, *Culture in the Plural*, 143.

23. Ibid.

24. Benjamin has the merit of linking these transformations to the fact that workers are able to express themselves: "As a specialist, which he had to become willy-nilly in an extremely specialized work process, even if only in some minor respect, the reader gains access to authorship." Walter Benjamin, "The Work of Art in the Age of Mechanical Reproduction," in *Illuminations* (New York: Schocken Books, 1968), 232.

25. We have directly translated the French here, but the English equivalent of this passage is to be found in Benjamin, "The Work of Art in the Age of Mechanical Reproduction," 235.

26. Marcel Duchamp, *Entretiens avec Pierre Cabanne* (Paris: Éditions Allia, 2014), 130. The intuitions contained in the concept of the

"creative process" makes it possible for us to leave the restricted concept of "production" as it has been developed by political economy and Marxism. The creative industries have a classical conception of production. They put the creator in the place of the worker, even though half the work, as Duchamp suggests, is actually done by the viewers. On could thus believe in the neoliberal ideology (Blairite in origin), which is theirs when it proposes, like Guattari and Jean-Luc Godard, to pay the spectators.

27. Duchamp has written on this subject, "posterity, that beautiful bitch."

28. Marcel Duchamp, "The Creative Act," in *The Essential Writings of Marcel Duchamp*, ed. Michel Sanouillet and Elmer Peterson (London: Thames & Hudson, 1975), 138.

29. Ibid.

30. For a critique of virtuosity, see appendix B.

31. Marcel Duchamp, *Duchamp du signe* (Paris: Flammarion, 1992), 185.

32. "Taste gives a sensual sentiment, not an aesthetic emotion. Taste presupposes an authoritative spectator who imposes what he likes and does not like, and translates into 'beautiful' and 'ugly' that which feels pleasant or unpleasant. In a completely different manner, the 'victim' of the aesthetic echo is in a position comparable to a man in love or a believer who spontaneously rejects the exigencies of his ego, and who, without any more support, submits himself to an agreeable and mysterious constraint. In exercising his taste, he adopts an attitude of authority, the same man, in a quasi-ecstatic mode, becomes receptive and humble."

33. Michel de Certeau, *L'invention du quotidien*, vol. 1, *Arts de faire* (Paris: Éditions Gallimard, 1990); Michel de Certeau, "Une pratique de la différence: croire," in *Actes dela table ronde organisée par l'École français de Rome* (Rome: École français de Rome, 1981), 360–383; William James, *The Will to Believe* (Mineola, NY: Dover Publications, 2003).

34. Guattari returns several times to what he calls the paradox of Tertullien, in order to account for the unreasonable existential force that deploys new universes of reference for the believer, the lover, and the militant. "The son of God is dead: it is a fact worthy of belief because it is so inept. Dead he is risen: it is certain because it is impossible." Félix Guattari, "Cracks in the Street," *Chimères* 3 (1987): 36.

35. "We believe and we scarcely know how or why," and "our reasons are ridiculously out of proportion with the extent of our feelings, but they are sufficient for us to act without hesitation" (ibid., 117). "In our universities, we all believe in molecules and in the conservation of energy, in democracy and the necessity of progress ... and all of these beliefs rest on no reason worthy of the name (ibid., 45).

36. "The event arrives as a rupture in relation to spatial and temporal coordinates. And Marcel Duchamp pushes the point of accommodation in order to demonstrate that there is always, in the retreat of the relationships of temporal discursivity, a possible index of the point of crystallization of the event outside of time, which traverses time, transversal to all measure of time." Guattari, quoted in Olivier Zahm, "Félix Guattari et l'art contemporain," *Chimères* 23 (1992): 63.

37. Nevertheless, Guattari distrusts the notion of act (and choice), since it "introduces a break between the field of the act and the nonact, a nondifferentiated field that the act would animate, overcode, organize, and program." Guattari's distrust of decisionism (for example, the idealistic decisionism of Badiou) sees the act "as something that falls from who knows where, making a connection, of some sort, between spirit and biological and material domains. ... The act ex nihilo in accord with divine powers, the word made flesh ... these result in a theology, from the ideas of freedom of choice, in an overall philosophy in this sense. In opposition to these conceptions, which avoid the problem of the act, I develop the idea that there is no act in itself, but degrees of consistency in the existence of the act—existential *thresholds* related to the act. In other words, *there are degrees of passage in the act. The act is always a passage between heterogeneous dimensions*. This is not a passage from "all or nothing," relevant to a binary or dialectical logic." See the

seminars of Guattari available on the site of the journal *Chimères*: www .revue-chimeres.fr.

38. This citation is given in the French original as Gilles Deleuze, *Cinema 2. L'image-temps* (Paris: Éditions de minuit, 1985), 164, although we are unable to trace any such citation to that page. The English edition of this work is published as Gilles Deleuze, *Cinema 2: The Time Image* (Minneapolis: University of Minnesota Press, 1989).

39. "Comparable to the duration of [Henri] Bergson, affect is not subsumed under extended categories, capable of being numbered, but under intensive and intentional categories, corresponding to an existential autopositioning." Félix Guattari, "Rittournelle and Existential Affects," *Chimères* 7 (1989): 2.

40. There is no vague spiritualism, nothing of the irrational in these concepts, since the new dimension of subjectivity is time itself, the nonchronological time of the event, the dimension where past, present, and future are copresent and constitute the extratemporal dimension of time.

41. One of the currents of Duchamp-inspired art works precisely on the nature of nonorganic affects: "Conceptual art produces the most deterritorialized sensations that it can engender. ... It works with a material that is a concept. But this is not a concept that makes concepts but a concept that makes sensations. It is especially in sensation that it deconstructs redundant sensations, the dominant sensations." Guattari, quoted in Zahm, "Félix Guattari et l'art contemporain," 53).

42. Félix Guattari, *Chaosmose* (Paris: Galilé, 1992). The equivalent passage in English can be found in Félix Guattari, *Chaosmosis: An Ethic-Aesthetic Paradigm* (Bloomington: Indiana University Press), 14. Note that in the present volume we have translated the French *subjectivation* as "subjectification," in line with the usage of a number of writers, whereas in the English edition of *Chaosmosis* the word is translated as "subjectivation," as it occasionally is in other texts. The meanings are to be understood as identical.

43. Deleuze, *Cinema 2*, 20 [English edition].

44. Guattari gives us, as is often the case, his political translation: "One must remember the passage in/to the void between February and March of 1968." Félix Guattari, "La Machine: Discussions," *Chimères*, http://www.revue-chimeres.fr/drupal_chimeres/files/840206b.pdf.

45. There are now too many things to believe and not enough credibility," says the narrator of Kafka's novel *America*.

46. But as de Certeau tells us, it is not a certainty that this belief will guarantee individual investment in neoliberal values. "Today, it is not enough to manipulate, transport, and refine belief; it must be ... artificially produced. Shell produces the *credo* of 'values' that inspire the administration, and that the managers and employees must adopt. ... One does not return belief easily to the administrations and enterprises that become in-credible. ... The sophistication of discipline does not compensate for the divestment of subjects." Michel de Certeau, *L'invention du quotidien*, 262–264. The English equivalent of this passage can be found in Michel de Certeau, *The Practice of Everyday Life* (Berkeley: University of California Press, 1984), 178–180.

47. Robert Lebel, *Sur Marcel Duchamp* (Paris: Éditions Trianon, 1959).

48. Ibid.

49. *Chimères* 48 (2002–2003): 69–94.

50. "We could say that contemporary art remains framed. There is a universe of reference, a universe of valorization, including economic valorization, which frames the work, qualifying it as such, placing it in the social field. There is an institutional cut out. Guattari, quoted in Zahm, "Félix Guattari et l'art contemporain," 56. On the page "Contemporary Art and Société Générale" of the daily planner that my bank generously offered me, one could read, "Being there where no one waits, suspending and creating creative attention outside the universe of daily traditions. Such is the task of the collection of contemporary art of Société Générale put together at its headquarters of Paris–La Défense. Poetry is everywhere, surprisingly everywhere, in this place dedicated to finance." Daily Planner of the Société Générale, 2007.

51. Guattari, *Chaosmose*, 185, 156; *Chaosmosis* 112, 101.

52. "Art here is not just the activity of established artists but of all subjective creativity," which traverses the most diverse milieus and domains, "the generations and oppressed peoples, ghettoes, minorities." *Chaosmose* 127; *Chaosmosis*, 91.

53. "The transformation of the work does not belong to the artist; she is carried along by its movement. There is not an operator and a material object of the operation but a collective assemblage that carries along the artist, individually, and her public, and all the institutions that surround her, critics, galleries, and museums included." Guattari, "La Vertige de l'immanence," 63.

54. Daniel Stern, cited often by Guattari in his last writings, demonstrates in *The Interpersonal World of the Infant* (New York: Basic Books, 1985) that before the acquisition of language, infants actively construct modalities of perception, communication, and experience of the world and others that are, at the same time, heterogeneous levels of semiotization and vectors of prelinguistic subjectification. Stern describes three distinct "senses of the self" (emergent sense of self, core sense of self, and intersubjective sense of self), which precede the "verbal sense of self." The emergent sense of self that Guattari constantly associates with the work of the artist is quite important for different reasons. It acts outside conscience and constitutes the "matrix" (Stern), the "existential dwelling" (Guattari), and the experiences from which thoughts, perceived forms, identifiable acts, and verbalized feelings will be born. It is also the source of affective appreciations of ongoing events. Finally, it is the foundational reservoir from which one draws all creative and artistic experiences. All learning experiences and all creative acts rely on this sense of emergent self. "This prediscursive domain of experience remains active during the formation process of each of the other senses of self," and during the later processes of creativity and learning experiences.

55. Guattari, *Chaosmose*, 43; *Chaosmosis*, 44.

56. The universities, the culture industry, the media, and so on, of the so-called knowledge societies are powerful apparatuses of standardization of the process of subjectification, since they reduce such a process to the production of knowledge or information.

57. In the phrase "collective assemblage of enunciation," collective does not refer to an intersubjectivity or a group of individuals but to a multiplicity that individuals are a part of, just as machines, objects, incorporeal universals, semiotics, and so on. Do not confuse collective assemblages of enunciation with collective enunciation.

58. Félix Guattari, *Les Années d'hiver, 1980–1985* (Paris: Les Prairies ordinaires, 1986), 94.

59. Guattari, "Cracks in the Street," 63.

60. Félix Guattari, "À propos des machines," *Chimères* 19 (1993): 94.

61. "Speech remains an essential medium, but it's not the only one; everything that short-circuits signifying chains, postures, facial traits, spatial dispositions, rhythms, a-signifying semiotic productions (relating, for example, to monetary exchange), and machinic sign-productions can be implicated in this type of assemblage. Speech itself—and I could never overemphasize this—only intervenes here inasmuch as it acts as a support for existential refrains." Guattari, *Chaosmose*, 177; *Chaosmosis*, 127–128.

62. Deleuze, *Cinema 2*, 171.

63. Ibid., 172–173.

64. Marcel Duchamp, quoted in Francis M. Naumann, *Marcel Duchamp: L'Art à l'ère de la reproduction mechanisé* (Paris: Hazan, 1999), 306.

Appendix A

1. Translators' note: Quote taken from Mark Harman's 1998 translation of *The Castle*.

2. Ibid.

3. This number, 3949, is that of the phone line that the French employment agency Pôle Emploi set up in 2009, and is contacted by job seekers and benefit claimants.

4. Translators' note: Six minutes is the maximum length of a call on the 3949 line.

Appendix B

1. Editor's note: A "differend" is a difference of expression and perception that cannot be "resolved" logically or transcendentally because it is the product of different "language games." See Jean-Francois Lyotard, *The Differend: Phrases in Dispute*, trans. Georges Van Den Abeele (Minneapolis: University of Minnesota Press, 1989).

Index